HONDA
250 & 350
CB - CL - SL
K0 - K5 & G
1968-1973

WORKSHOP MANUAL

A Floyd Clymer Publication
This edition published in 2022 by
www.VelocePress.com

All rights reserved. This work may not be reproduced or transmitted in any form without the express written consent of the publisher.

INTRODUCTION

Welcome to the world of digital publishing ~ the book you now hold in your hand was printed using the latest state of the art digital technology. The advent of print-on-demand has forever changed the publishing process, never has information been so accessible and it is our hope that this book serves your informational needs for years to come. If this is your first exposure to digital publishing, we hope that you are pleased with the results. Many more titles of interest to the classic automobile and motorcycle enthusiast, collector and restorer are available via our website at www.VelocePress.com.

NOTE FROM THE PUBLISHER

The information presented is true and complete to the best of our knowledge. All recommendations are made without any guarantees on the part of the author or the publisher, who also disclaims any and all liability incurred with the use of the information contained in this manual.

TRADEMARKS

We recognize that some words, model names and designations, for example, mentioned herein are the property of the trademark holder. We use them for identification purposes only. This is not an official publication.

INFORMATION ON THE USE OF THIS PUBLICATION

This manual is an invaluable resource for those interested in performing their own maintenance. However, in today's information age we are constantly subject to changes in common practice, new technology, availability of improved materials and increased awareness of chemical toxicity. As such, it is advised that the user consult with an experienced professional prior to undertaking any procedure described herein. While every care has been taken to ensure correctness of information, it is obviously not possible to guarantee complete freedom from errors or omissions or to accept liability arising from such errors or omissions. Therefore, any individual that uses the information contained within, or elects to perform or participate in do-it-yourself repairs or modifications acknowledges that there is a risk factor involved and that the publisher or its associates cannot be held responsible for personal injury or property damage resulting from the use of the information or the outcome of such procedures.

MEASUREMENT & VALUES

The metric system is the primary measurement method used in both the manufacture of these motorcycles and this reproduction of the Factory Workshop Manual. As such, the reader is urged to verify that the conversion of those metric measurements to other forms of measurement is correct. All measurements and values are made without any guarantees on behalf of the publisher.

WARNING!

One final word of advice, this publication is intended to be used as a reference guide, and when in doubt the reader should consult with a qualified technician.

FOREWORD

This Manual is a guide to the inspection and servicing of the Honda motorcycle, Honda 250/350, Model CB250/350, CL250/350 and SL350.

The CL350 is used as a base for this manual, therefore, the photographs and drawings are of this model. However, since all models are practically identical, the information contained will apply equally to the other models. The Minor Change (MMC) Table on page 19 shows the principal modifications of other models as compared to the CL350 Model (basic model). Major changes in construction and maintenance are given in the text of the manual and minor changes in those items are omitted.

Any information which is peculiar to any of the models will be identified to the applicable model by the use of the codes listed below:

Applicable to	Code
ALL CB/CL250, 350 models	Honda 250/350
ALL CB250, CB350 models	CB250/350
ALL CL250, CL350 models	CL250/350
ALL CB250, CL250 models	CB/CL250
ALL CB350, CL350 models	CB/CL350
ALL SL350 models	SL350

Service and maintenance procedures are outlined in detail to enable the shop personnel to locate the problems rapidly.

This manual has been prepared by major groups, assemblies and sections for easy use. Further, all work procedures are descriptive and accompanied by many photographs and drawings for clarity.

Following are the initial serial numbers of each model at the time of change.

Model	Frame No.	Model	Frame No.
CB250	1000001~1024626	CL250	1000001~1007711
CB250K2	3000001~3025222	CL250K2	3000001~3005079
CB250K3	4000001~4026057	CL350	1000001~1062293
CB250K4	5000001~	CL350K2	2000001~2030816
CB350	1000001~	CL350K3	3000001~3051361
CB350K2	2000001~2066494	CL350K4	4000001~
CB350K3	3000001~3103177	CL350K5	5000001~
CB350K4	4000001~	SL350	1000001~
CB350G	5000001~	SL350K1	2000001~2051661
		SL350K2	3000001~

MEMO

CONTENTS

1. TECHNICAL DATA 1
2. SPECIAL TOOLS 15
3. MINOR MODEL CHANGE TABLE OF PRINCIPAL MODIFICATIONS 19
4. ENGINE 29
    - 4·1 Main Features 29
    - 4·2 Power Transmission System 29
    - 4·3 Dismounting the Engine 29
    - 4·4 Remounting the Engine 30
    - 4·5 Valve Mechanism 31
        - A. Description 31
        - B. Disassembly 31
        - C. Inspection 33
        - D. Reassembly 38
    - 4·6 Pistons and Cylinders 39
        - A. Description 39
        - B. Disassembly 39
        - C. Inspection 39
        - D. Reassembly 41
    - 4·7 Cam Chain Tensioner 42
        - A. Description 42
        - B. Disassembly 43
        - C. Inspection 43
        - D. Reassembly 43
    - 4·8 Lubrication System 44
        - A. Description 44
        - B. Disassembly 45
        - C. Inspection 46
        - D. Reassembly 48
    - 4·9 Clutch 48
        - A. Description 48
        - B. Disassembly 49
        - C. Inspection 49
        - D. Reassembly 50
    - 4·10 Crankshaft and Connecting Rod 51
        - A. Description 51
        - B. Disassembly 51
        - C. Inspection 51
        - D. Reassembly 53
    - 4·11 Transmission 53

A.	Description	53
B.	Disassembly	53
C.	Inspection	54
D.	Reassembly	55

4·12 Gear Shift Mechanism 55
- A. Description 55
- B. Disassembly 56
- C. Inspection 56
- D. Reassembly 57

4·13 Kick Starter 57
- A. Description 57
- B. Disassembly 57
- C. Inspection 57
- D. Reassembly 57

4·14 Crankcases 58
- A. Description 58
- B. Disassembly 58
- C. Inspection 58
- D. Reassembly 59

4·15 Carburetor 59
- A. Description 59
- B. Disassembly 60
- C. Inspection 60

5. FRAME 61

5·1 Handlebar 61
- A. Description 61
- B. Disassembly 61
- C. Inspection 62
- D. Reassembly 62

5·2 Fork Top Bridge 63
- A. Description 63
- B. Disassembly 63
- C. Inspection 63
- D. Reassembly 63

5·3 Front Cushion 64
- A. Description 64
- B. Disassembly 65
- C. Inspection 66
- D. Reassembly 67

5·4 Steering Stem 71
- A. Description 71
- B. Disassembly 72
- C. Inspection 72
- D. Reassembly 72

5·5	**Fuel Tank**	72
	A. Description	72
	B. Disassembly	73
	C. Inspection	73
	D. Reassembly	73
5·6	**Frame Body**	73
	A. Description	74
	B. Disassembly	74
	C. Inspection	74
	D. Reassembly	74
5·7	**Seat**	74
	A. Description	75
	B. Disassembly	75
	C. Inspection	75
	D. Reassembly	75
5·8	**Stand and Brake Pedal**	75
	A. Description	75
	B. Disassembly	75
	C. Inspection	76
	D. Reassembly	76
5·9	**Exhaust Pipes and Mufflers**	76
	A. Description	76
	B. Disassembly	77
	C. Inspection	77
	D. Reassembly	77
5·10	**Air Cleaners**	77
	A. Description	77
	B. Disassembly	77
	C. Inspection	77
	D. Reassembly	77
5·11	**Rear Fork and Rear Fender**	78
	A. Description	78
	B. Disassembly	78
	C. Inspection	79
	D. Reassembly	79
5·12	**Rear Cushion**	80
	A. Description (De Carbon type)	80
	B. Operation	80
	A. Description (Double tube two-way valve)	81
	B. Operation	81
	B. Disassembly	82
	C. Inspection	82
	D. Reassembly	83
5·13	**Front Wheel**	83
	A. Description	83
	B. Disassembly	83

C. Inspection	84
D. Reassembly	85
Front Wheel (with disk brake system)	87
A. Disassembly	88
B. Inspection	89
C. Assembly	89
A. Disassembly of calipers and master cylinder	91
B. Inspection of calipers and master cylinder	93
C. Assembly of calipers and master cylinder	94
D. Adjustment of disk brake	95
5·14 **Rear Wheel**	96
A. Description	96
B. Disassembly	97
C. Inspection	98
D. Reassembly	99
6. ELECTRICAL PARTS	101
6·1 **Ignition System**	101
1. Ignition Coil	101
A. Description	101
B. Removal	101
C. Inspection	101
D. Reassembly	102
2. Spark Advancer	102
A. Description	102
B. Removal	102
C. Inspection	102
D. Reassembly	102
3. Breaker Point	103
A. Description	103
B. Disassembly	103
C. Inspection	103
D. Reassembly	105
4. Capacitor	105
A. Description	105
B. Removal	105
C. Inspection	105
5. Spark Plug	106
A. Description	106
B. Removal	107
C. Inspection	107
D. Installation	107
6. Noise Suppressor	108
A. Description	108
B. Removal	108
C. Inspection	108
D. Reinstallation	108

6·2 Generating System 108
1. A.C. Generator 108
   A. Description 108
   B. Disassembly 108
   C. Inspection 108
   D. Reassembly 109
2. Current Limiter (Regulator) 109
   A. Description 109
   B. Disassembly 109
   C. Inspection 110
   D. Reassembly 110

6·3 Rectifying System 110
A. Description 110
B. Disassembly 110
C. Inspection 110
D. Reassembly 111

6·4 Battery 111
A. Description 111
B. Removal 112
C. Inspection 112

6·5 Starting System 115
1. Starting Motor 115
   A. Description 115
   B. Disassembly 116
   C. Inspection 116
   D. Reassembly 117
2. Starting Clutch 117
   A. Description 117
   B. Disassembly 117
   C. Inspection 117
   D. Reassembly 118
3. Solenoid Switch 118
   A. Description 118
   B. Removal 118
   C. Inspection 118
   D. Reassembly 118

6·6 Safety Equipment 119
1. Horn 119
   A. Description 119
   B. Removal 119
   C. Inspection 119
   D. Reassembly 119
2. Speedometer and Tachometer 119
   A. Description 119

B.	Removal	119
C.	Reassembly	119
3.	Headlight	120
A.	Description	120
B.	Removal	120
C.	Inspection	120
D.	Reassembly	121
4.	Tail/Stop Light	121
A.	Description	121
B.	Removal	121
C.	Inspection	121
D.	Reassembly	121
5.	Turn Signal Light	121
A.	Description	121
B.	Removal	122
C.	Inspection	122
D.	Reassembly	122
6.	Flasher Relay	122
A.	Description	122
B.	Removal	122
C.	Inspection	122
D.	Reassembly	122

6・7 Switches ... 123

1.	Ignition Switch	123
A.	Description	123
B.	Removal	123
C.	Inspection	123
D.	Reassembly	123
2.	Stoplight Switch	123
A.	Description	123
B.	Removal	123
C.	Inspection	123
D.	Reassembly	124
3.	Starter Switch Button and Lighting Switch	124
A.	Description	124
B.	Removal	124
C.	Inspection	124
D.	Reassembly	124
4.	Turn Signal Control Switch and Horn Control Switch	124
A.	Description	124
B.	Disassembly	124
C.	Inspection	124
D.	Reassembly	124
5.	Neutral Switch	125
A.	Description	125
B.	Removal	125

  C. Inspection 125
  D. Reassembly 125
  6. Wiring Harness 126
  A. Description 126
  B. Removal 126
  C. Inspection 126
  D. Reassembly 126

7. ENGINE (SL350) 127

7·1 Dismounting the Engine 127
7·2 Remounting the Engine 127
7·3 Primary Kick Starter 128
  A. Disassembly 128
  B. Inspection 128
  C. Reassembly 128

7·4 Carburetor 129
  A. Specifications 129
  B. Carburetor Circuits 129

8. FRAME 132

8·1 Handlebar 132
  A. Description 132

8·2 Fork Top Bridge 132
  A. Description 132

8·3 Front Cushion 133
  A. Description 133
  B. Disassembly 133
  C. Inspection 134
  D. Reassembly 134

8·4 Steering Stem 135
  A. Description 135
  B. Disassembly 136
  C. Inspection 136
  D. Reassembly 136

8·5 Fuel Tank 137
  A. Description 137

8·6 Frame 137
  A. Description 137
  B. Disassembly 138
  C. Inspection 138
  D. Reassembly 138

8·7 Seat 138
  A. Description 138

8·8 Muffler 138
  A. Description 138

- 8·9 **Air Cleaner** ... 138
  - A. Description ... 138
  - B. Disassembly ... 138
  - C. Inspection ... 139
  - D. Reassembly ... 139
- 8·10 **Rear Fork** ... 139
  - A. Description ... 139
  - B. Disassembly ... 139
  - C. Inspection ... 139
  - D. Reassembly ... 139
- 8·11 **Rear Cushion** ... 140
  - A. Description ... 140
  - B. Disassembly ... 140
  - C. Inspection ... 140
  - D. Reassembly ... 141
- 8·12 **Front Wheel** ... 141
  - A. Description ... 141
  - B. Tire Recommendation ... 141
- 8·13 **Rear Wheel** ... 141
  - A. Description ... 141

9. **ELECTRICAL** ... 142
   - 9·1 **Ignition Coil** ... 142
   - 9·2 **Horn** ... 142
   - 9·3 **Speedometer** ... 142
   - 9·4 **Starter Lighting Emergency Switch** ... 142
     - A. Disassembly ... 142
     - B. Inspection ... 142
     - C. Reassembly ... 142
   - **WIRING DIAGRAM** ... 143
     - CB250K4 Wiring Diagram (U.K. Type) ... 143
     - CB350K4 Wiring Diagram (U.S.A. Type) ... 144
     - CB350K4 Wiring Diagram (General Type) ... 145
     - CL350K4 Wiring Diagram (U.S.A. Type) ... 146
     - CL350K4 Wiring Diagram (General Type) ... 147
     - SL350K2 Wiring Diagram (U.S.A. Type) ... 148
     - CB350G Wiring Diagram (U.S.A. Type) ... 149

10. **MAINTENANCE** ... 151
    - 10·1 **Maintenance Schedule** ... 151
    - 10·2 **Tightening Torque Standards** ... 152
    - 10·3 **Trouble Shooting** ... 153

1. TECHNICAL DATA
CB250K4, K5

Item \ Model	CB250 (U.S.A. Type)	CB250K4 (U.K. Type)	CB250K5
DIMENSIONS			
Overall length	2090 mm (82.3 in)	2040 mm (80.3 in)	2,040 mm
Overall width	775 mm (30.5 in)	690 mm (23.9 in)	775 mm
Overall height	1075 mm (42.3 in)	1025 mm (40.4 in)	1,125 mm
Wheel base	1320 mm (52.0 in)	1320 mm (52.0 in)	1,345 mm
Ground clearance	150 mm (5.9 in)	145 mm (5.7 in)	160 mm
Curb weight	160 kg (352.8 lb)	169 kg (372 lb)	172 kg
Weight distribution F/R	96/124 kg (211.7/273.8 lb) at loaded weight	13/83 kg (161/181 lb) at weight	79/93 kg
FRAME			
Type	Semi-double, cradle	Semi-double, cradle	Semi-double cradle type
Suspension, front	Telescopic fork	Telescopic fork	Telescopic fork 114.5 mm
Suspension, rear	Swinging arm	Swinging arm	Swing arm 77.6 mm
Tire size, front	3.00-18 (4 PR)	3.00-18 (4 PR)	3.00-18-4 PR Rib pattern
Tire size, rear	3.25-18 (4 PR)	3.25-18 (4 PR)	3.50-18-4 PR Block pattern
Brake, fronlt, ining area	Internal expansion, 52.2 cm²×2	Internal expansion, 169 cm², 26.2 sq. in	Internal expanding, 169 cm²
Brake, rear, lining area	Internal expansion, 51.0 cm²×2	Internal expansion, 150 cm², 23.3 sq. in	Internal expanding, 150 cm²
Fuel capacity	12 lit. (3.2 US gal., 2.6 Imp. gal.)	12 lit. (3.2 US gal., 2.6 Imp. gal.)	11.0 lit.
Caster angle	63°	63°	62°30′
Trail length	85 mm (3.35 in)	85 mm (3.35 in)	92 mm
ENGINE			
Type	O.H.C. twin cylinder, air-cooled 4-stroke	O.H.C. twin cylinder, air-cooled 4-stroke	Air cooled 4-stroke O.H.C. engine
Cylinder arrangement	Vertical, twin parallel	Vertical, twin parallel	Vertical twin parallel
Bore and stroke	56×50.6 mm (2.205×1.992 in)	56×50.6 mm (2.205×1.992 in)	56.0×50.6 mm
Displacement	249 cc (15.21 cu-in)	249 cc (15.21 cu-in)	249 cc
Compression ratio	9.5	9.5	9.5 : 1
Carburetor	Constant velocity type, Keihin	Constant velocity type, Keihin	Constant velocity type
Valve train	Chain driven overhead cam-shaft	Chain driven overhead cam-shaft	
Max. torque	2.14 kg-m/9,500 rpm (15.5 ft-lb/9,500 rpm)	2.14 kg-m/9,500 rpm (15.5 ft-lb/8,500 rpm)	20 kg-m/9,000 rpm

Item \ Model	CB250 (U.S.A. Type)	CB250K4 (U.K. Type)	CB250K5
Oil capacity	2 lit. (2.1 U.S. quart, 1.8 Imp. quart)	2 lit. (2.1 U.S. quart, 1.8 Imp. quart)	2.0 lit.
Lubrication system	Forced and wet sump	Forced and wet sump	Forced and wet sump
Fuel required	Octane number above 95	Octane number above 90	Low-lead gasoline with 91 octane number or higher
Engine weight (Include oil)	52.5 kg (115.5 lb)	52 kg (114.7 lb)	55 kg
DRIVE TRAIN			
Clutch	Wet, multi-plate type	Wet, multi-plate type	Wet multi-plate type
Transmission	5 speed forward, constant mesh	5 speed forward, constant mesh	5-speed constant mesh
Primary reduction	3.714	3.714	3.714
Gear ratio 1st	2.353	2.353	2.500
2nd	1.636	1.636	1.750
3rd	1.269	1.269	1.375
4th	1.036	1.036	1.111
5th	0.900	0.900	0.965
Final reduction	2.375	2.375	2.375
ELECTRICAL			
Ignition	Battery	Battery	Battery and ignition coil
Starting system	Motor and kick	Motor and kick	Starting motor and kick starter
Battery capacity	12V-12AH	12V-12AH	12V-12AH
Spark plug	NGK B-8ES	NGK B-8ES, ND W-24ES	NGK B8ES, ND W-24ES

CL350K4

Item \ Model	CL350 (U.S.A. Type)	CL350K4 (U.S.A. Type)
DIMENSIONS		
Overall length	2020 mm (79.5 in)	2.025 mm (79.7 in)
Overall width	830 mm (32.7 in)	830 mm (32.7 in)
Overall height	1090 mm (42.9 in)	1.100 mm (43.3 in)
Wheel base	1320 mm (52.0 in)	1.320 mm (52.0 in)
Ground clearance	180 mm (8.1 in)	160 mm (6.3 in)
Curb weight	157 kg 1345.4 lb)	169 kg (372.6 lb)
Weight distribution F/R	91/126 kg (200.7/277.8 lb)	91/126 kg (200.7/277.8 lb)
FRAME		
Type	Semi-double, cradle	Semi-double, cradle
Suspension, front	Telescopic fork	Telescopic fork
Suspension, rear	Swinging arm	Swinging arm
Tire size, front	3.00-19 (4 PR)	3.00-19 (4 PR)
Tire size, rear	3.50-18 (4 PR)	3.50-18 (4 PR)
Brake, front, lining area	Internal expansion, 52.2 cm$^2 \times 2$	Internal expansion, 52.2 cm$^2 \times 2$
Brake, rear, lining area	Internal expansion, 51.0 cm$^2 \times 2$	Internal expansion, 51.0 cm$^2 \times 2$
Fuel capacity	9 lit. (2.4 U.S. gal., 2.0 lmp. gal.)	9 lit. (2.4 U.S. gal., 2.0 Imp. gal.)
Caster angle	63°	63°
Trail length	95 mm (3.74 in)	95 mm (3.74 in)
ENGINE		
Type	O.H.C. twin cylinder, air-cooled 4-stroke	O.H.C. twin cylinder, air-cooled 4-stroke
Cylinder arrangement	Vertical, twin parallel	Vertical, twin parallel
Bore and stroke	64×50.6 mm (2.52×1.992 in)	64×50.6 mm (2.52×1.992 in)
Displacement	325 cc (19.8 cu-in)	325 cc (19.8 cu-in)
Compression ratio	9.5	9.5
Carburetor	Constant velocity type, Keihin	Constant velocity type, Keihin
Valve train	Chain driven overhead camshaft	Chain overhead camshaft
Max. torque	2.69 kg-m/8,000 rpm (19.5 ft-lb/8,000 rpm)	2.69 kg-m/8,000 rpm (19.5 ft-lb/8,000 rpm)

Item \ Model	CL350 (U.S.A. Type)	CL350K4 (U.S.A. Type)
Oil capacity	2 lit. (2.1 U.S. quart, 1.8 Imp. quart)	2 lit. (2.1 U.S. quart, 1.8 Imp. quart)
Lubrication system	Forced and wet sump	Forced and wet sump
Fuel required	Octane number above 95	Octane number above 90
Engine weight (Include oil)	52.5 kg (115.5 lb)	52 kg (114.7 lb)
DRIVE TRAIN		
Clutch	Wet, multi-plate type	Wet, multi-plate type
Transmission	5 speed forward, constant mesh	5 speed forward, constant mesh
Primary reduction	3.714	3.714
Gear ratio 1st	2.353	2.353
2nd	1.636	1.636
3rd	1.269	1.269
4th	1.036	1.036
5th	0.900	0.900
Final reduction	2.375	2.375
ELECTRICAL		
Ignition	Battery	Battery
Starting system	Motor and kick	Motor and kick
Battery capacity	12V-12AH	12V-12AH
Spark plug	NGK B-8ES	NGK B-8ES ND W-24ES

CL350K5 (U.S.A. Type)

	Item	Metric	English
Dimensions	Overall length	2,025 mm	79.7 in
	Overall width	810 mm	31.9 in
	Overall height	1,100 mm	43.3 in
	Wheel base	1,320 mm	52.0 in
	Seat height	820 mm	32.3 in
	Foot peg height	305 mm	12.0 in
	Ground clearance	160 mm	6.3 in
	Dry weight	162 kg	357 lb
Frame	Type	Semi-double cradle	
	F. suspension, travel	Telescopic fork, travel 114.6 mm (4.5 in)	
	R. suspension, travel	Swing arm, travel 77.6 mm (3.1 in)	
	F. tire size, pressure	3.00-19 (4 PR) Block pattern, tire air pressure 1.8 kg/cm² (26 psi)	
	R. tire size, pressure	3.50-18 (4 PR) Block pattern, tire air pressure 2.0 kg/cm² (28 psi)	
	F. brake, lining area	Internal expanding shoe, lining swept area 169 cm² (26.2 sq. in)	
	R. brake, lining area	Internal expanding shoe, lining swept area 150 cm² (23.3 sq. in)	
	Fuel capacity	8.5 lit	2.2 U.S. gal. 1.9 Imp. gal.
	Fuel reserve capacity	2.0 lit	0.5 U.S. gal. 0.4 Imp. gal.
	Caster angle	63°	
	Trail length	95 mm	3.7 in
	Front fork oil capacity	125–130 cc (to fill dry)	4.2–4.4 ozs
	Front fork oil capacity	105–110 cc (to fill after draining)	3.6–3.7 ozs
Engine	Type	Air-cooled, 4-stroke O.H.C. engine	
	Cylinder arrangement	Vertical twin parallel	
	Bore and Stroke	64.0 × 50.6 mm	2.520 × 1.992 in
	Displacement	325 cc	19.8 cu-in
	Compression ratio	9.5 : 1	
	Valve train	Chain driven over head camshaft	
	Oil capacity	2.0 lit	2.1 U.S. pt. 1.8 Imp. qt.
	Lubrication system	Forced and wet sump	
	Cylinder head compression pressure	12 kg/cm² (170.7 psi)	
	Intake valve Open	At 10° (before top dead center)	
	Intake valve Close	At 35° (after bottom dead center)	
	Exhaust valve Open	At 40° (before bottom dead center)	
	Exhaust valve Close	At 15° (after top dead center)	
	Valve tappet clearance	IN : 0.05, EX : 0.1 mm	IN : 0.002, EX : 0.004 in
	Idle speed	1,200 rpm	

	Item	Metric	English
Carburetor	Type		
	Setting mark	726A	
	Main jet		
	Slow jet		
	Air screw opening	$1 \pm 1/8$ turns	
	Float height		
Drive train	Clutch	Wet, multi plate type	
	Transmission	5-speed, constant mesh	
	Primary reduction	3.714	
	Gear ratio I	2.353	
	Gear ratio II	1.636	
	Gear ratio III	1.269	
	Gear ratio VI	1.036	
	Gear ratio V	0.900	
	Final reduction	2.375, drive sprocket 16T, driven 38T	
	Gear shift pattern	Left foot operated return system	
Electrical	Ignition	Battery and ignition coil	
	Starting system	Starting motor and kick starter	
	Alternator	A.C. generator 0.1 kw/5,000 rpm	
	Battery capacity	12V-12AH	
	Spark plug	NGK B8ES, NDW 24ES	
	Headlight	Low/high 12V-25W/35W	
	Tail/stoplight	Tail-stop 12V-3/32 CP (SAE TRADE No. 1157)	
	Turn signal light	Front/rear 12V-32/32 CP (SAE TRADE No. 1073)	
	Speedometer light	12V-2 CP (SAE TRADE No. 57)	
	Tachometer light	12V-2 CP (SAE TRADE No. 57)	
	Neutral indicator light	12V-2 CP (SAE TRADE No. 57)	
	Turn signal indicator light	12V-2 CP (SAE TRADE No. 57)	
	High beam indicator light	12V-2 CP (SAE TRADE No. 57)	

CB350K4

Item \ Model	CB350 (U.S.A. Type)	CB350K4 (U.S.A. Type)
DIMENSIONS		
Overall length	2.010 mm (79.2 in)	2.010 mm (79.1 in)
Overall width	775 mm (30.5 in)	765 mm (30.1 in)
Overall height	1.075 mm (42.3 in)	1.085 mm (42.7 in)
Wheel base	1.320 mm (52.0 in)	1.320 mm (52.0 in)
Ground clearance	150 mm (5.9 in)	150 mm (5.9 in)
Curb weight	160 kg (352.8 lb)	168 kg (372 lb)
Weight distribution F/R	96/124 kg (211.7/273.4 lb)	73/83 kg (161/183 lb)
FRAME		
Type	Semi-double, cradle	Semi-double, cradle
Suspension, front	Telescopic fork	Telescopic fork
Suspension, rear	Swinging arm	Swinging arm
Tire size, front	3.00–18 (4 PR)	3.00–18 (4 PR)
Tire size, rear	3.50–18 (4 PR)	3.50–18 (4 PR)
Brake, front, lining area	Internal expansion, 52.2 cm$^2\times$2	Internal expansion, 169 cm^2, 26 sq·in
Brake, rear, lining area	Internal expansion, 51.0 cm$^2\times$2	Internal expansion, 150 cm^2, 23 sq·in
Fuel capacity	12 lit. (3.2 U.S. gal., 2.6 Imp. gal.)	12 lit. (3.2 U.S. gal., 2.6 Imp. gal.)
Caster angle	63°	63°
Trail length	85 mm (3.35 in)	85 mm (3.35 in)
ENGINE		
Type	O.H.C. twin cylinder, air-cooled 4-stroke	O.H.C. twin cylinder, air-cooled 4-stroke
Cylinder arrangement	Vertical, twin parallel	Vertical, twin parallel
Bore and stroke	56$\times$50.6 mm (2.205$\times$1.992 in)	64$\times$50.6 mm (2.520$\times$1.992 in)
Displacement	325 cc (19.8 cu-in)	325 cc (19.8 cu-in)
Compression ratio	9.5	9.5
Carburetor	Constant velocity type, Keihin	Constant velocity type, Keihin
Valve train	Chain driven overhead camshaft	Chain driven overhead camshaft
Max. torque	2.14 kg-m/9,500 rpm (15.5 ft-lb/9,500 rpm)	2.14 kg-m/9,500 rpm (15.5 ft-lb/9,500 rpm)

Item \ Model	CB350 (U.S.A. Type)	CB350K4 (U.S.A. Type)
Oil capacity	2 lit. (2.1 U.S. quart, 1.8 Imp. quart)	2 lit. (2.1 U.S. quart, 1.8 Imp. quart)
Lubrication system	Forced and wet sump	Forced and wet sump
Fuel required	Octane number above 95	Octane number above 90
Engine weight (Include oil)	52.5 kg (115.5 lb)	52.0 kg (115 lb)
DRIVE TRAIN		
Clutch	Wet, multi-plate type	Wet, multi-plate type
Transmission	5 speed forward, constant mesh	5 speed forward, constant mesh
Primary reduction	3.714	3.714
Gear ratio 1st	2.353	2.353
2nd	1.636	1.636
3rd	1.269	1.269
4th	1.036	1.036
5th	0.900	0.900
Final reduction	2.250	2.250
ELECTRICAL		
Ignition	Battery	Battery
Starting system	Motor and kick	Motor and kick
Battery capacity	12V-12AH	12V-12AH
Spark plug	NGK B-8ES	NGK B-8ES ND W-24ES

CB350G

	Item	Metric	English
Dimensions	Overall length	2,010 mm	79.1 in
	Overall width	810 mm	31.9 in
	Overall height	1,115 mm	43.9 in
	Wheel base	1,320 mm	52.0 in
	Seat height	815 mm	32.1 in
	Foot peg height	305 mm	12.0 in
	Ground clearance	150 mm	5.9 in
	Dry weight	163 kg	359 lb
Frame	Type	Semi-double cradle type	
	F. suspension, travel	Telescopic fork, travel 114.6 mm (4.5 in)	
	R. suspension, travel	Swing arm, travel 77.6 mm (3.1 in)	
	F. tire size, pressure	3.00-18 (4 PR) Rib pattern, tire air pressure 1.8 kg/cm^2 (26 psi)	
	R. tire size, pressure	3.50-18 (4 PR) Block pattern, tire air pressure 2.0 kg/cm^2 (28 psi)	
	F. brake, lining area	Disk brake, lining swept area 38 cm^2 (5.9 sq. in)	
	R. brake, lining area	Internal expanding shoe, lining swept area 150 cm^2 (23.3 sq. in)	
	Fuel capacity	11 lit	2.9 U.S. gal. 2.4 Imp. gal.
	Fuel reserve capacity	2 lit	0.5 U.S. gal. 0.4 Imp. gal.
	Caster angle	63°	
	Trail length	85 mm	3.33 in
	Front fork oil capacity	125–130 cc (to fill dry)	4.2–4.4 ozs
	Front fork oil capacity	105–110 cc (to fill after draining)	3.6–3.7 ozs
Engine	Type	Air cooled, 4-stroke O.H.C. engine	
	Cylinder arrangement	Vertical twin parallel	
	Bore and stroke	64.0 × 50.6 mm	2.520 × 1.992 in
	Displacement	325 cc	19.8 cu-in
	Compression ratio	9.5 : 1	
	Valve train	Chain driven over head camshaft	
	Oil capacity	2.0 lit	2.1 U.S. qt. 1.8 Imp. qt.
	Lubrication system	Forced and wet sump	
	Cylinder head compression pressure	12 kg/cm^2 (160.7 psi)	
	Intake valve — Open	At 15° (before top dead center)	
	Intake valve — Close	At 40° (after bottom dead center)	
	Exhaust valve — Open	At 40° (before bottom dead center)	
	Exhaust valve — Close	At 15° (after top dead center)	
	Valve tappet clearance	IN : 0.05, EX : 0.1 mm	IN : 0.002, EX : 0.004 in
	Idle speed	1,200 rpm	

	Item	Metric	English
Carburetor	Type	Piston valve	
	Setting mark	722A	
	Main jet	Pri. #78, 2nd #105	
	Slow jet	#35	
	Air screwing opening	1⅛ ±⅜ turns	
	Float height	26	
Drive train	Clutch	Wet, multi-plate type	
	Transmission	5-speed, constant mesh	
	Primary reduction	3.714	
	Gear ratio I	2.353	
	Gear ratio II	1.636	
	Gear ratio III	1.269	
	Gear ratio VI	1.036	
	Gear ratio V	0.900	
	Final reduction	2.250, drive sprocket 16T, driven sprocket 36T	
	Gear shift pattern	Left foot operated return system	
Electrical	Ignition	Battery and ignition coil	
	Starting system	Starting motor and kick starter	
	Alternator	A.C. generator 0.1 kw/5,000 rpm	
	Battery capacity	12V-12AH	
	Spark plug	NGK 8ES, NDW 24ES	
	Headlight	Low/high 12V-25W/35W	
	Tail/stoplight	Tail/stop 12V-3/32 CP (SAE TRADE No. 1157)	
	Turn signal light	Front/rear 12V-32/32 CP (SAE TRADE No. 1073)	
	Speedometer light	12V-2 CP (SAE TRADE No. 57)	
	Tachometer light	12V-2 CP (SAE TRADE No. 57)	
	Neutral indicator light	12V-2 CP (SAE TRADE No. 57)	
	Turn signal indicator light	12V-2 CP (SAE TRADE No. 57)	
	High beam indicator light	12-V2 CP (SAE TRADE No. 57)	

CL250

Item \ Model	CL250 (U.S.A. Type)	
DIMENSIONS		
Overall length	2100 mm (82.7 in)	
Overall width	830 mm (32.7 in)	
Overall height	1090 mm (42.9 in)	
Wheel base		
Ground clearance	180 mm (7.1 in)	
Curb weight	157 kg (345.4 lb)	
Weight distribution F/R	91/126 kg (200.7/277.8 lb)	
FRAME		
Type	Semi-double, cradle	
Suspension, front	Telescopic fork	
Suspension, rear	Swinging arm	
Tire size, front	3.00-19 (4 PR)	
Tire size, rear	3.50-18 (4 PR)	
Brake, front, lining area	Internal expansion, 52.2 cm^2×2	
Brake, rear, lining area	Internal expansion, 51.0 cm^2×2	
Fuel capacity	9 lit. (2.4 U.S. gal., 2.0 Imp. gal.)	
Caster angle		
Trail length	95 mm (3.74 in)	
ENGINE		
Type	O.H.C. twin cylinder, air-cooled 4-stroke	
Cylinder arrangement	Vertical, twin parallel	
Bore and stroke	56×50.6 mm (2.205×1.992 in)	
Displacement	249 cc (15.21 cu-in)	
Compression ratio	9.5	
Carburetor	Constant velocity type, Keihin	
Valve train	Chain driven overhead camshaft	
Max. torque	2.07 kg-m/8,000 rpm (15 ft-lb/8,000 rpm)	

Item \ Model	CL250 (U.S.A. Type)	
Oil capacity	2 lit. (2.1 U.S. quart, 1.8 Imp. quart)	
Lubrication system	Forced and wet sump	
Fuel required	Octane number above 95	
Engine weight (Include oil)	52.5 kg (115.5 lb)	
DRIVE TRAIN		
Clutch	Wet, multi-plate type	
Transmission	5 speed forward, constant mesh	
Primary reduction	3.714	
Gear ratio 1st	2.353	
2nd	1.636	
3rd	1.269	
4th	1.036	
5th	0.900	
Final reduction	2.375	
ELECTRICAL		
Ignition	Battery	
Starting system	Motor and kick	
Battery capacity	12V-12AH	
Spark plug	NGK B-8ES	

Item \ Model	SL350K4 (U.S.A. Type)		SL350K2 (U.S.A. Type)	
DIMENSIONS				
Overall length	2,110 mm	83.07 in	2,165 mm	85.2 in
Overrll width	1,840 mm	33.07 in	870 mm	34.3 in
Overall height	1,145 mm	45.08 in	1,175 mm	46.3 in
Wheel base	1,390 mm	54.72 in	1,400 mm	55.1 in
Seat height	810 mm	31.89 in	845 mm	33.3 in
Foot peg height	300 mm	11.81 in	330 mm	13.0 in
Ground clearance	210 mm	8.3 in	230 mm	9.1 in
Curb weight	139 kg	306.5 lb	148 kg	326 lb
Weight distribution F/R	64/75 kg	141.1/165.4 lb	64.5/75.5 kg	142/166 lb
FRAME				
Type	Double cradle		Double cradle	
Suspension, F	Telescopic fork		Telescopic fork	
Suspension, R	Swinging arm, de carbon suspension		Swinging arm, de carbon suspension	
Tire size, F	3.25-19 (4 PR)		3.00-21 (4 PR)	
Tire size, R	4.00-18 (4 PR)		4.00-18 (4 PR)	
Brake, F, lining area	Internal expanding shoe, 7.21 sq. in × 2 (46.5 sq. cm × 2)		Internal expanding shoe, 7.21 sq. in × 2 (46.5 sq. cm × 2)	
Brake, R, lining area	Internal expanding shoe, 6.66 sq. in × 2 (42.9 sq. cm × 2)		Internal expanding shoe, 6.66 sq. in × 2 (42.9 sq. cm × 2)	
Fuel capacity	9.0 lit.	2.4 U.S. gal. 2.0 Imp. gal.	9.0 lit.	2.4 U.S. gal. 2.0 Imp. gal.
Fuel reserve capacity	2.0 lit.	4.2 U.S. pt. 3.5 Imp. pt.	2.0 lit.	4.2 U.S. pt. 3.5 Imp. pt.
Caster angle	62°		59°40′	
Trail length	110 mm	4.33 in	148 mm	5.8 in
ENGINE				
Type	O.H.C. twin-cylinder, air cooled, 4-cycle		O.H.C. twin-cylinder, air cooled, 4-cycle	
Cylinder arrangement	Two cylinders in tandem		Vertical, twin parallel	
Bore and Stroke	64 × 50.6 mm	2.52 × 1.992 in	64 × 50.6 mm	2.52 × 1.992 in
Displacement	325 cc	19.8 cu-in	325 cc	19.8 cu-in
Compression ratio	9.5		9.5	
Carburetor	Keihin, PW 24		Keihin, PW 24	
Valve train	Chain driven overhead camshaft		Chain driven overhead camshaft	
Maximum torque	2.5 kg-m/8,000 rpm	18.1 lb-ft/8,000 rpm	2.5 kg-m/8,000 rpm	18.1 lb-ft/8,000 rpm
Oil capacity	2.0 lit.	4.2 U.S. pt. 3.5 Imp. pt.	2.0 lit.	4.2 U.S. pt. 3.5 Imp. pt.
Lubrication system	Forced pressure and wet sump		Forced pressure and wet sump	
Engine weight (include oil)	47 kg	103.5 lb	47 kg	103.5 lb

Item \ Model	SL350K1 (U.S.A. Type)		SL350K2 (U.S.A. Type)	
DRIVE TRAIN				
Clutch	Multi-plate, wet type		Multi-plate, wet type	
Transmission	5 speed, constant mesh		5 speed, constant mesh	
Primary reduction	3.714		3.714	
Gear ratio 1st	2.353		2.866	
2nd	1.636		1.800	
3rd	1.280		1.333	
4th	1.036		1.035	
5th	0.900		0.870	
Final reduction	2.500		2.625	
Gear shift pattern	Left foot return type system		Left foot return type system	
ELECTRICAL				
Ignition	Battery and ignition coil		Battery and ignition coil	
Starting System	Starting motor and kick pedal		Kick starter	
Alternator	AC generator		AC generator	
Battery capacity	12 V–5.5 AH		12 V–5 AH	
Spark plug	NGK B–8ES, NDW–24 ES		NGK B–8 ES, NDW–24 ES	
PERFORMANCE				
Max speed in gear 1st	28 mph	44 kph	25 mph	40 kph
2nd	40 mph	64 kph	40 mph	60 kph
3rd	51 mph	81 kph	55 mph	85 kph
4th	63 mph	100 kph	68 mph	110 kph
5th	79 mph	127 kph	80 mph	128 kph
Fuel consumption	82 mile/U.S. gal. at 37.5 mph	25 km/lit. at 60 kph	82 mile/U.S. gal. at 37.5 mph	25 km/lit. at 60 kph
	98 mile/Imp. gal. at 37.5 mph		98 mile/Imp. gal. at 37.5 mph	
Climbing ability	25°		30°	
Turning circle	13.8 ft	4.2 m	7 ft	2.13 m
Braking distance	46 ft. at 31 mph	14 m at 50 kph	46 ft. at 31 mph	14 m at 50 kph
Special equipment	Headlight bulb: 12 V–35/25 W Tail/stoplight bulb: 12 V–8/23 W		Headlight bulb: 12 V–35/25 W Tail/stoplight bulb: 12 V–8/23 W	

2. SPECIAL TOOLS

CB/CL250 · 350

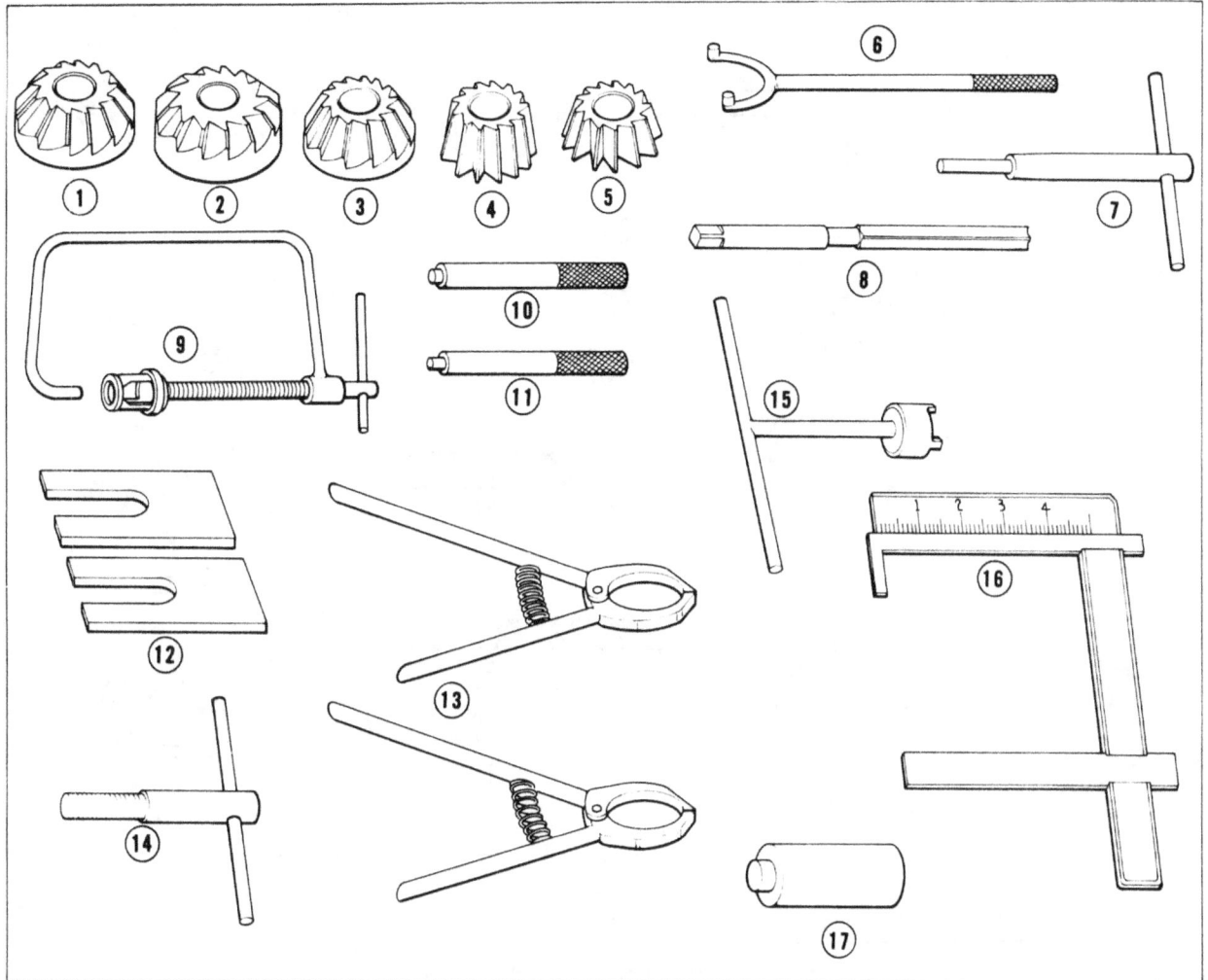

Ref. No.	Tool No.	Description
	07900-2860000	Special tool set for CB/CL250, 350
①	07980-2860100	Valve seat cutter 90°
②	07980-2860300	Inlet valve seat top cutter
③	07980-2860400	Exhaust valve seat top cutter
④	07980-2860500	Inlet valve seat interior cutter
⑤	07980-2860600	Exhaust valve seat interior cutter
⑥	07922-2870000	Drive sprocket holder
⑦	07981-2500000	Valve seat cutter holder
⑧	07984-5900000	Valve guide reamer, 7 mm
⑨	07957-3290000	Valve lifter
⑩	07942-2590100	Valve guide driving tool
⑪	07942-2590200	Valve guide removing tool
⑫	07958-2500000	Piston base (2 each)
⑬	07954-2510000	Piston ring compressor (CB/CL250)
⑬	07954-5510000	Piston ring compressor (CB/CL350)
⑭	07933-2160000	T-Handle dynamo rotor puller
⑮	07916-2830000	Lock nut wrench, 16 mm
⑯	07401-0010000	Carburetor float gauge (CB/CL250) (CB/CL350)
⑰	07945-2860100	Bearing driving tool
⑱	07902-2000000	Pin spanner, 48 mm

CB/CL250 · 350

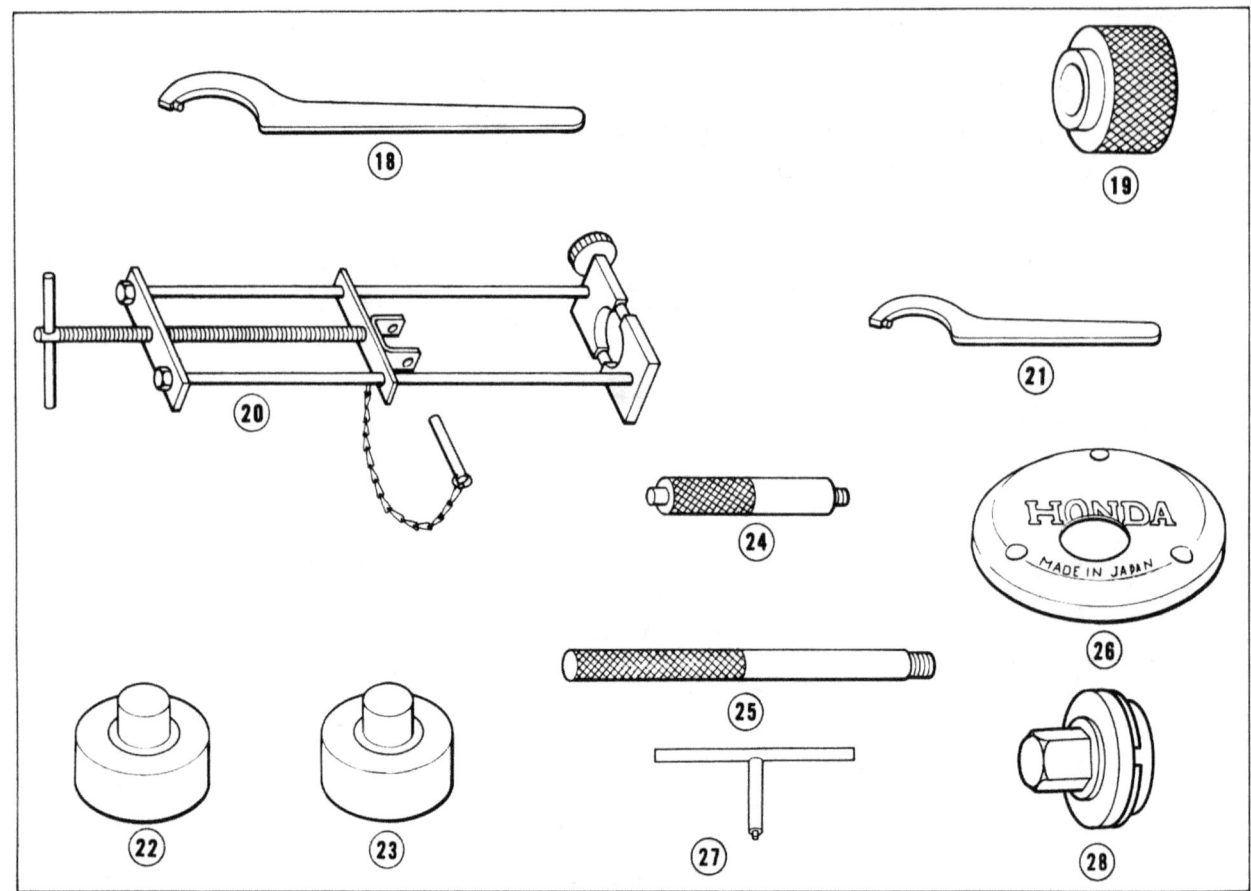

Ref. No.	Tool No.	Description
⑲	07947-2730100	Front fork oil seal driving guide
⑳	07959-3290000	Rear cushion assembling and disassembling tool
㉑	07902-2500000	Main switch pin spanner
㉒	07946-2860100	Front wheel bearing driver attachment
㉓	07946-2860200	Rear wheel bearing driver attachment
㉔	07949-2860000	Bearing driver handle
㉕	07965-2860000	Front fork assembling tool
㉖	07999-2860000	Dynamo inspection cover
㉗	07917-3230000	Wrench, hollow set 6 mm
㉘	07910-3290000	Rear wheel bearing retainer adjust wrench
	07797-2920300	Tool case (CB/CL250, 350)

SL350

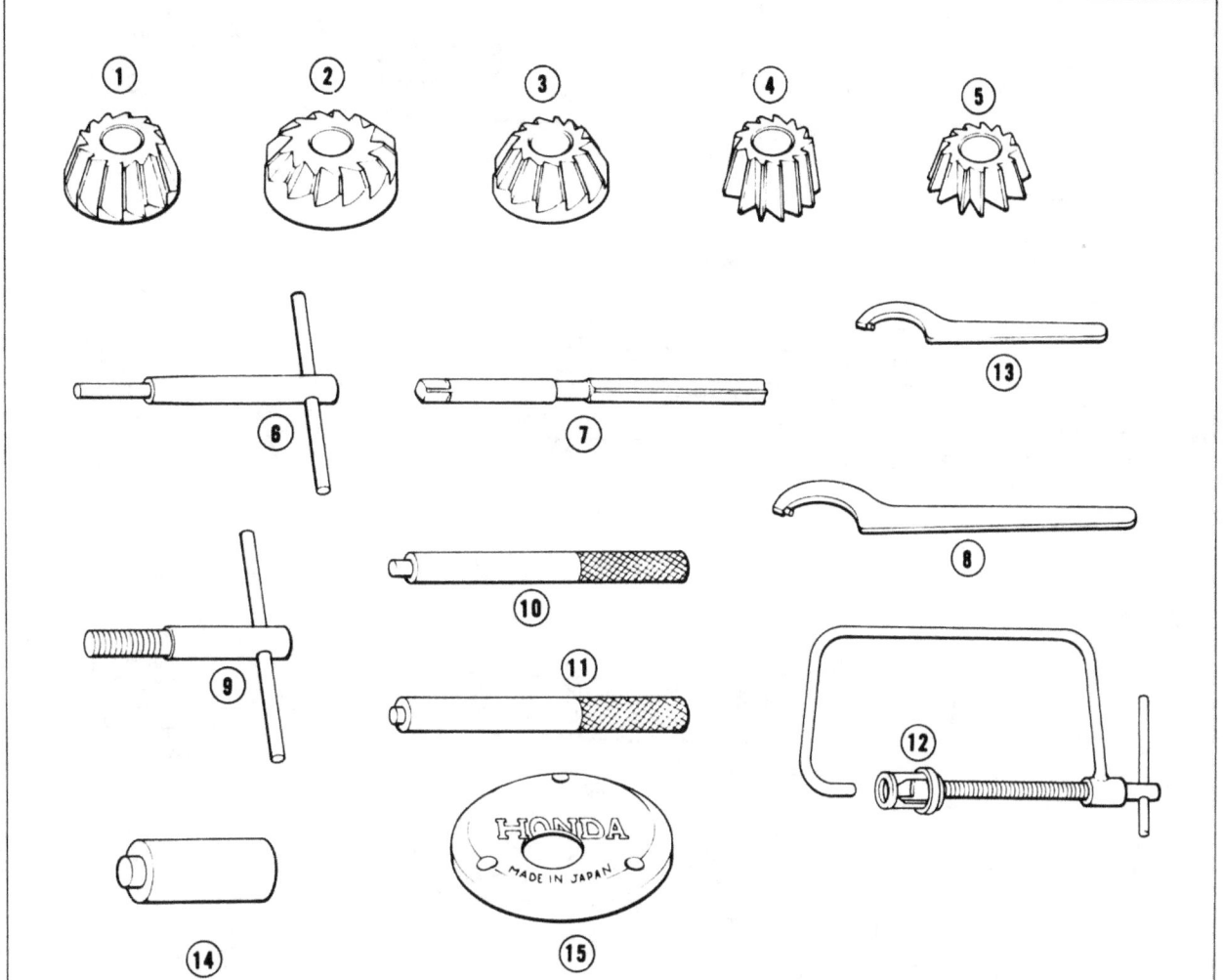

Ref. No.	Tool No.	Description
	07900-2860000	*Special tool set for SL350
①	07980-2860100	Inlet valve seat 90° cutter (IN. EX)
②	07980-2860300	Inlet valve seat top cutter
③	07980-2860400	Exhaust valve seat top cutter
④	07980-2860500	Inlet valve seat interior
⑤	07980-2860600	Exhaust valve seat interior cutter
⑥	07981-2500000	Valve seat cutter holder, 7 mm
⑦	07984-5900000	Valve guide reamer, 7 mm
⑧	07902-2000000	Pin spanner, 48 mm
⑨	07933-2160000	T-Handle dynamo rotor puller
⑩	07942-2590100	Valve guide driver
⑪	07942-2590200	Valve guide remover
⑫	07957-3290000	*Valve spring compressor
⑬	07902-2500000	Main switch pin spanner
⑭	07945-2860100	Bearing driver
⑮	07999-2860000	Dynamo inspection cover

*These tools are for use with the SL350 only, the others one common to all series.

SL350

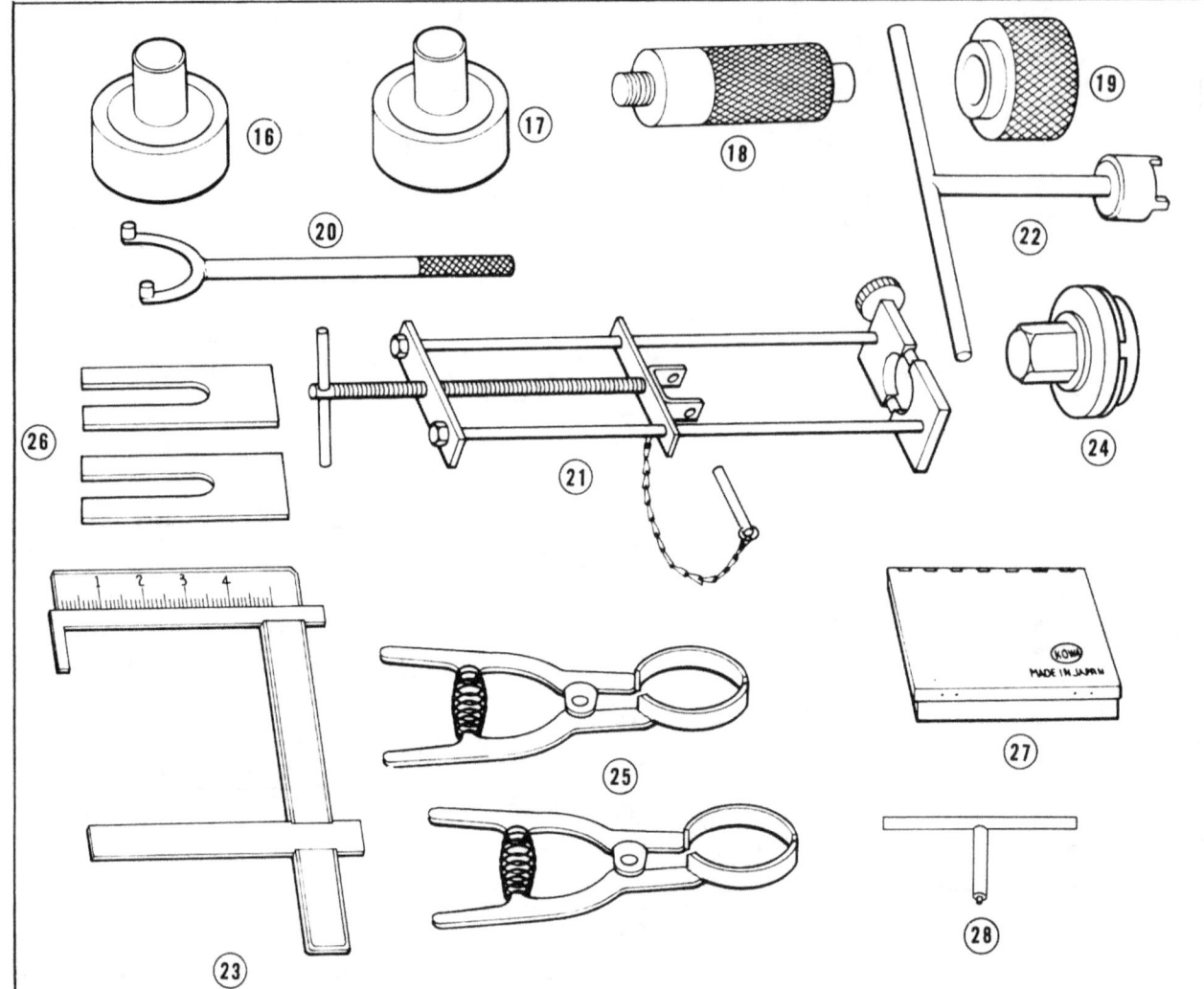

Ref. No.	Tool No.	Description
⑯	07946-2860100	*Front and R, Rear wheel bearing driver attachment
⑰	07946-2860200	*L, Rear wheel bearing driver attachment
⑱	07949-2860000	*Bearing driver handle
⑲	07949-2730100	Front fork oil seal driver guide
⑳	07922-2870000	Drive sprocket holder
㉑	07959-3290000	*Rear cushion disassembling and assembling tool
㉒	07916-2830000	T-handle box wrench, 16 mm
㉓	07401-0010000	Float level gauge
㉔	07910-3290000	Rear wheel bearing retainer adjusting wrench
㉕	07954-5510000	Piston ring compressor
㉖	07958-2500000	Piston base
㉗	07797-0510100	Valve seat cutter case
	07797-2920300	Tool case
㉘	07917-3230000	Wrench, hollow set 6 mm

*These tools are for use with the SL350 only, the others are common to all series.

3. MINOR MODEL CHANGE TABLE OF PRINCIPAL MODIFICATIONS

CB250.350

ITEM	CB250.350	CB250.350 K2	CB250.350 K3	CB250.350 K4
Fuel Tank Cap		For improved product quality	Change to painted strip and snap open fuel cap — For improved product quality	For improved product quality
Seat and Seat Locks	Rear hinged seat (lever relarse)		Side hinged seat (catch release) — For improved product quality	Side hinged seat (catch releace) and helmet holder installation — For improved product quality
Side Cover and Emblem			Exterior redesigh — For improved appearance	For improved appearance — Exterior redesign
Rear Brake Pedal			Brake pedal adjuster installation — For improved product quality	
Front Stop Switch	Front stop switch incorporated		Handle lever bracket incorporated — For improved product quality	
Tail Light Unit	None			Four point mounting

19

ITEM	CB250.350	CB250.350 K2	CB250.350 K3	CB250.350 K4
Front Wheel Assy. Rear Wheel	None		Balance weight installation	
			For better stability control	
Rear Cushion	Carbon type			Damper type (senior deversion)
				For better performance
Front Fork	Piston valve			Damper type (cross valve)
				For better stability control
Document Tray	None			Document tray installation
				For improved product quality
Side Reflector	None	Side reflector attached		Side reflector big type
				For improved product quality
		Safety precaution		Safety precaution
Tachometer		Trip meter attached		For improved product quality

ITEM	CB250.350	CB250.350 K2	CB250.350 K3	CB250.350 K4
Tire Pressure Caution Label		None		Safety precaution

CL250.350

ITEM	CL250.350	CL250.350 K2	CL 350 K3	CL 350 K4
Fuel tank			Change to painted strip and snap open fuel cap	Change to painted strip and snap open fuel cap
Rear Cushion	Upper cover attached		Upper cover not attached	
Battery Caution Mark	None		For improved appearance	
Seat			Redesign — For improved product quality, For improved appearance	Redesign — For improved product quality, For improved appearance, Improved safety feature
Helmet Holder	None			For improved product quality

SL350

ITEM	SL350	SL350 K1	SL350 K2
Front Fork	Piston valve (ultra oil S)		Free valve OIL : HONDA ATF Piston valve (Ultra oil S) Recommended oil Honda ultra #10~30 Oil capacity 180~190cc Stroke compression side 125mm extension side 45mm Total 170mm Free valve (Honda ATF) Manifold type free valve Oil capacity 100~175cc Stroke compression side 125mm extension side 46mm Total 171mm
Seat lock	None	None	For improved product quality
Seat Opening	Rear hinged seat (lever release)	Side hinged seat (catch release)	For improved product quality
Frame	Semi double cradle	Double cradle	For improved product quality
Fuel Tank and Capacity	Tank capacity 9.0 ℓ	Tank capacity 10 ℓ	Tank capacity 10 ℓ For improved appearance
Rear Fender	iron		aluminum To reduce weight

24

ITEM	SL350	SL350 K1	SL350 K2
Seat		Redesign	Redesign For improved appearance and
Tail Light Lens		Redesign	For safety in spite of increased size
Air Cleaner	Paper filter style	Urethane foam	Urethane foam
Document Tray	None	None	Document tray attached For improved convenience
Handlebar Pipe			30mm down For better stability control
Helmet Holder	None	None	Attached For improved product quality

ITEM	SL350	SL350 K1	SL350 K2
Carbureter		Redesign Piston valve used because of vehicle type	
Starting Motor		None	
Transmission Main Shaft	No. of teeth 17		No. of teeth 17 No. of teeth 15 for USA type
Main Shaft Second and Third Gear	No. of teeth 22 (second) No. of teeth 26 (third)		No. of teeth 22 (second) No. of teeth 25 (third) No. of teeth 20 (second) No. of teeth 24 (third) for U.S.A type
Main Shaft Top Gear	No. of teeth 30	No. of teeth 30 (top)	No. of teeth 30 (top) No. of teeth 31 (top) for U.S.A type
Counter Shaft Low Gear	No. of teeth 40		No. of teeth 40 No. of teeth 43 for U.S.A type

26

ITEM	SL350	SL350 K1	SL350 K2
Counter Shaft Second Gear		Redesign	
Counter Shaft Third Gear	No. of teeth 33	No. of teeth 32	

CB/CL350K4		CB350G/CL350K5	
Pattern on fuel tank changed.			
CB type	CL type	CB type	CL type

CB/CL350K4

Mounting angle of speedometer and tachometer changed and their dial plates changed to a transparent illumination type for better visibility.

CB350G/CL350K5

In conjunction with the change of mounting angle of the meters, retaining plate newly provided.

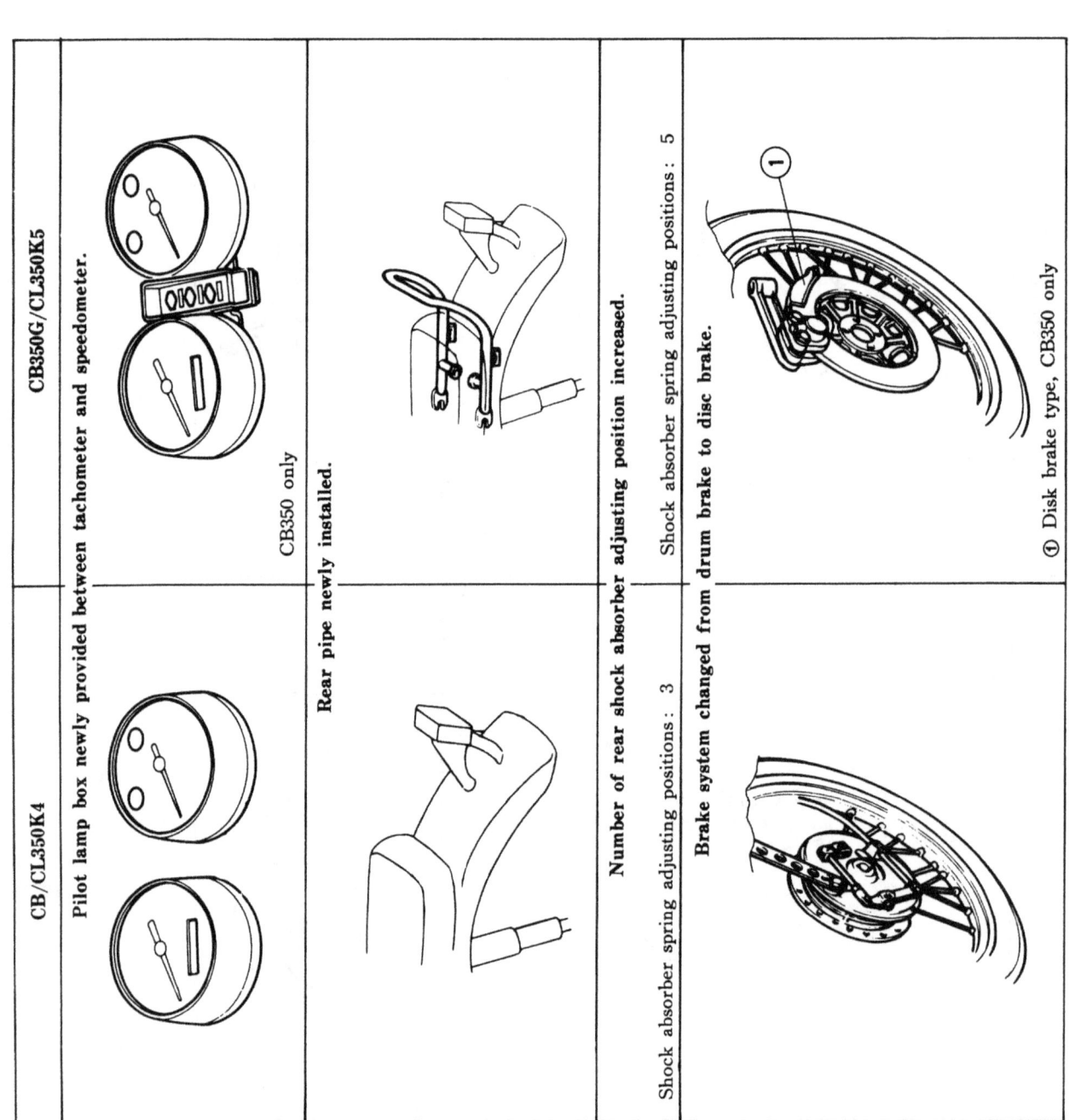

CB/CL350K4	CB350G/CL350K5
Pilot lamp box newly provided between tachometer and speedometer. CB350 only.	
Rear pipe newly installed.	
Number of rear shock absorber adjusting position increased.	
Shock absorber spring adjusting positions: 3	Shock absorber spring adjusting positions: 5
Brake system changed from drum brake to disc brake.	

① Disk brake type, CB350 only

4. ENGINE

4·1 MAIN FEATURES

The engine mounted on this motorcycle possesses the following features.
- Camshaft, rocker arm, etc. are contained within the cam case for greater rigidity and improve cooling. Further, by this construction, servicing of the engine is simplified.
- Valve tappet clearance adjustment is performed by the rocker arm pin which is mounted on an eccentric, simplifying the adjustment process.
- Heavy duty bearings are mounted on the crankshaft and transmission shaft.
- Redesign of the shift drum stopper and the neutral stopper provide improved gear change action as well as positive shifting.
- Use of the double spur gear for the primary reduction has reduced the gear noise and increased the durability.
- Employment of a dual filtering system using a metal screen strainer and a centrifugal filter vastly reduces the wear to the engine components.
- The two variable venturi system for the CV carburetor assures uniform fuel mixture independently to the respective cylinders to provide smooth power output at all speed ranges.

4·2 POWER TRANSMISSION SYSTEM

The power generation sequence and its transmission to at the rear wheel for performing useful work is as follows:

Combustion → piston → connecting rod → crankshaft → primary drive gear → (primary driven gear) clutch outer → eight friction disks → eight clutch plates → clutch center → transmission mainshaft → mainshaft gear → countershaft gear → countershaft → drive sprocket → drive chain → rear wheel. (Fig. 4-1)

NOTE:

The following parts can be disassembled from the engine without dismounting the engine from the frame.
- Crankcase cover (both right and left), left crankcase rear cover
- Clutch assembly
- Oil pump, oil filter
- A.C. generator assembly
- Neutral switch
- Cam chain tensioner holder

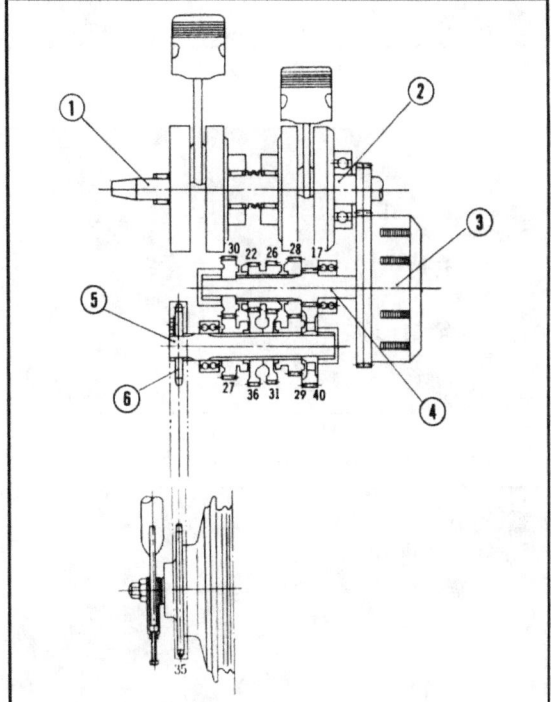

① L. crankshaft ② R. crankshaft ③ Clutch
④ Transmission mainshaft
⑤ Transmission countershaft ⑥ Drive sprocket
Fig. 4-1. Drive sequence

4·3 DISMOUNTING THE ENGINE

1. Fuel tank

   Turn the fuel cock to the "STOP" position; remove the fuel lines from the cock and the fuel level tube, and raise the seat to remove the tank.

2. Remove the mufflers.

3. Clutch cable

   Remove the gear change pedal and step bar, and take off the L. crankcase rear cover.

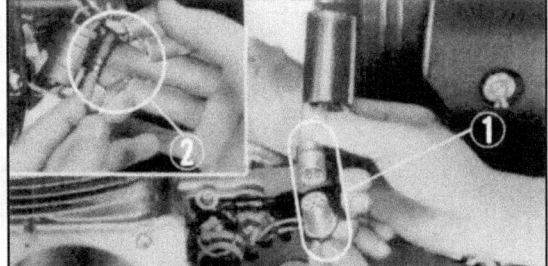

① Electrical leads connector
② Contact breaker leads
Fig. 4-2. Removing the electrical leads

① Starting motor cable
Fig. 4-3. Removing the starting motor cable

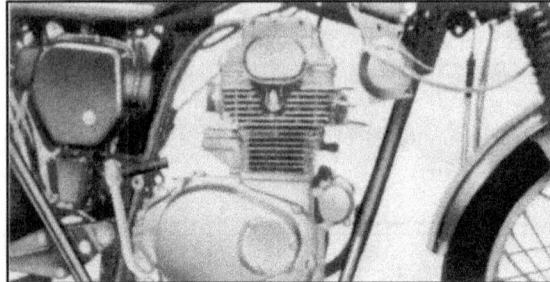

Fig. 4-4. Dismounting the engine

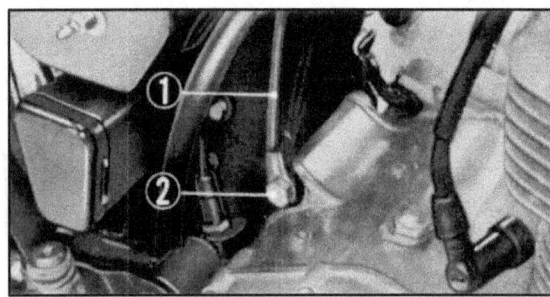

① Battery ground cable ② Engine hanger bolt
Fig. 4-5. Installing the battery ground cable

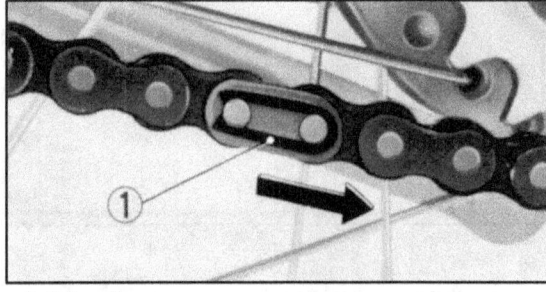

① Joint clip
Fig. 4-6. Drive chain joint clip direction

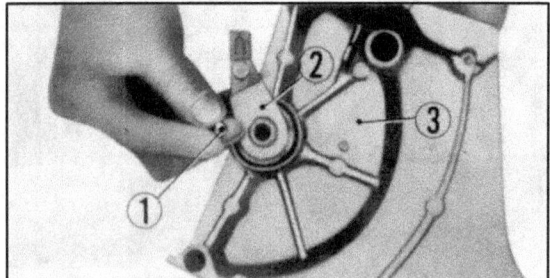

① Steel ball ② Clutch lever
③ Left crankcase rear cover
Fig. 4-7. Placing the steel ball

4. Remove the drive chain.
5. Remove the rear brake pedal.
6. Carburetor
   Remove the throttle control cables from the carburetor; remove the left and right air cleaner cases and loosen the carburetor insulating bands.
7. Unplug the electrical cable connection. (Fig. 4-2)
8. Remove the contact breaker cable connection.
9. Remove the high tension terminal assemblies from the spark plugs.
10. Remove the starting motor cable. (Fig. 4-3)
11. Disconnect the tachometer cable at the engine.
12. Remove the 7 engine hanger bolts and dismount the engine from the right side. (Fig. 4-4)

4·4 REMOUNTING THE ENGINE

Remount in the reverse sequence of dismounting.

NOTE:

- Insert the hanger bolts from the right side of the frame and tighten nuts from the left side. Install the battery ground cable from the right side. (Fig. 4-5)
- If the hanger bolts do not go in easily, do not force. Find the cause and make correction.
- When installing the battery ground cable, clean all rust and paint from the hanger bolt as well as from the terminal and the frame mounting area so that good contact is assured. (Fig. 4-5)

- Make sure that the drive chain joint link clip is facing in the correct direction, the opening must be opposite to the direction of chain movement. (Fig. 4-6)

- Make sure that the steel ball has been assembled in the clutch lever before installing the left crankcase rear cover. (Fig. 4-7)

4·5 VALVE MECHANISM

A. Description

The valve mechanism consists of a camshaft, rocker arms, intake and exhaust valves and their related parts and is housed within the cam case. Driven from the crankshaft through a loop of cam chain, the camshaft moves the valves through the rocker arms. This shaft is supported at two places and runs at 1/2 the crankshaft speed. The working surfaces of the cams are case-hardened by soft-nitriding (CLN) process to provide a greater wear resistance. The cam-side ends of the rocker arms are hard-faced with a special alloy. The valves are stellite-faced and their seats are made of a heat-resistant steel to minimize valve component wear. The tachometer drive is located at the right side of the camshaft and the spark advancer and contact breaker at the left side.

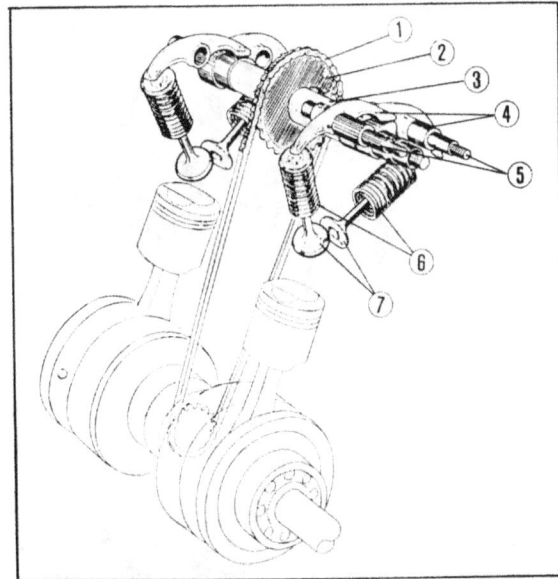

① Cam chain ② Cam sprocket ③ Camshaft
④ Valve rocker arm ⑤ Rocker arm pin
⑥ Valve spring ⑦ Valve
Fig. 4-8. Valve mechanism

B. Disassembly

1. Remove eight 8 mm cap nuts and remove the cylinder head cover.

2. Remove the dynamo cover, breaker point cover, contact breaker point assembly, and the spark advancer. (Fig. 4-9)

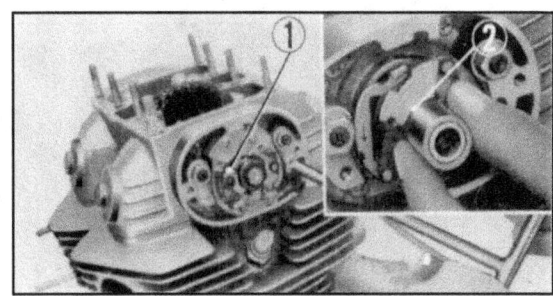

① Contact breaker assembly ② Spark advancer
Fig. 4-9. Removing the contact breaker and spark advancer

3. Remove the rocker arm pin lock nuts (both sides, 2 each), and the side covers and rocker arm pins. (Fig. 4-10)

4. Remove the cam chain tensioner.

① Rocker arm pin lock nuts ② Rocker arm pins
③ Side cover ④ Rocker arm
Fig. 4-10.

5. Align the stator index mark to the "LT" on the A.C. generator rotor (top dead center of the exhaust stroke) to approximately 10° ATDC and then remove the sprocket alignment bolt, followed by turning the rotor to align with a point approximately 10° ATDC of the compression stroke and then remove the remaining sprocket setting bolt. (Fig. 4-11, 12)

① Index mark ② "LT" mark
Fig. 4-11. Line up "LT" mark to the index mark

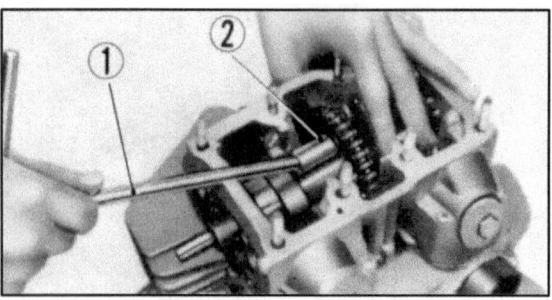

① 10 mm universal box wrench ② Cam sprocket
Fig. 4-12. Removing the cam sprocket

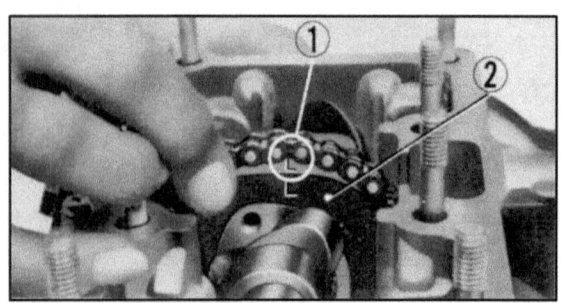

① "L" mark ② Cam sprocket
Fig. 4-13. Placing the "L" mark on the upper side

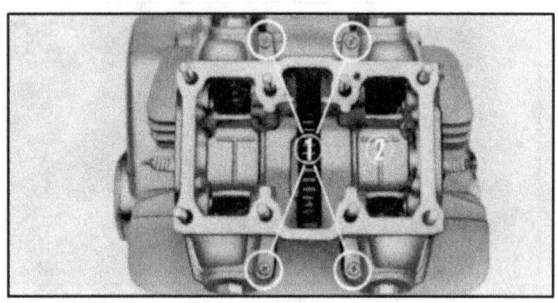

① 6 mm cross screws ② Cam case
Fig. 4-14. Removing the cam case

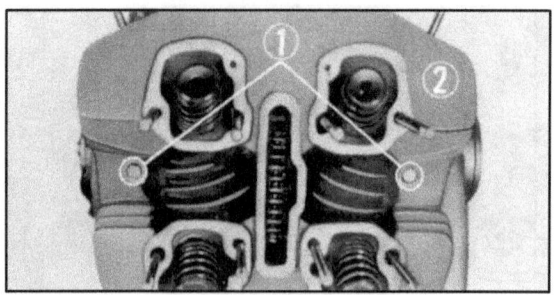

① 6 mm hex. bolts ② Cylinder head
Fig. 4-15. Removing the cylinder head

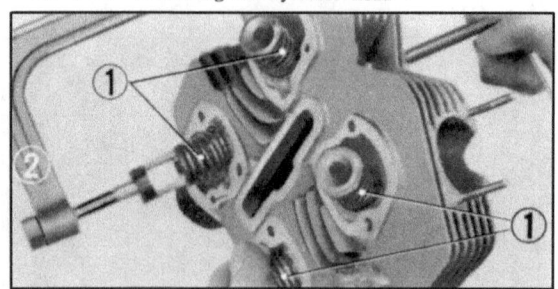

① Valve springs
② Valve assembly and disassembly tool
Fig. 4-16. Removing the valve

NOTE:
- Hook bolt and the sprocket setting bolt can be easily removed by using the 10 mm universal box wrench provided in the special tool kit. Tool No. 07093-28601) (Fig. 4-12)
- This is a special bolt and therefore it should not be lost or misplaced. It can be identified by the marking "9" stamp on the bolt head.

6. When removing the camshaft from the cam case, remove the camshaft through the openings for removing the cam sprocket and cam case, which are essentially provided to remove the camshaft, toward the right hand side while placing the "L" mark of cam sprocket on the upper side as for Fig. 4-13.

7. Remove the four 6 mm cross screws and separate the cam case. (Fig. 4-14)

8. Remove the spark plugs and unscrew the 6 mm bolts from both sides. (Fig. 4-15)

9. Separate the cylinder head from the cylinder.
10. Use the valve assembly and disassembly tool (Tool No. 07957-3290000) and disassemble the valve cotter, valve retainer, valve springs and valve spring seats.
(Fig. 4-16)

C. Inspection

1. Compression pressure (Fig. 4-17)

   - The engine does not have to be dismounted to check the cylinder head compression pressure. Perform the measurement while the engine is at operating temperature.

     1) Remove the spark plug.
     2) Fit the head of the compression gauge to the spark plug hole. Hold it firmly so that compression is not lost.
     3) Open the throttle grip and choke valve completely.

① Compression gauge
Fig. 4-17. Measuring compression pressure

     4) Kick the starter pedal repeatedly, quickly and powerfully, and read the maximum value on the gauge.
     5) The rated compression is **12 kg/sq-cm (170 psil)**.

2. Adjusting the engine to the proper compression pressure.

   - The engine must be dismounted for this operation.

     If the compression measures **over 12 kg/sq-cm (170 psi)**, the combustion chamber wall and/or piston head probably have carbon deposit.

     Remove the carbon deposits from the combustion chamber (refer to page 35) or piston head.

   - When the compression is **below 10.5 kg/sq-cm (150 psi)**, perform the following operation.

     1) Lap the valves (refer to page 36).
     2) Check piston and piston rings (refer to page 40).
     3) Check cylinder head gasketing surface (refer to page 35).

3. Valve tappet clearance inspection and adjustment

   This operation can be performed without dismounting the engine. Further, make the check with a cold engine. Perform the check and adjustment in accordance with the following procedures.

     1) Remove the tappet hole caps.
     2) Remove the contact breaker cover and dynamo cover.

     3) Turn the generator rotor counterclockwise and align the "LT" timing mark with the index mark on the stator. (Fig. 4-18)

        With the finger, check to make sure that both rocker arms of the left side in the cam case is free, this indicates that the piston for this cylinder is at top-dead-center of the compression stroke. If the valves are tight, turn the generator rotor counterclockwise 360° and realign the timing mark. Insert the thickness gauge between the valve stem and rocker arm to check the tappet clearance. If adjustment is required, turn the rocker arm pin in either the right or left with the screwdriver to obtain the proper clearance. After completing the adjustment, tighten the adjuster lock nut and the recheck tappet clearance to assure that the clearance has not changed during locking. (Fig. 4-19)

① Index mark ② Generator rotor
Fig. 4-18. Aligning the "LT" mark

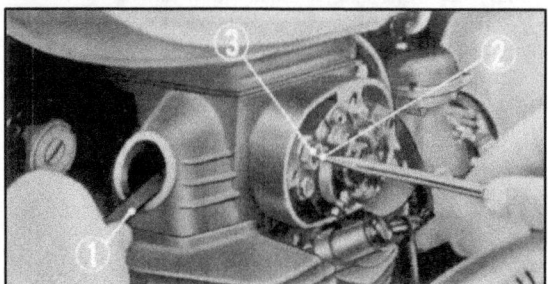

① Thickness gauge ② Rocker arm pin
③ Rocker arm pin lock nut
Fig. 4-19. Adjusting tappet clearance

mm (inch)

Tappet Clearance	Standard Value
Inlet	0.05 (0.002)
Exhaust	0.10 (0.004)

34

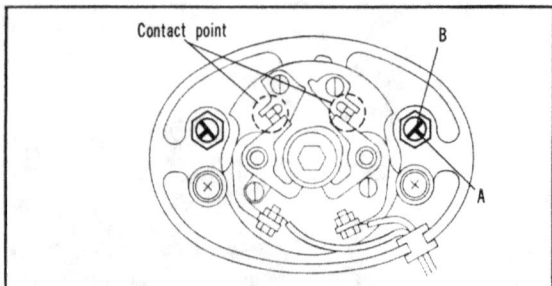

Fig. 4-20.

NOTE

1. Two thickness gauges of 0.05 mm (0.002 in) thickness are included in the tool kit. Stack the two gauges when checking the tappet clearance of the exhaust valve.
2. The eccentric indicator cutout "A" of the rocker arm pin must be rotated so that it is to the outside of the screwdriver slot "B" (opposite the contact points) as shown in Fig. 4-20.

   This setting is the same for both the right and left cylinders.

4) After completing the check of the left cylinder, turn the generator rotor counterclockwise 180° and align the "L" timing mark with the stator index mark and perform the check and adjustment in the same manner as described in 3 above.

NOTE:

Refer to Fig. 4-21 for adjusting the tappet clearance.

⊕ Increase ⊖ Decrease
Fig. 4-21. Rocker arm pin turning direction

① Small dial gauge ② Camshaft
Fig. 4-22. Checking camshaft side clearance

4. Camshaft side clearance

   If the side clearance is excessively large, noise will develop between 5,000 to 6,000 rpm.
   Attach a dial indicator to the side of the cam sprocket and check the side clearance of the camshaft.
   If the side clearance is over 1.0 mm (0.04 in), install 0.2 mm (0.008 in) shim which are available. The standard side clearance is 0.2~0.6 mm (0.008~0.024 in).
   (Fig. 4-22)

5. Cam diameter

   Measure the diameter using a micrometer. (Fig. 4-23)

   mm (inch)

	Standard Value	Serviceable Limit
Inlet and exhaust cam	36.858~36.898 (1.451~1.453)	Replace if under 36.68 (1.444)

NOTE:

Minor defects on the cam may be reworked using a fine oil stone.

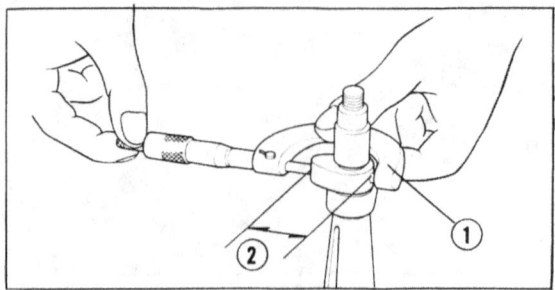

① Micrometer ② Cam diameter
Fig. 4-23. Measuring cam diameter

6. Camshaft mounting end

    Measure both the right and left ends of the camshaft with a micrometer. (Fig. 4-24)

    mm (inch)

	Standard Value	Serviceable Limit
End diameter	21.939~21.960 (0.864~0.865)	Replace if under 21.920 (0.863)

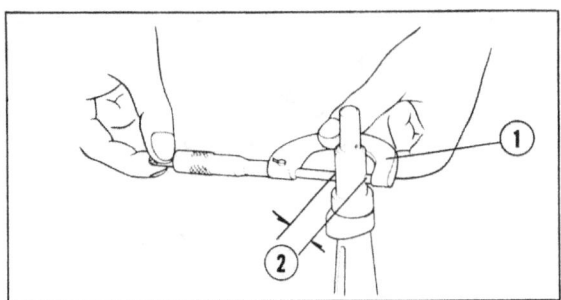

① Micrometer ② Mounting end diameter
Fig. 4-24. Measuring diameter

7. Rocker arm pin diameter

    Measure the rocker arm pin pivot diameter with a micrometer. (Fig. 4-25)

    mm (inch)

	Standard Value	Serviceable Limit
Rocker arm pin pivot diameter	12.950~12.968 (0.510~0.511)	Replace if under 12.9 (0.508)

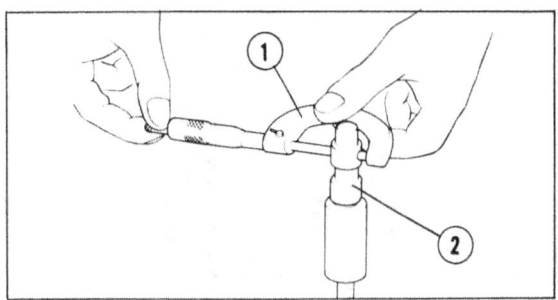

① Micrometer ② Rocker arm pin
Fig. 4-25. Measuring rocker arm pin

8. Right and left cylinder head side cover internal diameter

    Measure the camshaft mounting holes in both the X and Y axis, with a cylinder gauge. (Fig. 4-26)

    mm (inch)

	Standard Value	Serviceable Limit
Mounting hole diameter	22.000~22.021 (0.866~0.867)	Replace if over 20.050 (0.868)

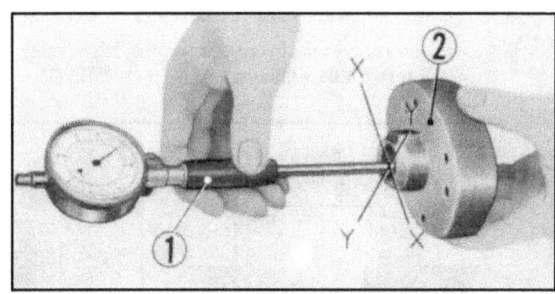

① Cylinder gauge ② Cylinder head side cover
Fig. 4-26. Measuring cylinder head side cover

9. Deformation of the gasketing surface

    Check the gasketing surface for deformation or warpage using a straight edge or a square bar and a thickness gauge. If there is any clearance between the measuring tool and the surface which is greater than **0.05 mm (0.002 in)** the part should be either repaired or replaced. (Fig. 4-27)

    (Repair)

    Apply a thin coating of red lead or bluing on a surface plate and rub the gasketing surface over the surface plate to determine the area of deformation. With a flat oilstone, lap the high areas using a figure 8 motion. Occasionally check the lapping progress with the coated surface plate. Finally check with a straight edge or square bar and thickness gauge.

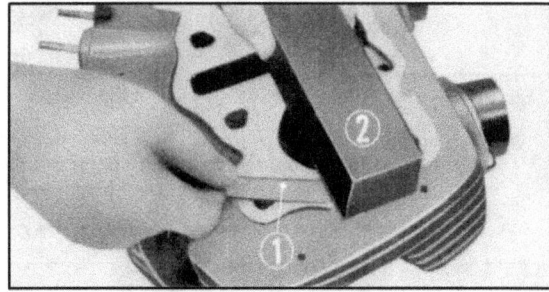

① Thickness gauge ② Stretch
Fig. 4-27. Checking warpage of gasket surface

10. Carbon removal

    Remove the carbon with a carbon remover brush, being careful not to scratch or damage the combustion chamber surface. (Fig. 4-28)

    NOTE:

    Performing this operation with the valves installed will facilitate the work and prevent the valve seats from getting scratched.

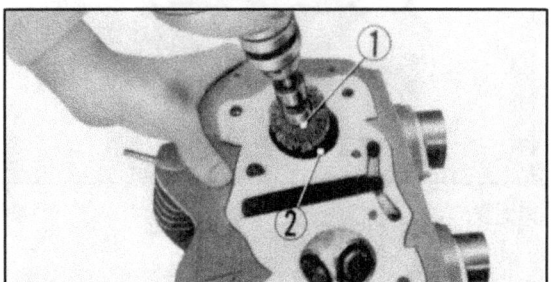

① Wire brush ② Combustion chamber
Fig. 4-28. Removing the carbon

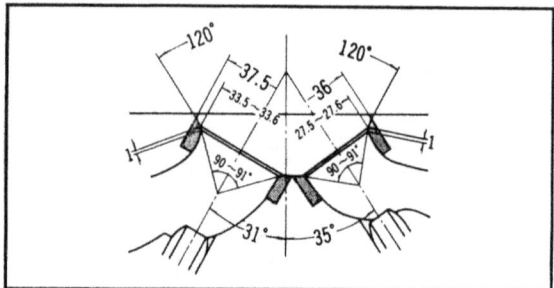

Fig. 4-29. Sectional view of valve seat

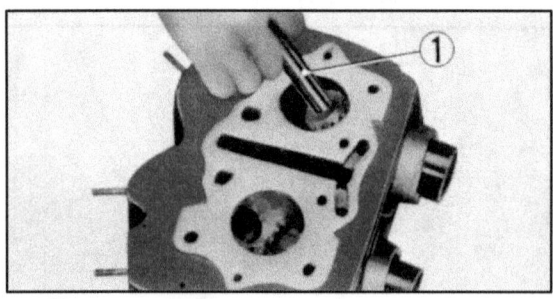

① Valve seat cutter
Fig. 4-30. Re-forming valve seat with cutter

11. Valve seat contact

   Apply a thin coating of red lead or bluing on the valve seat, install the valve into the guide and rotate the valve while applying a slight pressure to the valve head. Inspect the impression of the coating.

   Measure the valve face contact width using a vernier caliper.

mm (inch)

	Standard Value	Serviceable Limit
Contact width	1.0~1.3 (0.040~0.051)	Replace or repair if over 2.0 (0.08)

(Repair)

Repair the valve seat using a special tool valve seat cutters. (Fig. 4-30)

(Refer to special tools on page 15~18)

Description	Tool No.
Valve seat cutter, 90°	07980-2860100
Inlet valve seat top cutter	07980-2860300
Exhaust valve seat top cutter	07980-2860400
Inlet valve seat interior cutter	07980-2860500
Exhaust valve seat interior cutter	07980-2860600
Valve seat cutter holder	07981-2500000

1) Use the 90° valve seat cutter and cut the seat enough to obtain a continuous seating surface. (Fig. 4-31A)
2) Use the valve seat top cutter and the valve seat interior cutter to narrow the width of the valve seat to **1~1.3 mm (0.04~0.05 in)**. (Fig. 4-31B, C)

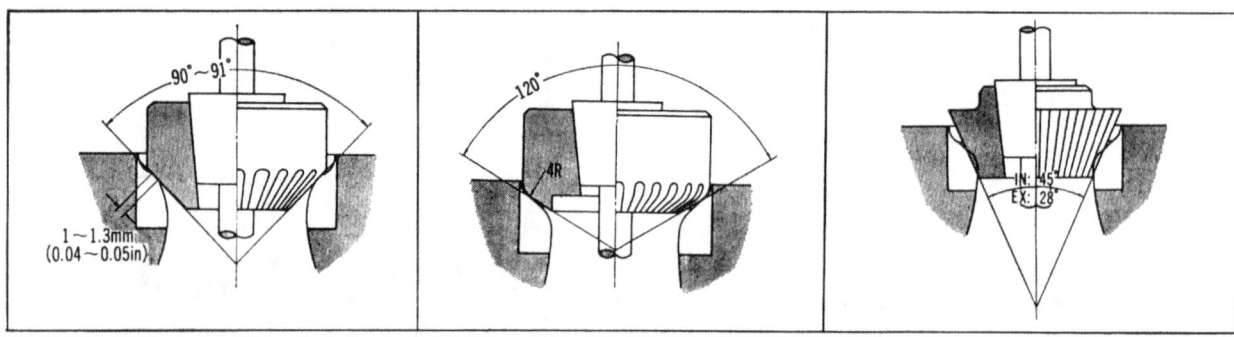

Fig. 4-31A.   **Fig. 3-41B.**   **Fig. 4-31C.**

3) For lapping the valve with the valve seat, use a sucker (a suction cup lapping tool). After applying a small amount of fine lapping compound on the valve seat face, lap the valves while holding the sucker with both hands, and apply a slight pressure by tapping while rotating to the right and left. (Fig. 4-32)
4) After completing the lapping operation, wash off all trace of the lapping compound with kerosene or solvent.

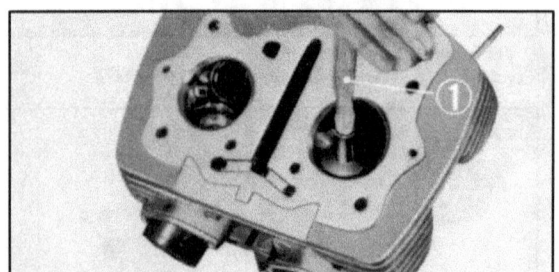

① Valve seat lapping tool
Fig. 4-32. Performing valve seat lapping

NOTE:
· When assembling the valve into the head, apply a liberal amount of engine oil on the valve stem.

CAUTION:
Use the valve seat grinder (tool No. 07782-0020000, A set) to correct the valve seat width and contact from the following serial number.

E No. {CB250E-5025978~ / CB350E-4171086~ / CB350E-5073078~}   E No. {SL350E-3024698~ / CL350E-4171086~ / CL350E-5073078~}

Read carefully the instruction provided with the valve seat grinder.

5) After lapping the valve, pour a small amount of engine oil into the combustion chamber and blast air **2 kg/sq-cm (28.4 psi)** in from the inlet and exhaust ports. If no bubbles appear in the valve seat area, it is an indication that the valves are well seated.

12. Valve stem clearance

    Inspect the valve into the valve guide and measure the clearance by placing a small dial gauge against the valve. (Fig. 4-33)

    mm (inch)

	Standard Value	Serviceable Limit
Inlet valve	0.01~0.035 (0.0004~0.0014)	Replace if over 0.08 (0.0031)
Exhaust valve	0.03~0.055 (0.0012~0.0022)	Replace if over 0.09 (0.0035)

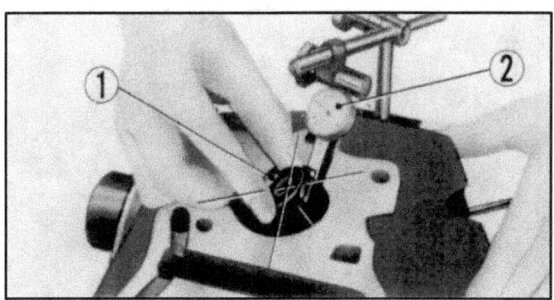

① Valve ② Small dial gauge
Fig. 4-33. Checking valve guide clearance

13. Valve stem diameter

    Measure the valve stem at the top, bottom and intermediate points using a micrometer. (Fig. 4-34)

    mm (inch)

	Standard Value	Serviceable Limit
Inlet valve	6.975~6.990 (0.2746~0.2752)	Replace if under 6.955 (0.2738)
Exhaust valve	6.955~6.970 (0.2738~0.2744)	Replace if under 6.935 (0.2730)

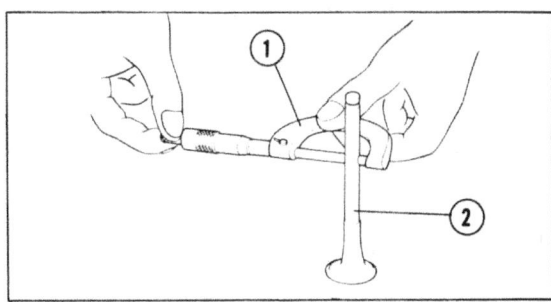

① Micrometer ② Valve stem
Fig. 4-34. Measuring valve stem diameter

14. Valve guide replacement

    When replacing valves, it is recommended that the guides also be replaced. Valve guides can be removed by installing the Valve Guide Removing Tool (Tool No. 07942-2590200) from the combustion chamber side and tapping lightly with a hammer. (Fig. 4-35)

    Install the valve guide in from the valve compartment side using a Valve Guide Driving Tool (Tool No. 07942-2590100), exercising care to install the guide straight. An oversize guide (oversize guide interference of 0.072~0.1 mm compared to a standard guide interference of 0.042~0.070 mm) should be used when replacing. After installing the guide, use a Valve Guide Reamer (Tool No. 07984-5900000) and slowly ream out the guide. Perform this operation carefully using sufficient oil to prevent reamer from binding; if the reamer starts to bind, remove and clean off the metal shavings before continuing to ream. (Fig. 4-36)

    NOTE:

    Upon completing the valve guide reaming, install the valve and check the valve clearance.

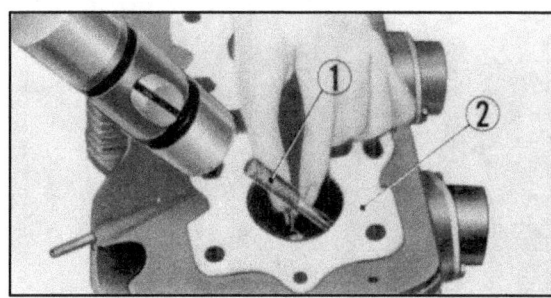

① Valve guide removing tool ② Cylinder head
Fig. 4-35. Removing the valve guide

15. Valve spring dimension

    Measure the free length of the valve spring using a vernier caliper. (Fig. 4-37)

    mm (inch)

	Standard Value	Serviceable Limit
Free length of outer spring	49.0 (1.929)	Replace if under 47.8 (1.882)
Free length of inner spring	39.8 (1.567)	Replace if under 39.3 (1.547)

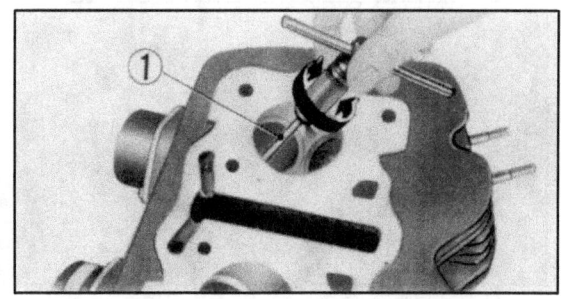

① Reamer
Fig. 4-36. Performing reaming

16. Valve spring force

    Measure the valve spring compression force using a spring compression tester.

	Standard Value
Outer spring compressive force	62.6~72.0 kg @ 31 mm (138.0~158.8 lb @ 1.22 in)
Inner spring compressive force	30.5~35.1 kg @ 26 mm (67.3~77.4 lb @ 1.02 in)

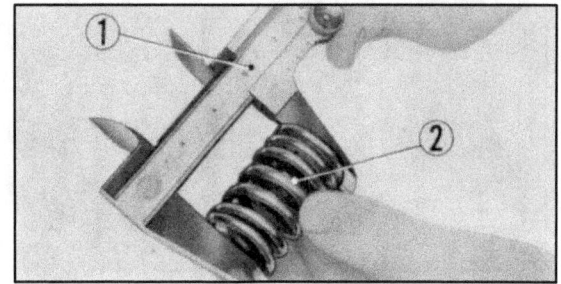

① Vernier caliper ② Valve spring
Fig. 4-37. Measuring valve spring length

38

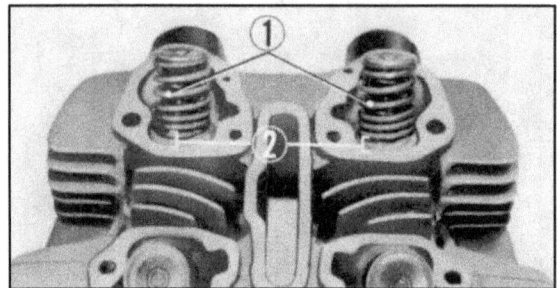

① Valve springs   ② Smaller pitch
Fig. 4-38. Installing valve spring

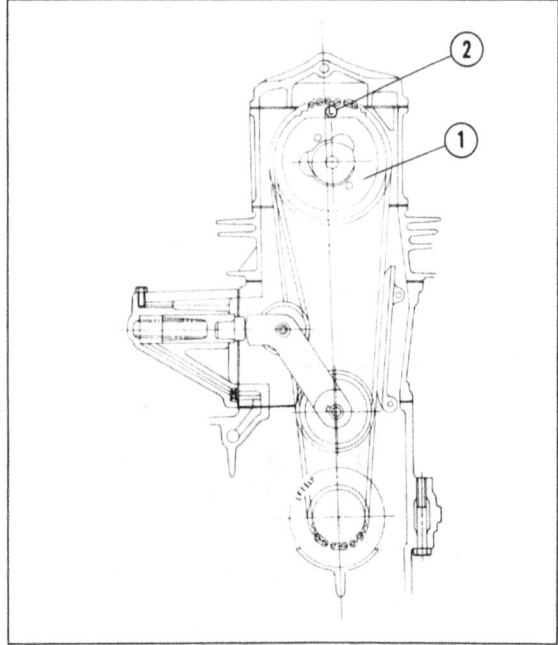

① Cam sprocket   ② "L" mark
Fig. 4-39. Valve timing

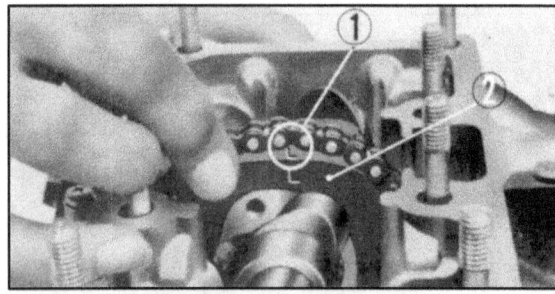

① "L" mark   ② Cam sprocket
Fig. 4-40. Placing the "L" mark on the upper side

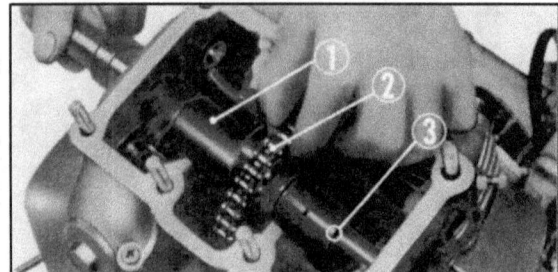

① Camshaft   ② Cam sprocket   ③ Pin
Fig. 4-41. Assembling the camshaft

D. Reassembly

1. The valve spring has a dual pitch; make sure that the end with the smaller pitch is installed toward the seat. (Fig. 4-38)

2. When installing the cylinder head, make sure that the two hollow pins are installed in the correct locations.

3. After assembling the component parts into the cylinder head, mount the head to the cylinder with two 6 mm bolts and torque to 85~100 kg-cm (6.15~7.23 lb-ft).

4. Do not forget to install the cam case gasket, two guide pins.

5. Mount the cam case on the cylinder head with four 6 mm cross screws and torque to **60 to 75 kg-cm (4.34–5.24 lb-ft)**.

6. Raise the cam sprocket as shown in Fig. 4-39 and insert the camshaft by working it back and forth. Refer to the Section 4·7, valve timing.

7. Valve timing
   1) Align the "LT" marking on the rotor to the index mark on the stator. The left cylinder will be on top-dead-center.
   2) Align the cutout of the cam sprocket rubber damper to the cam case mating surface. (Fig. 4-40)
   3) When assembling the cam sprocket on the camshaft, slightly raise the governor alignment pin on the camshaft from the right side and make the assembly. (Fig. 4-41)

8. Mount the cam sprocket on the camshaft with two 6 mm bolts.

NOTE :

The bolts used are of different types, setting dowel bolt and setting bolt, do not reverse their installation.

(Fig. 4-42)

9. Install the rocker arm on the cam case with the rocker arm pin, on both sides.
10. Install the side covers on both sides.
11. Assemble the spark advancer assembly, contact breaker assembly, and the point cover on the left side.
12. Install the cylinder head cover with the eight 8 mm cap nuts and torque the nuts uniformly.

NOTE :

- Torque the cylinder head starting from the inside and working out in the diagonal sequence. Use a torque wrench and torque to **180~200 kg-cm (13-14.5 ft-lbs)**.

(Fig. 4-43)

- The two holes on the cylinder head inlet side are oil holes, therefore, all the nuts must be properly torqued to prevent oil leaks.

13. Install the cam chain tensioner on the cylinder.

4·6 PISTONS AND CYLINDERS

A. Description

The pistons are made from a heat-resistant aluminum alloy and are fitted with three rings, top, second and oil. Their skirts are finished to an elliptical shape, or "cam grind" to provide for unequal expansion that occurs at operating temperature. Another design feature that each piston is set off-center of its connecting rod to prevent the piston skirt being pressed against the cylinder wall by a resultant horizontal or side force acting at the center of the piston pin.

B. Disassembly

1. Remove the cam case in accordance with section 4·5B on page 31.
2. Remove the cylinder head in accordance with section 4·5B on page 31.
3. Remove the cylinder from the crankcase.
4. Remove the piston clip and push out the piston pin. Disassemble the piston from the connecting rod.

NOTE :

When removing the piston pin clip, care should be exercised so that the clip is not dropped into the crankcase. (Fig. 4-45)

C. Inspection

1. Measure the cylinder bore, taper and out-of-round with a precision cylinder gauge. Take measurements at the top, middle and bottom in both diametrical axis.

(Fig. 4-46)

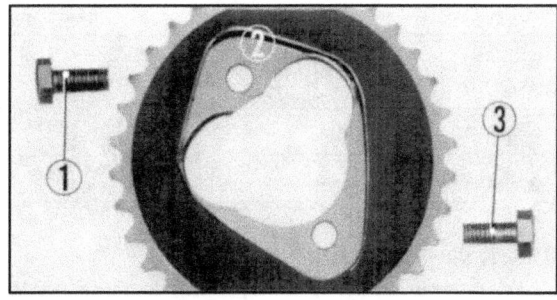

① 6 mm setting bolt ② Cam sprocket
③ 6 mm setting dowel bolt
Fig. 4-42.

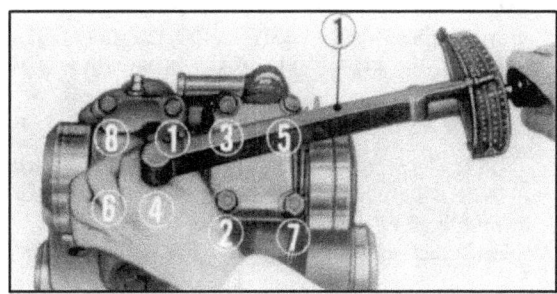

① Torque wrench
Fig. 4-43. Tightening sequence

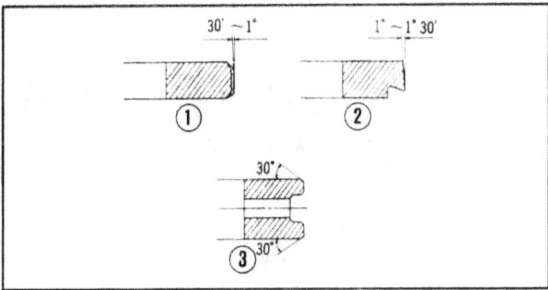

① Top ring ② Second ring ③ Oil ring
Fig. 4-44. Sectional view of piston rings

① Piston pin clip ② Pliers
Fig. 4-45. Removing the piston pin clip

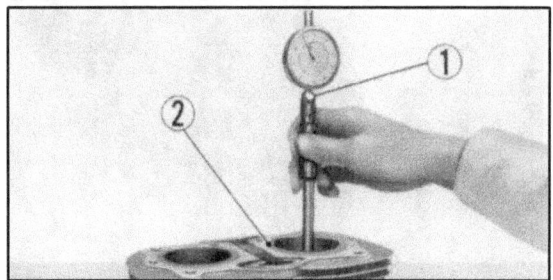

① Cylinder gauge ② Cylinder
Fig. 4-46. Measuring the inner diameter

CB/CL250   mm (inch)

Item	Standard Value	Serviceable Limit
Bore	56.01~56.02 (2.205~2.206)	Replace if over 56.1 (2.209)
Taper	0.005 (0.0002)	Replace if over 0.05 (0.002)
Out of round	0.005 (0.0002)	Replace if over 0.05 (0.002)

CB/CL350   mm (inch)

Item	Standard Value	Serviceable Limit
Bore	64.01~64.02 (2.5201~2.5205)	Replace if over 64.1 (2.524)
Taper	0.005 (0.0002)	Replace if over 0.05 (0.002)
Out of round	0.005 (0.0002)	Replace if over 0.05 (0.002)

2. Cylinder boring and honing

After reboring the cylinder, finish honing must be performed to provide 0.8S~1.5S surface finish. The permissible stock removal during the honing operation is approximately 0.01 mm (0.0004 in).

NOTE:

Surface finish 0.8S~1.5S refers to the JIS (Japanese Industrial Standard) surface roughness designation. The value indicates the mean depth of the groove over a definate area and this value is expressed in μ (micron is 1/1000 of a millimeter).

The "S" designates a JIS measuring unit. Surface finish value 0.8S indicates the average depth of the roughness over a length of 0.3 mm perpendicular to the lay is 0.8μ; 1.5S indicates the average depth of the roughness over a length of 1.0 mm perpendicular to the lay.

The values are determined by visual comparison against master sample.

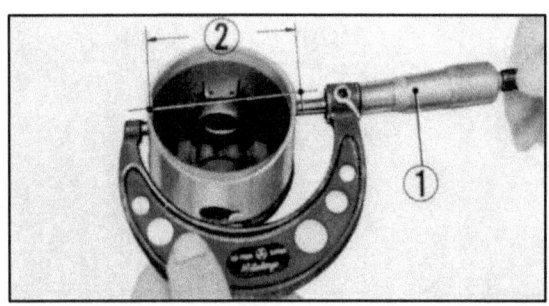

① Micrometer ② Outside diameter
Fig. 4-47. Measuring piston diameter

3. Piston dimension

   Measure the diameter of the piston skirt perpendicular to the piston pin. (Fig. 4-47)

   mm (inch)

	Standard Value	Serviceable Limit
CB/CL250	55.97~55.99 (2.2035~2.2043)	Replace if under 55.9 (2.20)
CB/CL350	63.97~63.99 (2.5185~2.5193)	Replace if under 63.9 (2.51)

NOTE:
- The "d" dimension is smaller than "D" dimension by **0.22~0.24 mm (0.0087~0.0095 in)**.
- Oversize pistons are available in four different sizes at increments of **0.25 mm (0.009 in)**.

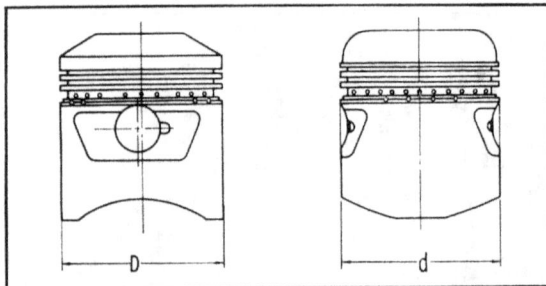

Fig. 4-48. Dimension of piston

4. Piston ring side clearance

   Measure the piston ring side clearance at four points, 90° apart using a thickness gauge. (Fig. 4-49)

   CB/CL250   mm (inch)

Item	Standard Value	Serviceable Limit
Top	0.030~0.060 (0.0012~0.0024)	Replace if over 0.18 (0.007)
Second	0.015~0.045 (0.0006~0.0018)	Replace if over 0.165 (0.0065)
Oil	0.010~0.045 (0.0004~0.0018)	Replace if over 0.170 (0.0067)

   CB/CL350   mm (inch)

Item	Standard Value	Serviceable Limit
Top	0.030~0.060 (0.0012~0.0024)	Replace if over 0.18 (0.007)
Second	0.015~0.045 (0.0006~0.0018)	Replace if over 0.165 (0.0065)
Oil	0.015~0.045 (0.0004~0.0018)	Replace if over 0.170 (0.0067)

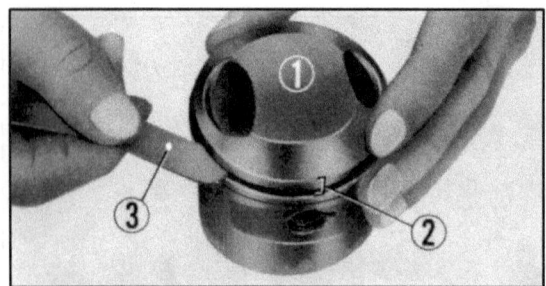

① Piston ② Piston ring ③ Thickness gauge
Fig. 4-49. Piston groove and piston ring clearance

5. Piston ring end gap

    Measure the ring gap by inserting the piston ring into the cylinder so that the ring is at right angle to the cylinder axis, the gap should be measured with a thickness gauge. (Fig. 4-50)

    CB/CL250   mm (inch)

Item	Standard Value	Serviceable Limit
Ring end gap	0.15~0.35 (0.006~0.014)	Replace if over 0.75 (0.030)

    CB/CL350   mm (inch)

Item	Standard Value	Serviceable Limit
Ring end gap	0.2~0.4 (0.008~0.016)	Replace if over 0.8 (0.032)

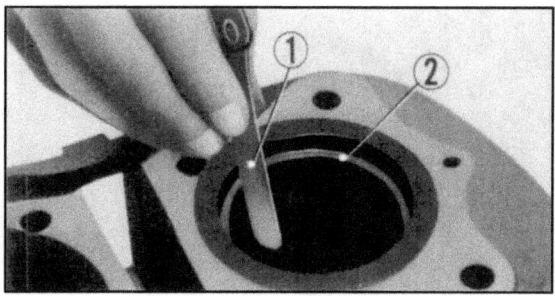

① Thickness gauge ② Piston ring
Fig. 4-50. Measuring end gap of piston ring

6. Piston ring thickness

    Measure the thickness of the ring using a micrometer. (Fig. 4-51)

    mm (inch)

Item	Standard Value	Serviceable Limit
Top	1.460~1.475 (0.057~0.058)	Replace if under 1.435 (0.0564)
Second	1.475~1.490 (0.058~0.059)	Replace if under 1.435 (0.0564)
Oil	2.475~2.490 (0.097~0.098)	Replace if under 2.430 (0.096)

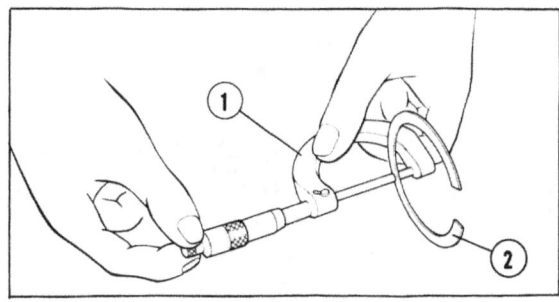

① Micrometer ② Piston ring
Fig. 4-51. Measuring thickness of piston ring

7. Piston pin bore

    Measure the piston pin bore at both ends and at 90° apart. (Fig. 4-52)

    mm (inch)

Standard Value	Serviceable Limit
15.002~15.008 (0.5906~0.5909)	Replace if over 15.08 (0.5937)

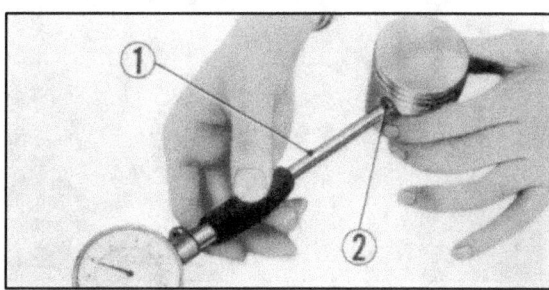

① Cylinder gauge ② Piston pin bore
Fig. 4-52. Measuring piston pin bore

8. Piston pin diameter

    Measure the piston pin diameter at both ends and center. (Fig. 4-53)

Standard Value	Serviceable Limit
14.994~15.000 (0.590~0.5906)	Replace if under 14.96 (0.5889)

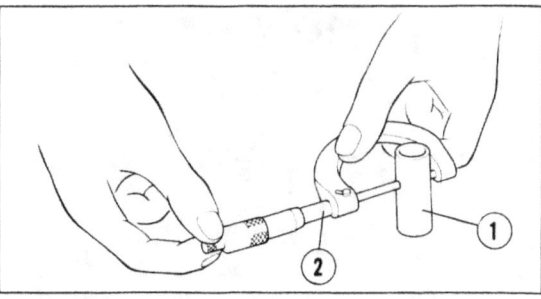

① Piston pin ② Micrometer
Fig. 4-53. Measuring piston pin diameter

D. Reassembly

1. Install the piston rings on the piston in the reverse order of disassembly.

NOTE:

- When a new piston ring is installed, a check should be made to assure that the ring fits freely in the groove. This can be done by rolling the piston ring externally in the piston groove. (Fig. 4-54)

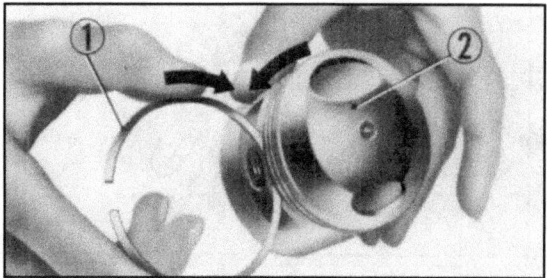

① Piston ring ② Piston
Fig. 4-54. Rolling the piston ring in the piston groove

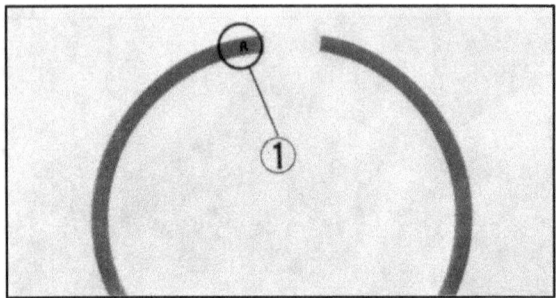

① Manufacturer's mark
Fig. 4-55.

- The rings must not be installed upside down; this will cause oil pumping. The top side of the ring is etched at the opening with the initial of the manufacturer's name. (Fig. 4-55)

2. Assemble the piston to the small end of the connecting rod. Only a slight hand pressure should be required to insert the piston pin. Always install a new piston pin clip.

① Piston pin clip
Fig. 4-56. Setting the piston pin clip

NOTE:
- Cover the crankcase with a rag to prevent possibility of the pin clip from dropping into the crankcase.
- Set the clip so that the opening is away from the groove cutout. (Fig. 4-56)

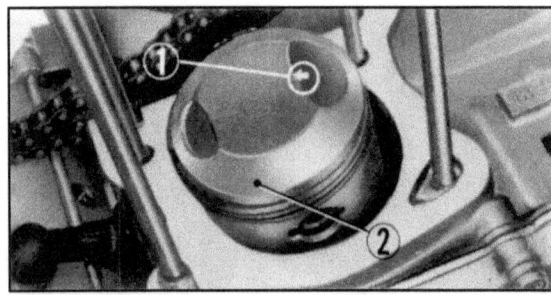

① Arrow mark ② Piston
Fig. 4-57. Assembling the piston

- The piston must be assembled so that the arrow marking stamped on the piston head is toward the front when the engine is in the normal attitude. (Fig. 4-57)

3. Assemble the cam chain guide to the cylinder.
4. Install the cylinder.

NOTE:
- The ring gap of the three piston rings should be staggered 120° apart.
- Use of the piston ring compressor tool (Tool No. 07954-2510000 (CB/CL250), 07954-5510000 (CB/CL350) for installing the cylinder will prevent breakage of the piston ring and, further, it will simplify the work. (Fig. 4-58)
- Check to make sure that the cylinder gasket and the two locating pins on the crankcase are installed in place; also check to make sure that the O ring and cam chain guide are installed on the cylinder skirt.

① Cylinder ② Piston ③ Piston ring compressor
Fig. 4-58. Installing the cylinder

4·7 CAM CHAIN TENSIONER (hydraulic type)

A. Description

The cam chain tensioner is, as shown in the figure at left, of a hydraulic type and provides a mean of maintaining the cam chain tension constant at all times. In operating principle, it is based on a condition of equilibrium sought by the two forces, one by the hydraulic force and the other by the chain tension. Oil delivered under pressure from the pump flows through orifice ① provided in the upper crankcase and check valve ⑦ built in the lower section of cam chain tensioner holder ②, and then enters a chamber provided in the holder. As the oil enters the chamber, the pressure increases therein and pushes one end of tensioner push rod ④ and in turn tensioner roller ⑤ against cam chain. When the chain tension overcomes the hydraulic force, the check valve opens to reduce the pressure in the chamber, permitting the roller to move away from the cam chain until the chain tension is balanced with the force of the spring ③. (Fig. 4-59)

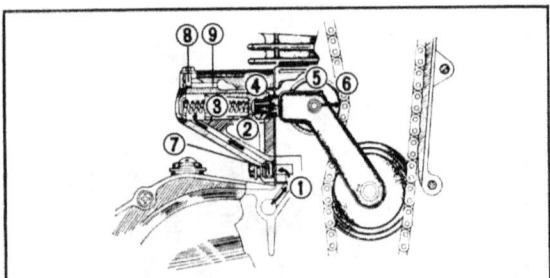

① Orifice ② Cam chain tensioner holder ③ Spring
④ Tensioner push rod ⑤ Tensioner roller
⑥ Cam chain ⑦ Check valve ⑧ Bolt ⑨ Air passage
Fig. 4-59. Cam chain tensioner mechanism

B. Disassembly

1. Cam chain tensioner holder assembly can be disassembled from the cylinder by removing the four mounting bolts. (Dismounting of the engine from the frame is not necessary when disassembling only the cam chain tensioner holder).
2. Disassemble the cylinder from the crankcase in accordance with section 4·6B on page 39.
3. Remove the cam chain roller pin rubber which holds the cam chain tensioner from the crankcase. (Fig. 4-60)

NOTE:

When disassembling, exercise care so that the small cam chain roller pin rubber will not be dropped in the crankcase.

4. Remove the cam chain tensioner

   Separate the cam chain tensioner from the case.
5. By removing the cam chain roller pin the cam chain guide roller can be removed from the cam chain tensioner. (Fig. 4-61)

C. Inspection

1. Immerse the cam chain tensioner holder in engine oil, operate the tensioner pushrod in the direction indicated by the arrow in Fig. 4-62. If the pressure is maintained, the pushrod should hydraulically lock and should not move or it may move very minutely. This indicates that the cam chain tensioner holder assembly is in good condition.
2. Cam chain tensioner (manual type)

   An improved cam chain tensioner is installed on CB (CL) 250E-1013001, CB (CL) 350E-1079079, SL350E-1000001~ and subsequent. The adjustment of cam chain tensioner is performed in the following manner.

   A loose cam chain will cause the valve timing to change, resulting in poor performance. It will also cause excessive engine noise.

   1) Adjustment must be made when the four valves are closed completely and the tappets are free. This position occurs 90° A.T.D.C. on the compression stroke of the left side cylinder. Rotate the generator rotor counterclockwise until index mark on the stator is 90° A.T.D.C. (after 90° "LT" mark). If the valves are still lifted, rotate the generator rotor 360° and realign same above.(Fig. 4-62A)
   2) Loosen the lock nut ③ and the tensioner lock bolt ②. When the lock bolts is loosened, this allows an internal, spring loaded plunger to reposition itself and automatically provide correct tension.
   3) Tighten the lock bolt and lock nut. This locks the internal plunger in position.

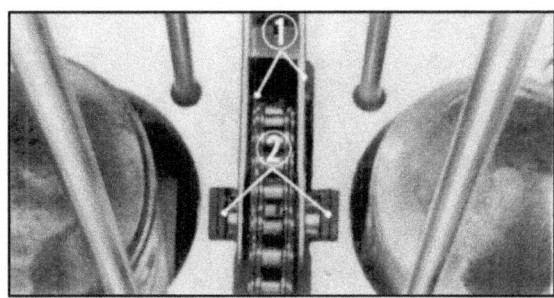

① Cam chain tensioner ② Cam chain roller pin rubber
Fig. 4-60. Removing the cam chain roller pin rubber

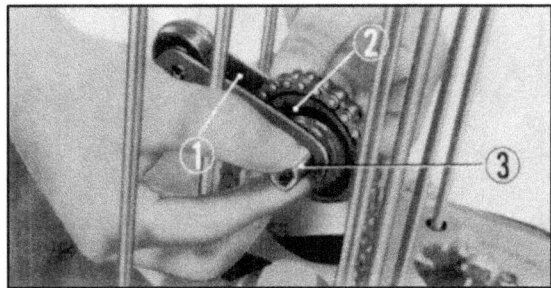

① Cam chain tensioner ② Cam chain guide roller
③ Cam chain roller pin
Fig. 4-61. Removing the cam chain guide roller

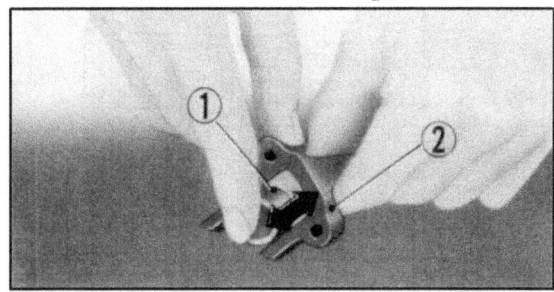

① Tensioner pushrod ② Tensioner holder
Fig. 4-62. Checking pushrod operation

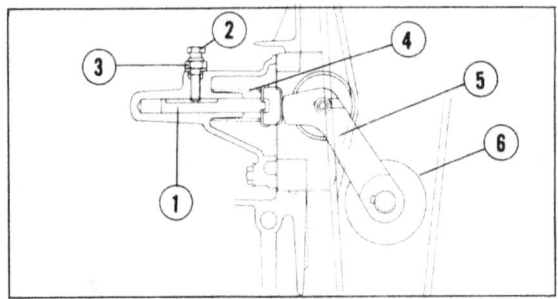

① Push bar ② Tensioner lock bolt
③ Tensioner lock nut ④ Tensioner spring
⑤ Cam chain tensioner ⑥ Cam chain guide roller
Fig. 4-62A.

D. Reassembly

1. After checking all the parts for damage and distortion, perform the assembly in the reverse order of removal.

NOTE:

When installing the cam chain tensioner into the case, the cutout on the cam chain roller pin must be positioned toward the top; then install the roller pin rubber.

4·8 LUBRICATING SYSTEM

A. Description

The lubricating system is of a pressure-feed type using a plunger type pump. The oil circuits of the system are schematically illustrated in the figure at left.

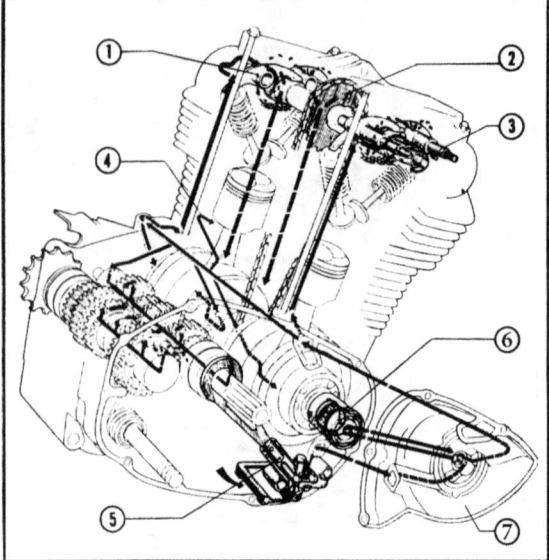

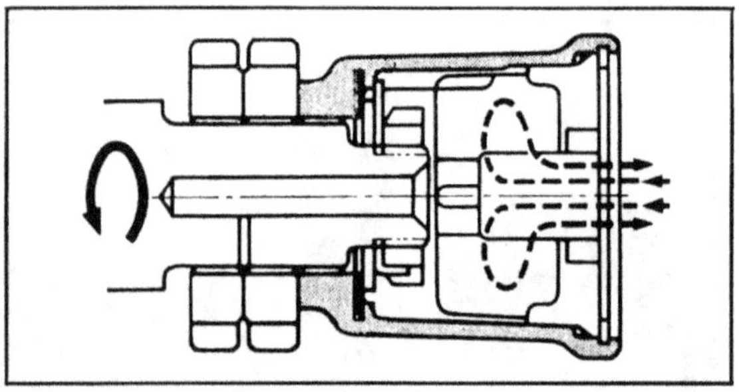

① Rocker arm ② Cam sprocket ③ Rocker arm pin
④ To cam chain tensioner ⑤ Plunger oil pump
⑥ Centrifugal oil filter ⑦ R. crankcase cover
Fig. 4-63. Oil lubrication system

The oil filter is of a centrifugal type. As the oil enters the filter and is picked up by the spinning vanes of the filter cover, foreign matter such as metallic dust and carbon particles are separated from the oil by centrifugal force. The oil is cleaned in this manner and fed to the engine parts through the outlet port in the center section of the filter cover.

Fig. 4-64. Cross section of oil filter

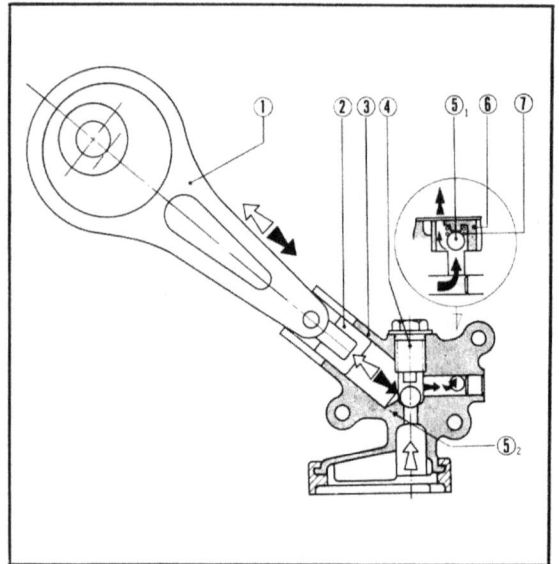

The oil pump, as shown in the figure at left, consists of a pump rod (drive rod) ①, a pump plunger ②, a pump body ③ and steel-ball type suction and delivery valves. The pump rod input end is eccentrically mounted on the clutch outer and is driven at the outer end in a reciprocating motion to the plunger ② for pumping operation. Delivery valve steel ball ⑤ is spring-loaded.

Fig. 4-65.

B. Disassembly

1. Drain the engine oil.
2. Remove the kick starter pedal from the kick starter pinion shaft.
3. Remove the mounting screws and disassemble R. crankcase cover. (Fig. 4-66)

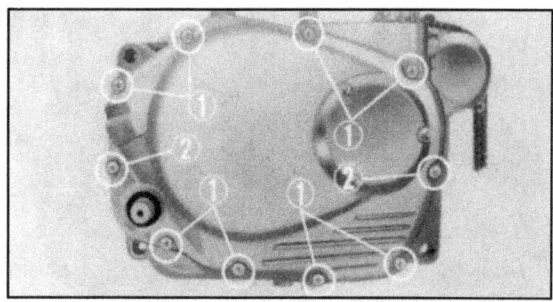

① 6×28 cross screws ② 6×36 cross screws
Fig. 4-66. Removing R. crankcase cover

4. Remove the circlip and filter cap. (Fig. 4-67)

① Circlip ② Oil filter cap ③ Pliers ④ 6 mm hex. bolt
Fig. 4-67. Removing the oil filter cap

5. Straighten the tongue of the spring, washer pawls and remove the 16 mm lock nut by using the T-handle lock nut wrench (Tool No. 07916-2830000). The filter rotor can then be removed. (Fig. 4-68)

① Oil filter rotor ② T-handle lock nut wrench
③ Block
Fig. 4-68. Removing the oil filter rotor

6. Unscrew the four 6 mm bolts and remove the clutch springs, pressure plates, friction discs and clutch plates. (Fig. 4-69)

① Clutch plate and friction disks
Fig. 4-69. Removing the clutch plates and friction disks

7. Remove the 25 mm circlip and disassemble the clutch center. (Fig. 4-70)
8. Unlock the oil pump bolt locking washer and remove the bolts.

① 25 mm circlip ② Clutch center ③ Pliers
Fig. 4-70. Removing the clutch center

46

① Clutch outer ② Oil pump
Fig. 4-71. Removing the clutch outer

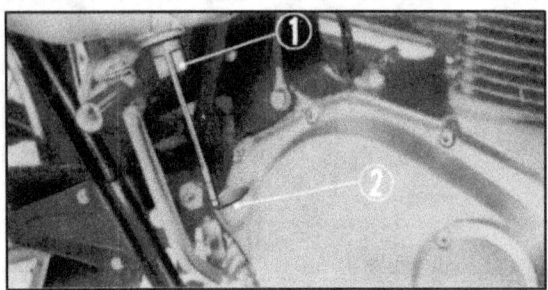

① Oil filler cap ② Oil filler opening
Fig. 4-72. Oil filler cap

① Drain plug
Fig. 4-73. Oil drain plug

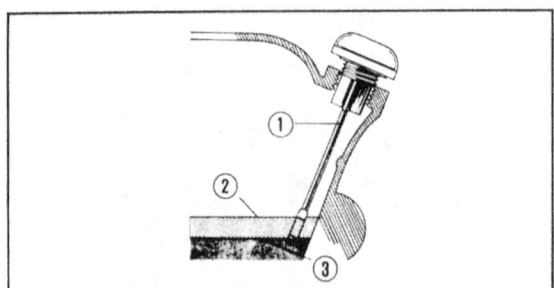

① Level gauge ② Upper limit ③ Lower limit
Fig. 4-74. Oil level

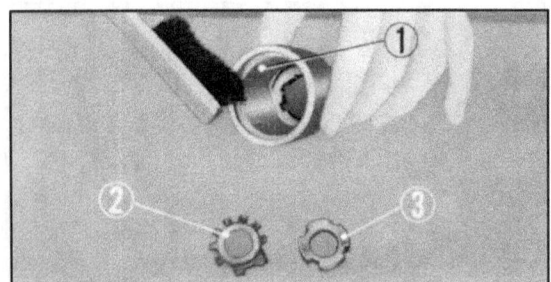

① Oil filter rotor ② Lock washer ③ Lock nut
Fig. 4-75. Cleaning oil filter

9. Remove the oil pump together with the clutch outer. (Fig. 4-71)

C. Inspection

1. Engine oil check and change

   The engine oil should be changed after the initial 500 miles and then every 1500 km (1000 miles).

   1) Remove the oil filler cap and drain plug on the bottom of the crankcase and drain all the engine oil. Draining will be hastened if oil filler cap is removed. (Fig. 4-72)

   2) After draining, retighten the drain plug and pour new oil into the engine through the oil filler opening.

   3) If the oil level is between lower and upper limits on the oil level gauge dipstick with the filler cap not threaded in but just inserted, it indicates that the oil level is correct. (Fig. 4-74)

   NOTE :
   - If the oil level falls below the upper limit mark on the oil level gauge dipstick, add oil through the filler up to the upper limit mark to keep the engine in good condition.
   - Do not overfill the crankcase with oil otherwise, the excessive oil flows out of the breather.
   - When driving the motorcycle in unusually dusty condition, it is recommended that oil changes be performed at more frequent intervals than what is specified in the maintenance schedule ; this will have a very beneficial effect on the performance and serviceable life of the engine.
   - Always use only the oils classified for A.P.I. service M.S.-D.G. (and/or D.M.) or the use of all season SAE group 20W-40 oil is recommended.

2. Cleaning oil filter

   (The oil filter can be removed without dismounting the engine from the frame.)

   Clean the inside of the filter rotor and remove all dirt, metal particles and any other foreign objects. (Fig. 4-75)

   1) Remove the oil filter cover, unfasten the circlip which mounts the oil filter rotor in place and pull off the rotor cap.

   2) Wash off the accumulation of dirt from within the rotor with kerosene or solvent.

NOTE:

- When reinstalling the rotor cap, the rotor cap vane should be matched to the groove on the inside wall of the rotor. (Fig. 4-76)

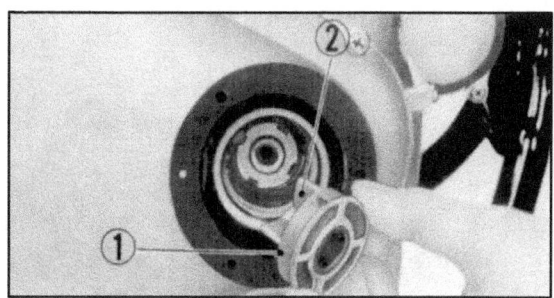

① Rotor cap ② Vane
Fig. 4-76. Rotor cap installation

- Before installing the oil filter cover, check to make sure that the oil guide is operating smoothly. (Fig. 4-77)

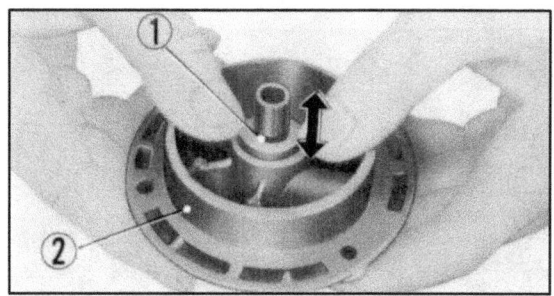

① Oil guide ② Oil filter cover
Fig. 4-77. Checking guide operation

- When installing the oil filter cover, make sure to position it properly. (Fig. 4-78)

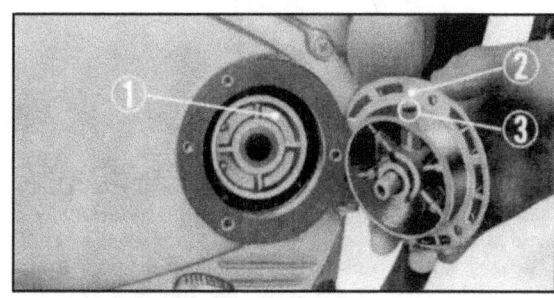

① Rotor cap ② Oil filter cover ③ Oil filter opening
Fig. 4-78. Oil filter cover installation

3. R. crankcase and oil filter inspection

   Inspect the crankcase and oil filter covers for cracks and also for any damage to the mating surfaces since they may cause oil leaks. The damaged areas may be reworked with fine oilstone if not excessively damaged.

4. Oil pump body bore dimension

   Inspect the bore of the oil pump body for any damage and measure the diameter at 90° apart at both top and bottom. (Fig. 4-79)

mm (inch)

	Standard Value	Serviceable Limit
Bore diameter	16.000~16.018 (0.630~0.631)	Replace if over 16.1 (0.634)

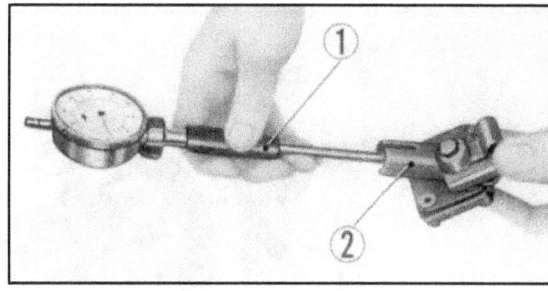

① Cylinder gauge ② Oil pump body
Fig. 4-79. Measuring pump body bore

5. Oil pump plunger dimension

   Measure the diameter of the oil pump plunger with a micrometer. (Fig. 4-80)

mm (inch)

	Standard Value	Serviceable Limit
Plunger diameter	15.955~15.970 (0.628~0.629)	Replace if under 15.930 (0.627)

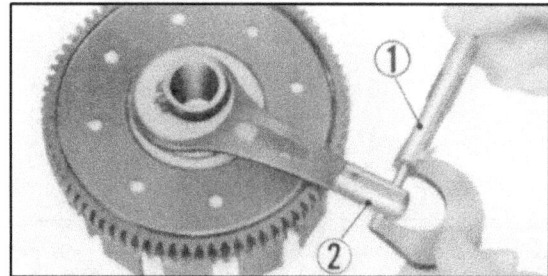

① Micrometer ② Oil pump plunger
Fig. 4-80. Measuring pump plunger

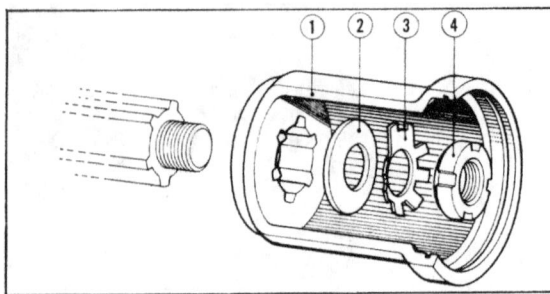

① Oil filter rotor   ② Oil filter rotor lock washer
③ 16 mm lock washer   ④ 16 mm lock nut
Fig. 4-81. Assembling oil filter rotor lock washer

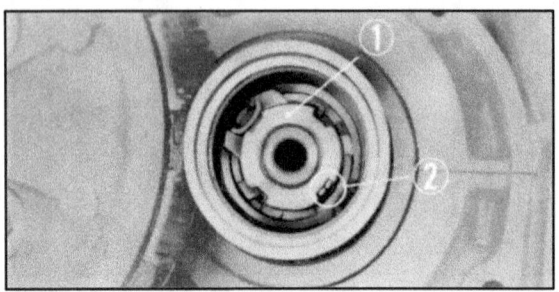

① Lock nut   ② Lock washer
Fig. 4-82. Tightening the lock nut

D. Reassembly

1. Reassemble the oil pump in the reverse procedure of disassembly 4.8B on page 45.

NOTE:
- The oil pump lock washer should be replaced with a new item.
- The circlip used to set the clutch center is of a special dimension (25×1.5 mm) therefore exercise care that the standard 25 mm circlip is not used.

2. When assembling the oil filter rotor on the crankshaft, assemble the oil filter rotor lock washer, 16 mm lock washer and the lock nut in that order. The oil filter rotor lock washer should be assembled with the tab toward the outside. (Fig. 4-81)

3. Make sure that the 16 mm lock nut is properly torqued and locked to prevent loosening.

   Standard torque:
   300–320 kg-cm (21.7–23.1 ft-lbs)

   (Fig. 4-82)

4. Align filter cap head to the groove incorporated within the rotor wall, assemble the filter cap install and set the circlip.

4·9 CLUTCH

A. Description

The clutch is of a wet, multiple-disc type. As shown in the figures below, clutch plates A ④$_1$ and B ④$_2$ ("drive plates"), which are capable of sliding axially on clutch center ⑤, are "sandwiched" between friction discs ③ ("driven discs") engaged in clutch outer ②$_2$. In normal engaged condition of the clutch, pressure plate ⑦, upon which the force of clutch springs ⑥ is acting, presses the stack of the disks and the plates against the clutch outer. Under this condition, engine power is transmitted through primary drive gears ②$_1$ to the transmission main shaft. As the clutch lever is squeezed to disengage the clutch, lifter rod ⑨ is moved in such a direction as to push the pressure plate away from the discs and the plates, opposing the force of the clutch springs. Now the pressure at the friction surfaces of the power transmitting parts is reduced to zero, resulting in disengagement of the clutch.

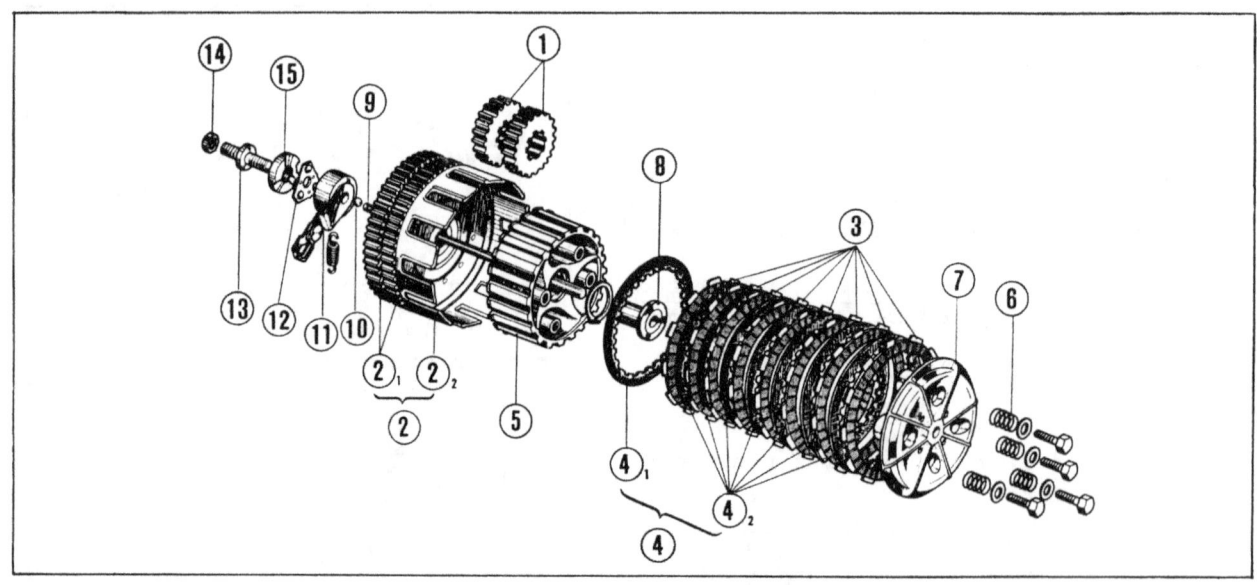

① Primary drive gear   ② Clutch outer complete   (②$_1$ Primary driven gear   ②$_2$ Clutch outer)   ③ Clutch friction disk (8 ea.)
④ Clutch plate   (④$_1$ Clutch plate A   ④$_2$ Clutch plate B)   ⑤ Clutch center   ⑥ Clutch spring   ⑦ Clutch pressure plate
⑧ Clutch lifter joint piece   ⑨ Clutch lifter rod   ⑩ #10 Steel ball   ⑪ Clutch lever   ⑫ Steel ball (clutch ball retainer)
⑬ Clutch adjuster   ⑭ Clutch adjuster lock nut   ⑮ Clutch adjusting cam
Fig. 4-83A.

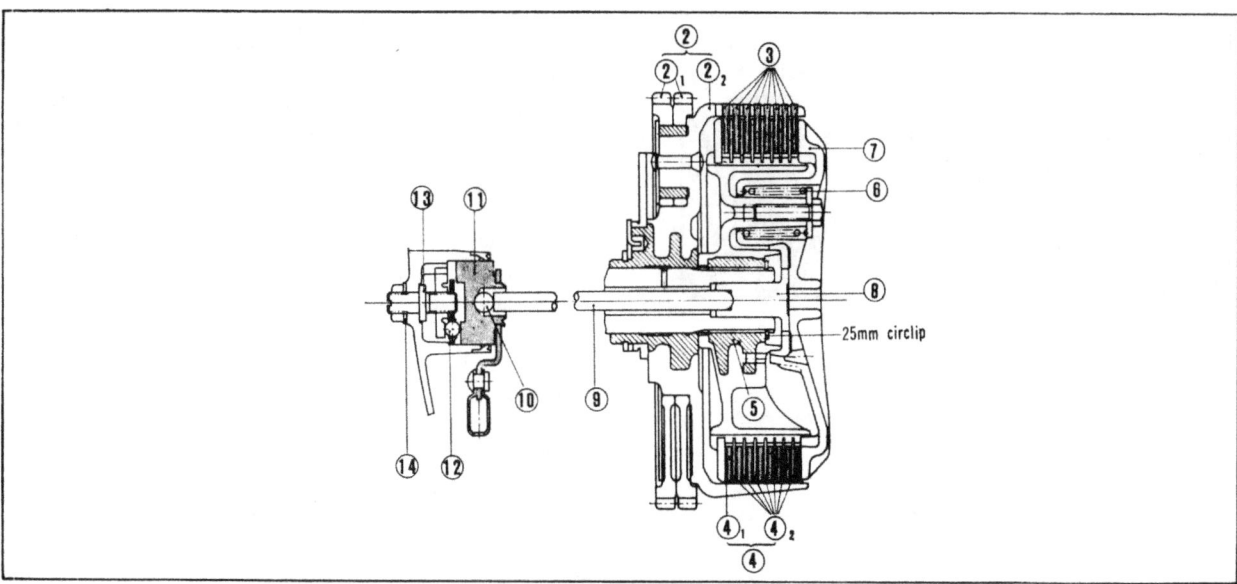

Fig. 4-83B. Sectional view of clutch

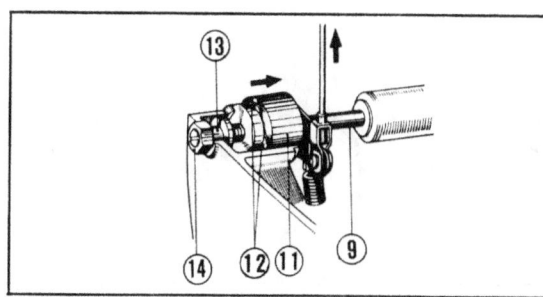

Fig. 4-83C. Clutch adjusting mechanism

B. Disassembly

Disassemble the clutch in accordance with 4·8B on page 45.

C. Inspection

1. Clutch adjustment

1) Screw the clutch cable adjusting bolt A, located on the clutch lever, all the way into the clutch lever bracket. (Fig. 4-84)

2) Turn the clutch cable adjusting bolt B, located on the drive chain cover, in the direction Ⓐ to loosen the clutch cable. (Fig. 4-85)

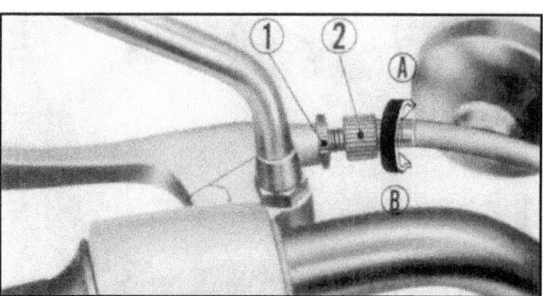

① Circular lock nut ② Clutch cable adjusting bolt A
Fig. 4-84.

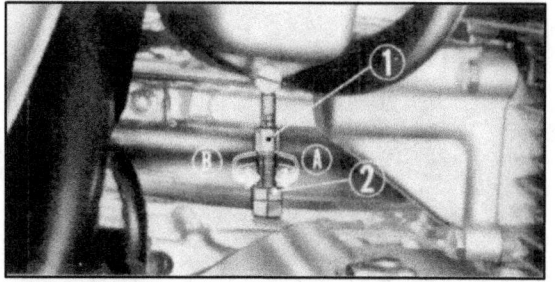

① Clutch cable adjusting bolt B ② Lock nut
Fig. 4-85.

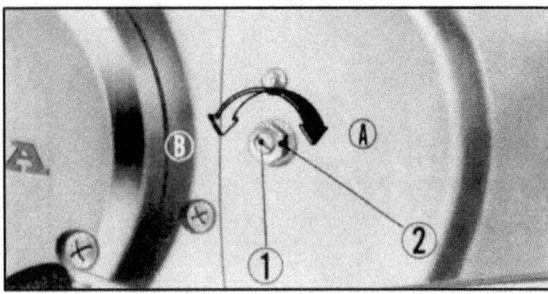

① Clutch adjusting screw
② Clutch adjusting screw lock nut
Fig. 4-86.

3) Loosen the clutch adjusting screw lock nut, turn the clutch adjusting screw in the counterclockwise direction until a slight resistance is felt. From this position turn the adjusting screw in the clockwise by 1/4 turn and tighten the clutch adjusting screw lock nut. (**Fig. 4-86**)

4) Turn the clutch cable adjusting bolt B, located on the drive chain cover, in the ⓑ direction so that there is approximately 3/4 in of free play at the clutch lever; then tighten the lock nut. (**Fig. 4-85**)

5) The remaining clutch lever free play is obtained by the clutch cable adjusting bolt A. (**Fig. 4-84**)

6) After the adjustment had been made, check to see that the clutch is not slipping or that the clutch is properly disengaging.

    a. When the kick starter is used, does the engine easily start without the clutch, slipping.

    b. After the engine starts, pull the clutch lever and shift into gear, and make sure that the engine does not stall, nor the motorcycle start to creep.

    c. Gradually release the clutch lever and open the throttle, the motorcycle should start smoothly and gradually accelerate.

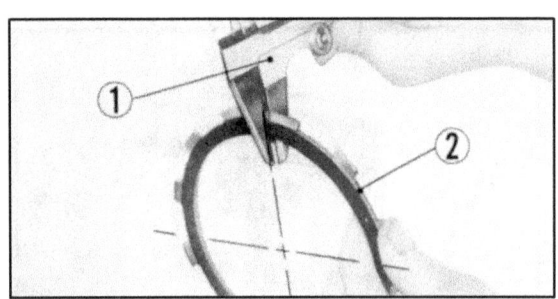

① Vernier caliper ② Friction disk
Fig. 4-87. Measuring thickness of friction disk

2. Friction disc dimension

Measure the thickness of the friction disc with a vernier caliper. (**Fig. 4-87**)

mm (inch)

Standard Value	Serviceable Limit
2.62～2.78 (0.031～0.110)	Replace if under 2.3 (0.906)

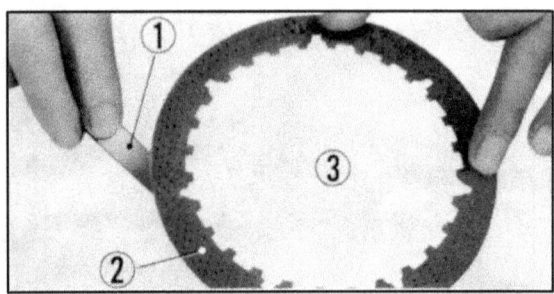

① Thickness gauge ② Clutch plate ③ Surface plate
Fig. 4-88. Measuring the warpage of clutch plate

3. Clutch plate warpage

Measure the warpage of the clutch plate on the surface plate using a thickness gauge. (**Fig. 4-88**)

mm (inch)

Standard Value	Serviceable Limit
0.15 max. (0.006)	Replace or repair if over 0.3 (0.012)

4. Clutch spring dimension

Measure the free length of the clutch spring with a vernier caliper. (**Fig. 4-89**)

mm (inch)

	Standard Value	Serviceable Limit
Spring free length CB/CL250	35.5 (1.390)	Replace if under 34.20 (1.345)
Spring free length CB/CL350	31.9 (1.258)	Replace if under 30.50 (1.200)

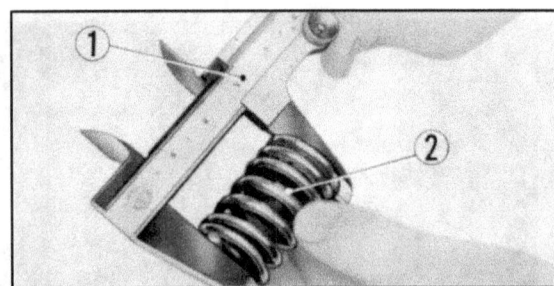

① Vernier caliper ② Clutch spring
Fig. 4-89. Measuring free length of clutch spring

D. Reassembly

Reassemble the clutch in the reverse procedure of disassembly 4·8B on page 45.

4·10 CRANKSHAFT AND CONNECTING RODS

A. Description

The crankshaft is made from high carbon steel and consists of three sections such as left, center and right sections and counterweights, which are put together by press-fitting. It is supported at four places by antifriction bearings – three roller bearings and one ball bearing of heavy duty type – so that it is fully balanced both statically and dynamically. Mounted on the crankshaft is a starting sprocket, an a-c generator and a cam chain drive sprocket. The connecting rods are of chrome-molybdenum material and are made by die-forging. Their big ends are supported by needle roller bearings.

Fig. 4-90. Crankshaft

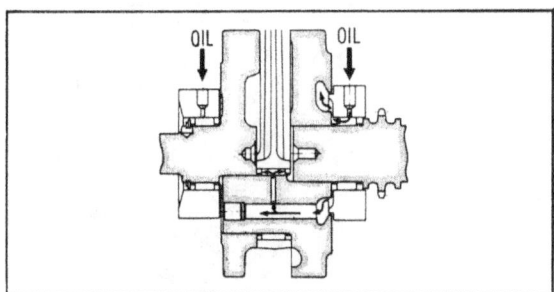

Fig. 4-91. Oil channel

B. Disassembly

1. Disassemble the cam case in accordance with section 4·8B on page 45.
2. Disassemble the cylinder head in accordance with section 4·5B on page 31.
3. Disassemble the cylinder in accordance with 4·6B on page 39.
4. Disassemble cam chain tensioner in accordance with section 4·7B on page 43.
5. Remove oil filter, oil pump, clutch in accordance with section 4·8B on page 45.
6. Remove the gear shift spindle.
7. Remove the neutral lead connection from the neutral switch (Fig. 4-92)

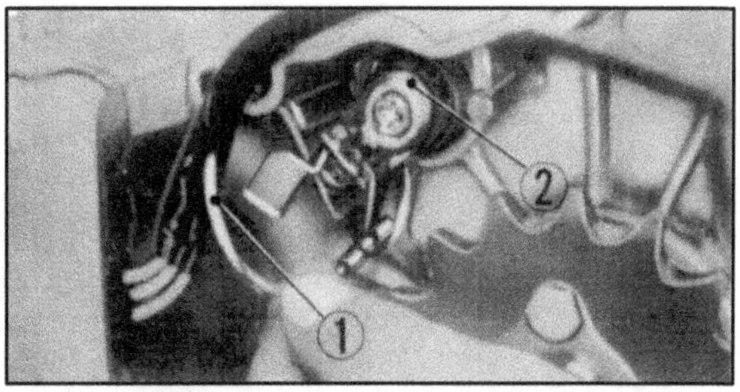

① Neutral lead connection ② Neutral switch
Fig. 4-92. Removing the neutral lead connection

8. Remove the left crankcase cover. (Fig. 4-93)

① L. crankcase cover
Fig. 4-93. Removing the L. crankcase cover

9. Remove the generator rotor by using a generator rotor puller (Tool No.07933-2160000). (Fig. 4-94)

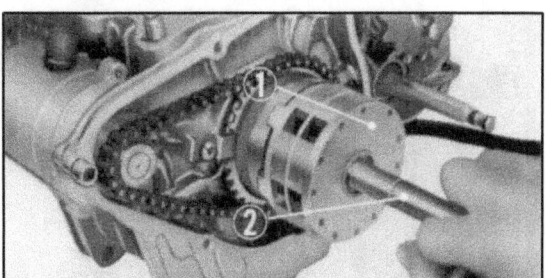

① Generator rotor ② Generator rotor puller
Fig. 4-94. Removing the generator rotor

52

① Starting motor sprocket ② Starting sprocket
③ Starting chain
Fig. 4-95. Removing the starting sprocket

10. Remove the starting sprocket set plate and take out the starting sprocket together with the starting motor sprocket. (Fig. 4-95)
11. Separate the lower crankcase by removing the case fixing bolts.
12. Unscrew the center bearing cap bolts and remove the crankshaft.

C. Inspection

1. Measure amount of bend

   Support the crankshaft by the center bearing on V-block. Rotate the crankshaft with the right and left connecting rod and measure the amount of runout with a dial gauge. (Fig. 4-96)

   mm (inch)

	Standard Value	Serviceable Limit
Shaft	0.02 (0.0008)	Repair or replace if over 0.15 (0.006)
Counter weight	0.10 (0.004)	Repair or replace if over 0.3 (0.012)

① Small dial gauge ② Crankshaft ③ V-block
Fig. 4-96. Measuring runout of crankshaft

2. Main bearing diametrical clearance

   Support the crankshaft on V-blocks at two points and measure the amount of clearance by setting the dial gauge on top of the outer race. (Fig. 4-97)

   mm (inch)

Standard Value	Serviceable Limit
0.012~0.020 (0.0005~0.0008)	Replace if over 0.05 (0.002)

① Dial gauge ② Bearing outer race
Fig. 4-97. Measuring the diametrical clearance

3. Connecting rod diametrical clearance

   Support the crankshaft on V-block at two points, move the connecting rod in the vertical direction and measure the amount of clearance with a dial gauge. (Fig. 4-98)

   mm (inch)

Standard Value	Serviceable Limit
0.004~0.012 (0.0002~0.0005)	Replace if over 0.05 (0.002)

① Dial gauge ② Connecting rod
Fig. 4-98. Measuring the connecting rod diametrical clearance

4. Connecting rod side clearance

   Measure the amount of side clearance of the connecting rod with a thickness gauge. (Fig. 4-99)

   mm (inch)

Standard Value	Serviceable Limit
0.07~0.33 (0.0028~0.0130)	Replace if over 0.60 (0.023)

① Thickness gauge ② Connecting rod
Fig. 4-99. Measuring the connecting rod side clearance

5. Connecting rod small end bore

Measure the small end bore with a cylinder gauge. (Fig. 4-100)

mm (inch)

Standard Value	Serviceable Limit
15.016~15.034 (0.591~0.592)	Replace if over 15.07 (0.593)

① Connecting rod ② Cylinder gauge
Fig. 4-100. Measuring small end bore

D. Reassembly

1. The dowel pin on the bearing outer race is firmly installed into the grooves of the crankcase. (Fig. 4-101)
2. Assemble the crankshaft in the reverse procedure of disassembly in accordance with 4·10B on page 51.

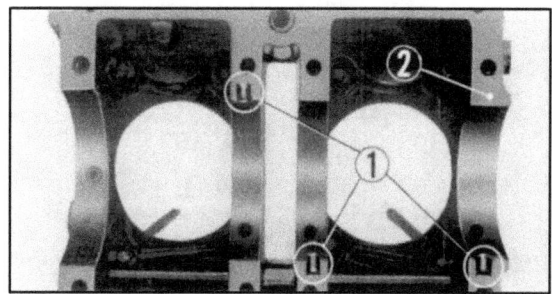

① Dowel pin grooves ② Upper crankcase
Fig. 4-101.

NOTE:

- Uniformly tighten the four center bearing cap bolts in a diagonal sequence to **220–240 kg-cm (15.9~17.4 ft-lbs)** torque. (Fig. 4-102)
- Tighten the A.C. generator rotor setting bolt to **220~240 kg-cm (15.9~17.4 ft-lbs)** torque.

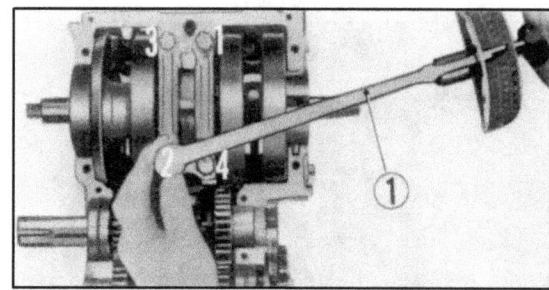

① Torque wrench
Fig. 4-102. Tightening the bearing cap bolts

4·11 TRANSMISSION

A. Description

The transmission is of a constant-mesh type and provides a selection of five speeds – the flow of power in the respective gear positions are illustrated in Fig. 4-103 through Fig. 4-108. It has two shafts; namely, a main shaft (input shaft) and a countershaft (output shaft) on which various speed gears are spline-mounted, with dog engagement for the main shaft second/third and fourth gears and the countershaft third and fourth gears. The shafts are supported by ball bearings. On the output end of the countershaft is mounted the drive sprocket.

B. Disassembly

1. Disassemble the cam case in accordance with section 4·8B on page 45.
2. Disassemble the cylinder head in accordance with section 4·5B on page 31.
3. Disassemble the cylinder in accordance with section 4·6B on page 39.
4. Disassemble the cam chain tensioner in accordance with section 4·7B on page 43.

Fig. 4-103. Neutral

Fig. 4-104. Low gear (C4 is shifted)

Fig. 4-105. Second gear (C4 is shifted)

Fig. 4-106. Third gear (C4 is shifted)

Fig. 4-107. Fourth gear (M2-M3 is shifted)

① Small dial gauge
Fig. 4-109. Measuring the gear backlash

5. Disassemble the oil pump and clutch in accordance with section 4·8B on page 45.
6. Disassemble the crankshaft in accordance with section 4·10B on page 52.
7. Disassemble the transmission gear shift assembly from the upper crankcase.
8. Remove from the main shaft, the respective needle roller bearing and the M5, M2-M3 gears; remove the circlip and thrust washer and then remove the M4 gear.
9. Remove from the countershaft the respective needle roller bearings and the C1, C4 gears; remove the circlip thrust washer which retains the C3 gear and remove C3 and C2 gears. Remove the circlip and thrust washer retaining C5 gear; remove C5 gear from the shaft.

Note: a 25 mm thrust washer and lock washer are employed in between the C2 and C3 gears for engines manufactured after engine serial No. **CB/CL250E-1005974 or CB/CL350E-1042395,** after removing the C3 gear remove the lock washer and thrust washer.

Refer to Service Bulletin No. 012 for CB/CL250 & 350 and Parts News No. 8034 for CB250 concerning the details of the subject matter.

Fig. 4-108. Top gear (M2-M3 is shifted)

C. Inspection

1. Measuring backlash

   Hold the mating gear so that it does not move and lightly rock the gear being measured. Measure the amount of backlash using a small dial gauge.

   mm (inch)

Item	Standard Value	Serviceable Limit
Low, 2nd	0.044~0.133 (0.0017~0.0052)	Replace if over 0.2 (0.008)
3rd, 4th, 5th	0.046~0.14 (0.0018~0.0055)	Replace if over 0.2 (0.008)

	Standard Value	Serviceable Limit
M4, M5	0.02~0.062 (0.0008~0.0024)	Replace if over 0.1 (0.0039)
C1	0.02~0.054 (0.000~0.002)	Replace if over 0.1 (0.0039)
C2, C3	0.04~0.084 (0.0016~0.002)	Replace if over 0.1 (0.0047)

2. Wear to transmission gear

   Gears after long period of use will develop wear to the teeth and dogs resulting in uneven contact which produces noise or cause the dogs to disengage. To correct this condition, the mating gears must be replaced in sets.

3. Clearance between gear and shaft

   Measure the bore of the gear with a cylinder gauge or an inside micrometer; measure the shaft diameter with a micrometer and compute the clearance. (Refer to the above table)

4. Place the gears in neutral position and check to assure that the dogs are not clashing and the respective gears are operating smoothly.

① Bearing setting ring ② Bearing dowel pin
③ 5205 HS, ball bearing ④ 8×34×8, oil seal
⑤ 20 mm, needle bearing ⑥ Mainshaft top gear
⑦ Mainshaft second & third gear ⑧ 25 mm, circlip
⑨ 25 mm, thrust washer ⑩ Mainshaft fourth gear
⑪ Transmission mainshaft ⑫ 20 mm, needle bearing
⑬ Countershaft low gear ⑭ Countershaft fourth gear
⑮ Countershaft third gear ⑯ Countershaft second gear
⑰ Countershaft top gear ⑱ Drive sprocket fixing plate
⑲ Drive sprocket ⑳ 33×52×7, oil seal
㉑ Transmission countershaft ㉒ 24.5 mm, O ring
㉓ Transmission countershaft only ㉔ 6 mm, hex., bolt
㉕ 20 mm, thrust washer ㉖ 25 mm, lock washer
㉗ 25 mm, thrust washer B

D. Reassembly

Reassemble in the reverse sequence of disassembly in accordance with 4·11B on page 53.

NOTE:

- Make sure that the thrust washers and circlips are installed on the M4, C2 and C3 gears.
- Use only new circlips and properly installed in the groove.
- When assembling the bearings to the mainshaft and countershaft, make sure that the bearing with the oil groove is installed on the countershaft and the bearing without the oil groove on the main shaft.
- The installation of the bearing set rings and the dowel pins must not be forgotten.
- Assemble the left shift fork on gear C4, right shift fork on gear C5 and the center shift fork on gear M2-M3, and then assemble the mainshaft and the countershaft as a set. (Fig. 4-111)

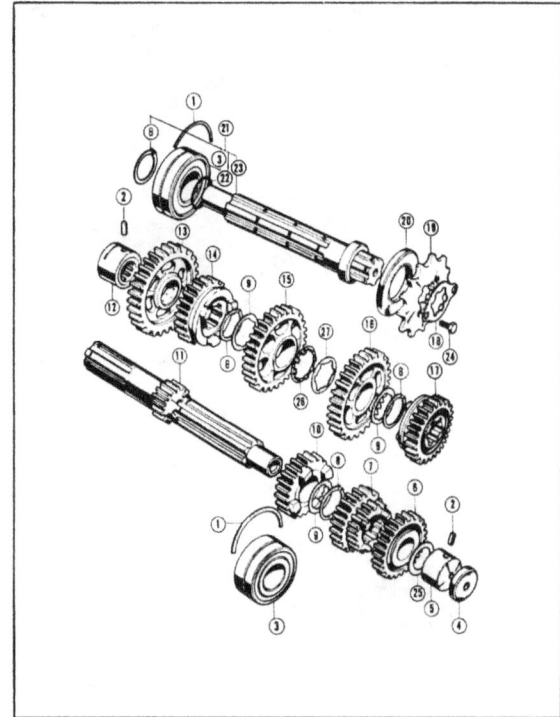

Fig. 4-110. Transmission

① Mainshaft ② Countershaft
Fig. 4-111. Assembling the gears

4·12 GEAR SHIFT MECHANISM

A. Description

The gear shift mechanism is a linkage arranged between the gear change pedal and the shift forks and includes a shift arm ②, a shift drum ④, a neutral stopper ①, a drum stopper ③, etc. as shown in Fig. 4-112.

When the pedal is depressed, the shift spindle rotates, causing the arm to rotate the drum. As the drum is so rotated, the fork is moved by the cam action of a groove cut in the drum to shift a gear. The drum stopper is provided to prevent unintentional gear engagement. Return spring is used to return the pedal to its original position when released and to place it in the neutral position for subsequent shifting.

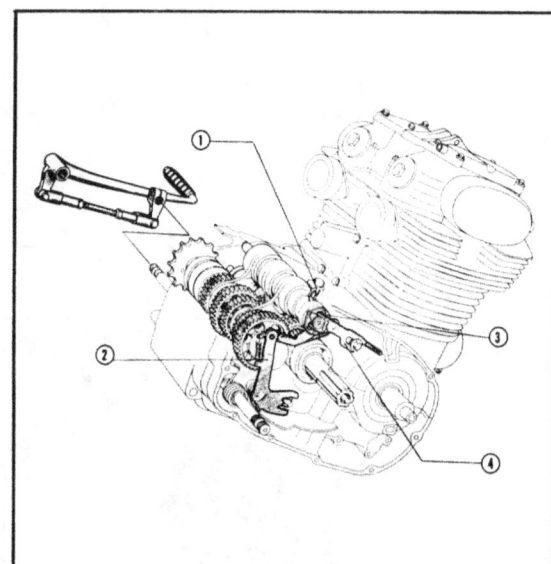

① Neutral stopper ② Gear shift arm
③ Drum stopper plate ④ Shift drum stopper
Fig. 4-112. Gear shift mechanism

① Gear shift drum ② Gear shift forks
Fig. 4-113. Removing the gear shift drum

① Dial gauge ② Gear shift fork
Fig. 4-114. Measuring the flatness of gear shift fork

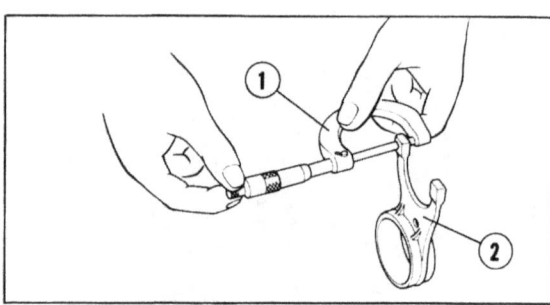

① Micrometer ② Gear shift fork
Fig. 4-115. Measuring the thickness of gear shift fork

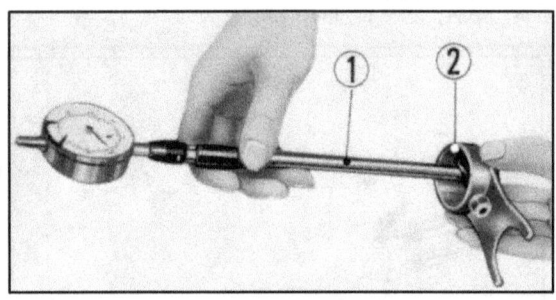

① Cylinder gauge ② Gear shift fork
Fig. 4-116. Measuring shift fork bore

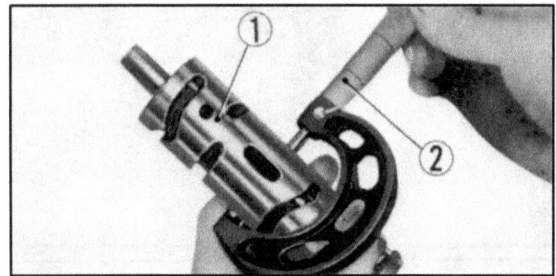

① Gear shift drum ② Micrometer
Fig. 4-117. Measuring the outer diameter

B. Disassembly

1. Separate the transmission gear assembly from the upper crankcase in accordance with 4·11B on page 53.
2. Remove the neutral switch rotor and then separate the shift drum stopper.
3. Remove the shift fork guide pin clip and then pull out guide pin.
4. Remove the gear shift drum by lightly tapping the case on the side of the neutral switch mounting.
(Fig. 4-113)

C. Inspection

1. Measure the amount of wear to the dog on the gear shift fork.

   Position the gear shift drum vertically on the V-block, measure the shift drum fork dog at two points.
   (Fig. 4-114)

   mm (inch)

Standard Value	Serviceable Limit
0.1 (0.004) max.	Replace if over 0.2 (0.008)

2. Measure the thickness of the gear shift fork dog.
   (Fig. 4-115)

   mm (inch)

	Standard Value	Serviceable Limit
A (fitted to C4, C5)	4.93~5.0 (0.94~0.197)	Replace if under 4.6 (0.181)
B (fitted to M2-M3)	6.93~6.0 (0.233~0.236)	Replace if under 5.6 (0.22)

3. Gear shift fork bore diameter

   Measure the bore with a cylinder gauge or an inside micrometer. (Fig. 4-116)

   mm (inch)

Standard Value	Serviceable Limit
40.0~40.025 (1.575~1.576)	Replace if over 40.075 (1.577)

4. Gear shift drum outside diameter

   Measure the gear shift drum using a micrometer.
   (Fig. 4-117)

   mm (inch)

Standard Value	Serviceable Limit
39.95~39.975 (1.5689~1.5738)	Replace if under 39.9 (1.571)

D. Reassembly

1. Assemble the gear shift drum into the upper case. At this time make sure that the location of the shift forks are in their respective position.

   The two outside and the center gear shift forks are different.

   NOTE:

   When assembling the gear shift drum, exercise care not to damage the oil seal fitted into the crankcase.

2. Install the shift fork guide pin into the shift fork and lock with a clip. (Fig. 4-118)

   NOTE:

   Check to make sure the clip is set securely.

3. Reassemble the remaining parts in the reverse sequence of disassembly.

   NOTE:

   Check to make sure that the action of the gear shift fork is smooth.

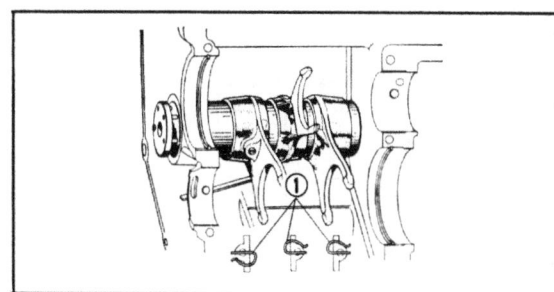

① Guide pin clip
Fig. 4-118.

4·13 KICK STARTER

A. Description

The kick starter is a device used to crank the engine for start-up, and consists essentially of a pinion, a spindle ④ and a return spring. When the starter pedal is depressed with a full kick stroke, the spindle is rotated in the direction of arrow (counterclockwise) within the pinion and the screw threads provided on the spindle cause the pinion, stationary because of its inertia, to move in the direction of arrow, engaging the countershaft low gear. Upon engagement, the torque or drive is transmitted through the clutch to the engine crankshaft, cranking the engine. When the pedal is released, the spindle rotates in the reverse direction (clockwise), causing the pinion to move away from the gear, disengaging the drive.

B. Disassembly

1. Disassemble the upper and lower crankcase.
2. Disassemble the kick starter spindle.

C. Inspection

Check the kick starter spindle and pinion, if damaged or worn, replace with a new part.

D. Reassembly

Reassemble the kick starter components in the reverse order of disassembly.

NOTE:

Do not forget to install the 18 mm circlip and the 18 mm washer. (Fig. 4-121)

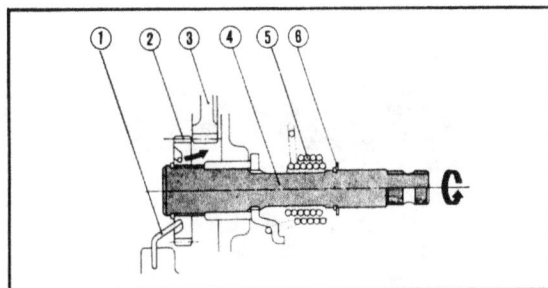

① Friction spring ② Kick starter pinion
③ Countershaft low gear ④ Kick starter spindle
⑤ Kick starter spring ⑥ 18 mm washer
Fig. 4-119. Kick starter mechanism

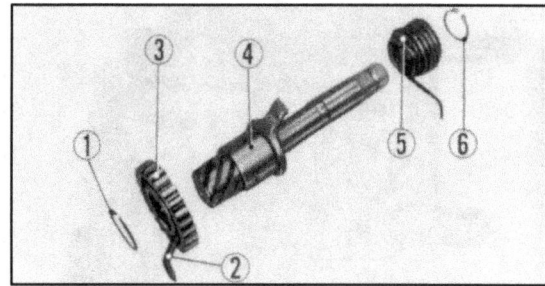

① 25 mm circlip ② Friction spring
③ Kick starter pinion ④ Kick starter spindle
⑤ Kick starter spring ⑥ 18 mm circlip
Fig. 4-120. Component parts of kick spindle

① 18 mm washer ② Kick starter spindle
Fig. 4-121. Installing the 18 mm washer

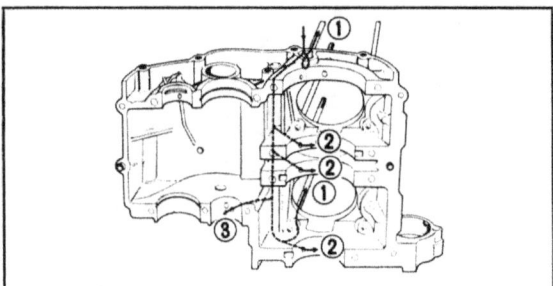

① To camshaft　② To crankshaft　③ To mainshaft
Fig. 4-122. Upper crankcase oil passage

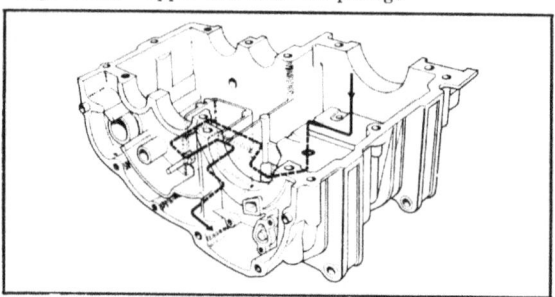

Fig. 4-123. Oil flow in the lower crankcase

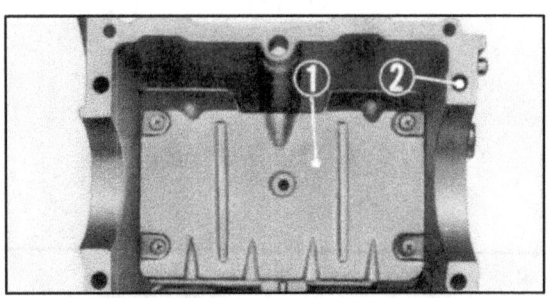

① Separator　② Lower crankcase
Fig. 4-124. Oil separator

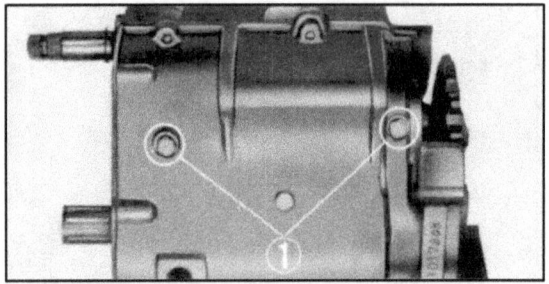

① 6 mm hex. bolts
Fig. 4-125. Tightening upper crankcase

① 8×97 hex. bolt　② 8×115 hex. bolt
③ 8×150 hex. bolt　④ 6×56 hex. bolt
⑤ 6×45 hex. bolt　⑥ 6×100 hex. bolt
⑦ 6×140 hex. bolt
Fig. 4-126. Tightening lower crankcase

4·14　CRANKCASES

A. Description

The upper and lower crankcases are a aluminium-alloy material and are one piece castings. They can be separated from each other and are internally provided with oil passages through which lubricating oil is fed to the crankshaft, camshaft, transmission etc.

Oil Separator Operation

The lower crankcase is provided with the oil separator which serves as baffle plate to prevent lubricating oil from splashing the crankshaft.

B. Disassembly

1. Disassemble the cam case in accordance with section 4·5B on page 31.
2. Disassemble the cylinder head and cylinder in accordance with section 4·5B on page 31.
3. Disassemble the cylinder in accordance with section 4·6B on page 39.
4. Disassemble the cam chain tensioner in accordance with section 4·6B on page 39.
5. Remove the R. crackcase cover, oil filter, oil pump and clutch in accordance with section 4·8B on page 45~46.
6. Remove the L. crankcase cover, A.C. generator rotor and starting clutch in accordance with 4·10B on page 51.
7. Loosen the two 6 mm hex. bolts on the upper side, the four 8 mm hex. bolts and eight 6 mm hex. bolts on the lower side, and remove the lower case.

C. Inspection

Check for damage especially around mating surfaces since even a small defect such as scratch will cause oil leaks. Repair should be made with an oil stone.

D. Reassembly

1. Check to make sure that the kick starter is properly engaged in the lower crankcase. Apply liquid gasket to the mating surface of the lower crankcase.

NOTE:
- Oil, solvent, stuck gasket should be completely removed from the mating machine surface.
- Do not permit the liquid gasket to get on the dowel pin hole or on surfaces other than the mating parts.
- Apply the liquid gasket evenly and smoothly.
- Allow the liquid gasket to set before joining the two crankcase halves.

2. Assemble the lower case.
3. Handle the starting motor cable and dynamo cable with care so as not to damage the clamps; tighten the bolts.

4·15 CARBURETOR

A. Description

The outstanding feature of the CV carburetor is a constant pressure, single barrel, compound carburetors brought about by the automatic changing of the venturi area by the vacuum pressure of the engine. Each cylinder is equipped with a single carburetor of this type which provides the following advantages to engines having a broad speed range and a high power output.

1. Because of the variable venturi design, the transition between the first and second stage is exceptionally smooth.
2. The construction is very simple due to the single barrel feature.
3. Excellent acceleration and good economy is assured.

The air passing through the cleaner flows through the air inlet ①, venturi ②, throttle valve ③ and enters the cylinder through the inlet port. The vacuum piston ④ is protruding into the venturi area ② and by the action of the vacuum piston spring ⑤ the venturi is restricted by the piston ④. When there is only a small amount of air being taken into the engine, the vacuum piston ④ is in the lowered position, forming the primary venturi ⑥. The air velocity in the venturi area ② is maintained constant, affording good atomization of the fuel. With an increase in the air flow, the vacuum pressure in the venturi increases, causing the vacuum piston to rise due to the pressure applied to the top of the piston. The venturi area is increased by the amount the piston rises which is proportional to the vacuum pressure.

When the engine reaches maximum rpm, the vacuum piston reaches the top and becomes the secondary venturi to provide sufficient venturi area for maximum power output.

(Refer to Carburetor Manual for details).

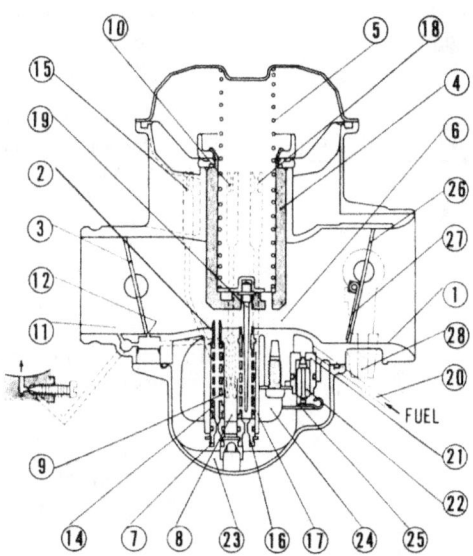

Fig. 4-127. Sectional view of carburetor

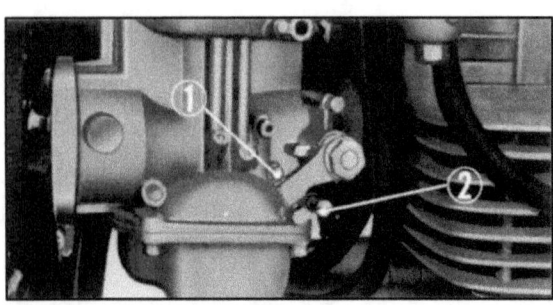

① Stop screw ② Pilot screw
Fig. 4-128. Adjusting idling speed

① Throttle cable adjust bolt ② Lock nut
Fig. 4-129. Throttle cable adjustment

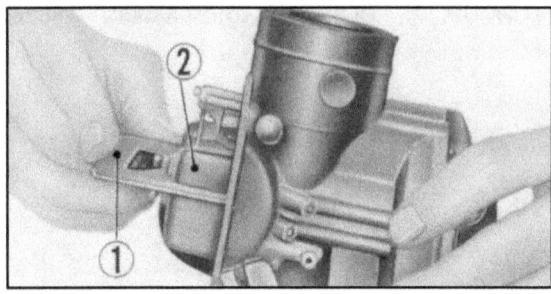

① Float level gauge ② Float
Fig. 4-130. Checking float level

B. Disassembly

1. Remove both left and right air cleaner covers.
2. Loosen the throttle cable adjusting bolt and nut, and remove the throttle cable from the carburetor.
3. Loosen the carburetor bands and remove the carburetors.

C. Inspection

1. Idling adjustment

    1) Adjust the stop screw ① so that the exhaust pressure is the same for both the right and left side.
    (Fig. 4-128)

    If the engine speed does not decrease when the stop screw is screwed out, loosen the lock nut ② and screw in the cable adjusting bolt ① by about one turn. The engine rpm at this point should be **between 1,100~1,300 rpm.** (Fig. 4-129)

    2) Starting with either the right or left carburetor, manipulate the pilot screw ② and find the point of highest rpm; the same should be done with the opposite carburetor. Turning the pilot screw in will give a lean fuel air mixture, turning the screw out will give a rich mixture. The pilot screw ② should be set at one turn out (3/4 of a turn for 350) from fully closed.
    (Fig. 4-128)

    3) After completeting the adjustment in paragraph 2 above, recheck the exhaust pipe pressure on both the right and left sides and if necessary, readjust the stop screws as was done in paragraph 1.

    4) Repeat the procedures from paragraph 1 through 3 several times so that the pilot screw is set to give optimum mixture, while the stop screws are set to provide the specified rpm and the same exhaust pressure on both the right and left sides.

2. Synchronizing the throttle valve

    Make the adjustment so that the right and left throttle valves will both move by the same amount when the throttle grip is moved slightly. This adjustment can be made by placing a hand under the carburetor and noting the movement of the throttle lever, or by observing the movement while the throttle grip is slowly moved and checking to see that the throttle levers start moving at the same time. If adjustment is required, loosen the lock nut ② and perform the adjustment with the cable adjust bolt ①. (Fig. 4-129)

3. Float level check

    Remove the float chamber cover, position the float to the point where the float arm barely touches the float valve. In this position, set the float level gauge vertically on the float. (Carburetor tilt of 10° is normal).
    (Fig. 4-130)

4. If adjustment is necessary, make the adjustment by bending the float arm.

5. FRAME

5·1 HANDLEBAR

A. Description

The handlebar is specially designed with the up-to-date engineering techniques of Honda to provide maximum riding comfort and minimum steering difficulty. It is mounted on the fork top bridge with two clamps. A fully-raised type handlebar is mounted on the CL-series machines and a semi-raised type handlebar on the CB-series machines.

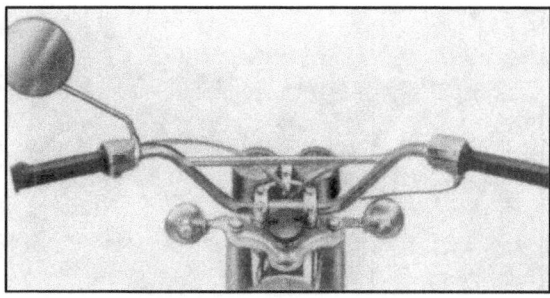

Fig. 5-1. External view of handlebar

B. Disassembly

1. Disconnect the front brake cable at the lower end by loosening the front brake adjusting bolt nut, move the brake arm toward the braking position to providing slack to the cable, and then disconnect the cable from the brake arm. (Fig. 5-2, 5-3)

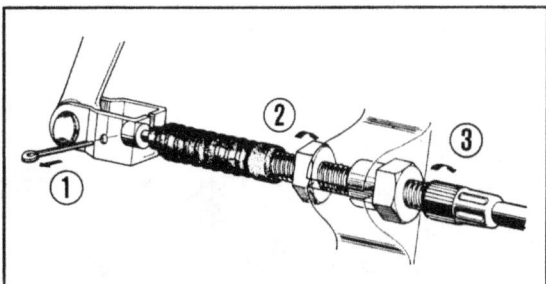

Fig. 5-2. Removing brake cable

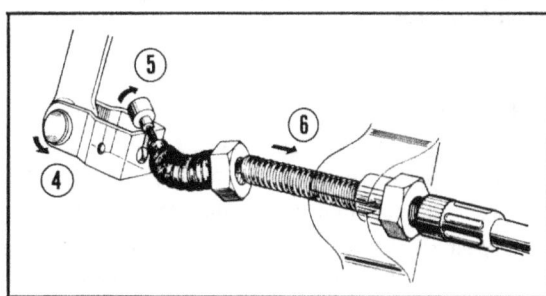

Fig. 5-3. Removing brake cable

2. Remove the brake and clutch cables from the handlebar by turning the slotted ring adjusting bolt so that the slots in the holder and the fixing nut are aligned. Remove inner cable and slide the end off of the handle lever. (Fig. 5-4)

NOTE:

When disconnecting the clutch cable at the lower end, remove the gear shift pedal, drive chain cover, and then remove the cable end from clutch lever.

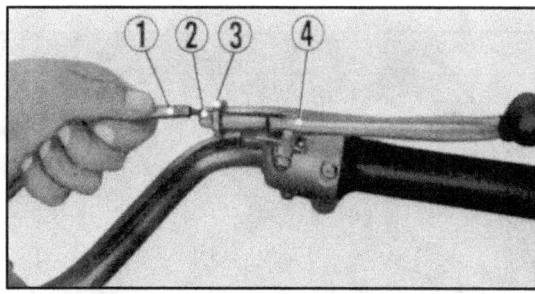

① Clutch cable ② Clutch cable adjusting bolt
③ Fixing nut ④ Clutch lever
Fig. 5-4. Removing cable from the handle

3. To remove throttle cable from the handle lever, unscrew the setting screw on the starter switch assembly and separate the two halves of the starter switch. The throttle cable will be exposed and can be removed from throttle grip. (Fig. 5-5)

① Throttle grip ② Throttle cable
③ Starter lighting switch assembly
Fig. 5-5. Removing the throttle cable

① Throttle cable ② Throttle cable adjuster
③ Lock nut
Fig. 5-6. Removing the throttle cable

4. Disconnect the throttle cable at the lower end by loosening the lock nut at the cable support arm on the carburetor and then disconnect the throttle cable from the carburetor. (Fig. 5-6)

① Steering handle pipe ② 8 mm hex. bolt
Fig. 5-7. Removing the handlebar

5. The electrical wiring for the horn, starting motor switch and the light dimmer switch can be disconnected by uncoupling the cable junctions from the wire harness located within headlight case.
6. Remove handlebar by unscrewing the four 8 mm bolts from the handlebar clamps. (Fig. 5-7)

C. Inspection

1. Inspect the throttle, clutch and front brake cable for damage to the housing and inner cable, also check to see that the cable is operating smoothly. Apply grease before reassembly.
2. Check the operation of the throttle grip; make sure that the action of the grip is smooth through the entire range.
3. Inspect the hand lever operation for lightness.
4. Inspect the handlebar for twist, bends or other damage.
5. Inspect the switches on the handlebar for proper operation and also the lead wires for breaks and frayed covering.

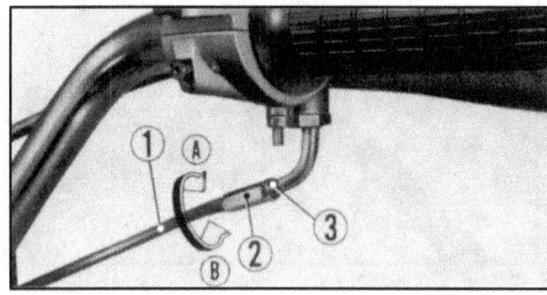

① Throttle cable ② Throttle cable adjust nut "A"
③ Lock nut Ⓐ Decrease Ⓑ Increase
Fig. 5-8. Throttle cable play adjustment

D. Reassembly

1. Route the electrical leads from the handlebar through the center hole in the top bridge and mount the handlebar on the top bridge. Fix in place with the handlebar holder and lock with the four 8 mm bolts.
2. Connect the throttle cable to the throttle grip and adjust the play with the nut ②. (Fig. 5-8)

① Front brake cable
Fig. 5-9. Adjusting the front brake

3. Connect the clutch cable to the left hand lever and the front brake cable to the right hand lever. The adjustment of the clutch cable is made at the crankcase (Refer to page 21), whereas, the adjustment for the front brake is made with nut "b" and "c" at the lower end of the front brake cable. (Fig. 5-9)

4. Connect the electrical leads from the handlebar at the headlight case. (Fig. 5-10)

① Wire connectors ② Headlight
Fig. 5-10. Connecting electrical leads

5·2 FORK TOP BRIDGE

A. Description

The fork top bridge is mounted on the top of the fork with two bolts and is secured to the steering stem with stem nut, as illustrated in the figure at right. To this bridge is mounted the handlebar with cushion rubber to resist shocks to the rider's hands.

B. Disassembly

1. Remove the handlebar in accordance with section 5·1B on page 61~62.
2. Extract the 6 mm lock pin and remove steering damper by pulling upward.
3. Disconnect the speedometer and the tachometer cables from the respective meters (the meters may be removed from the fork top bridge by unscrewing the 6 mm nuts).
4. Separate the fork top bridge from the front fork by unscrewing the two front fork bolts and loosening the steering stem nut. (Fig. 5-12)
5. Unscrew the 8 mm hex. nuts and remove the front fork washer, handlebar cushion rubbers and the handlebar lower holders from the fork top bridge. (Fig. 5-13)

NOTE:

If the handlebar lower holders are to be removed, it is recommended that the 8 mm hex. nuts on the holders are unscrewed before removing the handlebar. This prevents the handlebar holders from turning. (Fig. 5-14)

C. Inspection

1. Inspect the fork top bridge for cracks and other damage.
2. Inspect the handlebar cushion rubber for damage or wear.

D. Reassembly

1. Mount the fork top bridge on the front fork, install the front fork bolts and steering stem nut.
2. Assemble the handlebar in accordance with section 5·1B on page 61~62.
3. After completing the installation, check to make sure that the electrical equipment is operating properly.

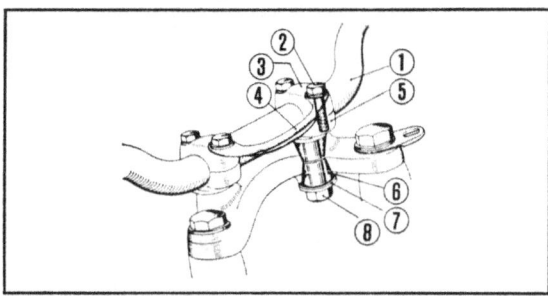

① Steering handle ② 8 mm hex. bolt
③ Handle pipe upper holder ④ Cable holder
⑤ Handle pipe under holder ⑥ Handle cushion rubber
⑦ Handle cushion washer ⑧ 8 mm hex. nut
Fig. 5-11.

① Front fork bolt ② Steering stem nut
③ Damper lock spring set bolt
④ Steering damper lock spring ⑤ Fork top bridge
Fig. 5-12. Removing the fork top bridge

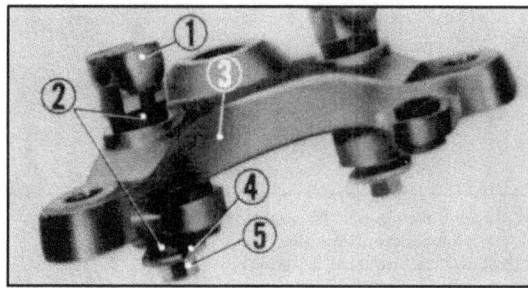

① Under handlebar holder ② Handlebar cushion rubber
③ Fork top bridge ④ Handle cushion washer
⑤ 8 mm hex. nut
Fig. 5-13. Component parts of fork top bridge

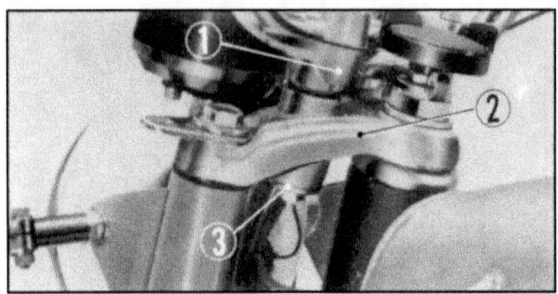

① Handle pipe under holder ② Fork top bridge
③ 8 mm nut
Fig. 5-14. Top bridge holder installing 8 mm nut

• The models CB/CL250, 350K2 thru K5 are not provided with a steering damper.

5·3 FRONT CUSHION (Piston type)

A. Description

The front fork is of a hydraulically-damped telescopic type. It consists mainly of a fork pipe ① complete with piston ④, a fork bottom case ② and a cushion spring. On "compression", that is, when any downward load is imposed on the front fork, for example, under heavy front braking, the piston moves down, compressing the oil in chamber "A" and forcing it into chamber "B" through orifices "a" in the periphery of the fork pipe to lift damper valve ⑤ off its seat. On the other hand, the cushion spring, now compressed, exerts an upward reaction to move the piston up. The piston when so moved compresses the oil in chamber "B" and forces it back into chamber "A" through orifice "b" to provide damping action. On "full bump", or bump overcoming the capacity of the cushion spring, the pipe is moved down toward the bottom end of the bottom case, trapping the oil in the space between the pipe and tapered lock piece ⑥ to provide maximum damping. On "full rebound", the orifice "b" is covered by guide ③ and the oil is trapped within chamber "B" to provide extension damping. (Fig. 5-16C & D)

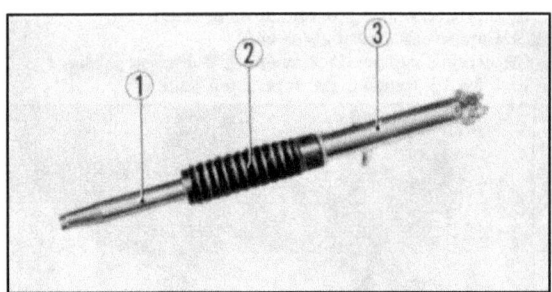

① Front fork pipe ② Front fork boot (CL250/350)
③ Front fork bottom case
Fig. 5-15. Front fork assembly

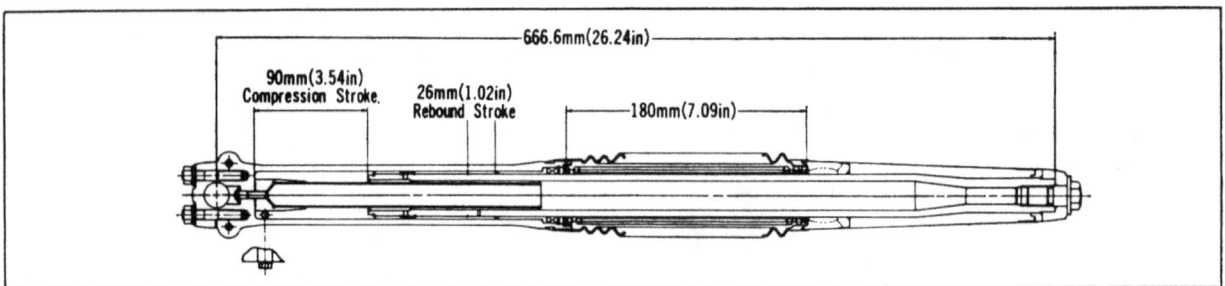

Fig. 5-16A. CL250/350

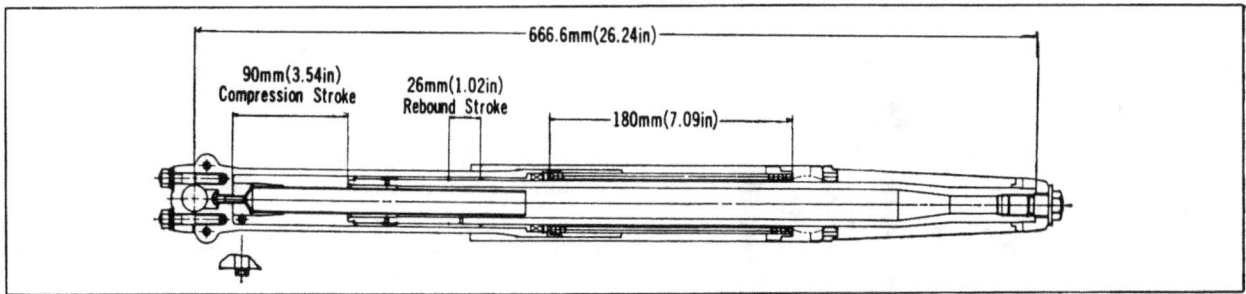

Fig. 5-16B. CB250/350

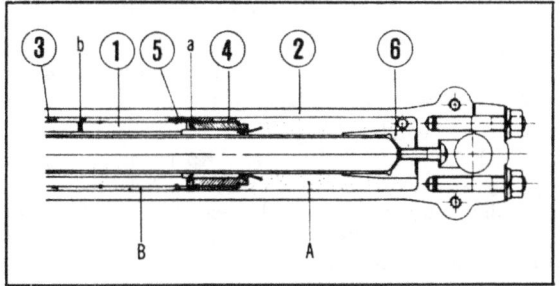
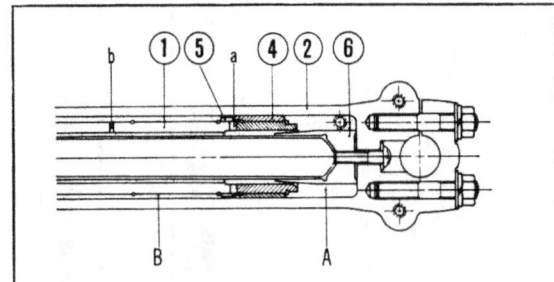

① Front fork pipe complete ② Front fork bottom case complete ③ Front fork pipe guide ④ Front fork piston
⑤ Front damper valve ⑥ Oil lock piece

Fig. 5-16C. Front cushion operation

Fig. 5-16D.

(Rod type)

A. Description

The rod type telescopic shock absorber is the most advanced absorber ever produced—so called because the spring lower seat incorporates a damper actuated by a long rod. The rod is held in the bottom of the fork by a bolt. One of the distinguishing features of this latest unit is its higher ability to absorb shocks and vibrations.

The fork pipe is in direct contact with the cylinder without the use of a piston.

The rod type unit consist of a lightweight aluminum front fork bottom case with a dual action telescoping shock absorber oil damper. Cushioning travel is 90 mm (3.5 in.) on compression and 27.6 mm (1.08 in.) on extension strokes.

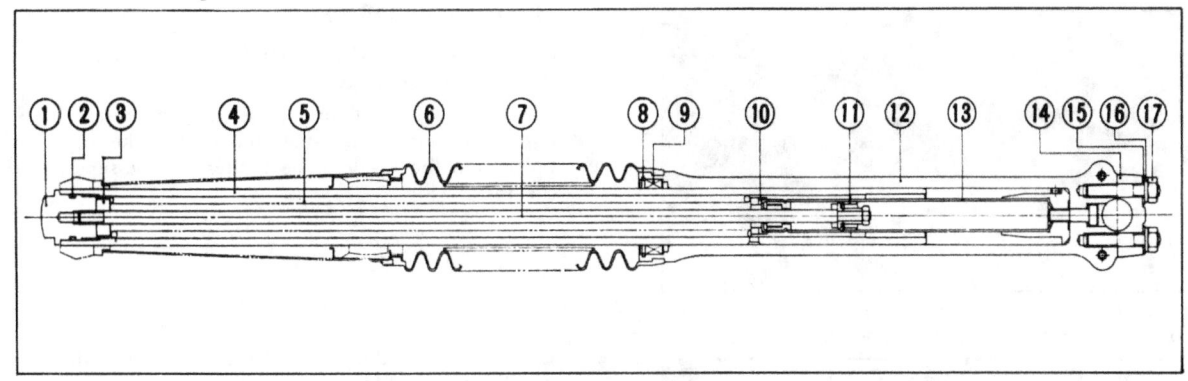

Fig. 5-17A. Front fork unit

① Front fork bolt
② O-ring
③ Lock nut
④ Front fork pipe
⑤ Front suspension spring
⑥ Front fork boot
⑦ Damper rod
⑧ Snap ring
⑨ Oil seal
⑩ Holder
⑪ Collar
⑫ Front fork bottom case
⑬ Damper case
⑭ Axle holder
⑮ Plain washer
⑯ Spring washer
⑰ Nut

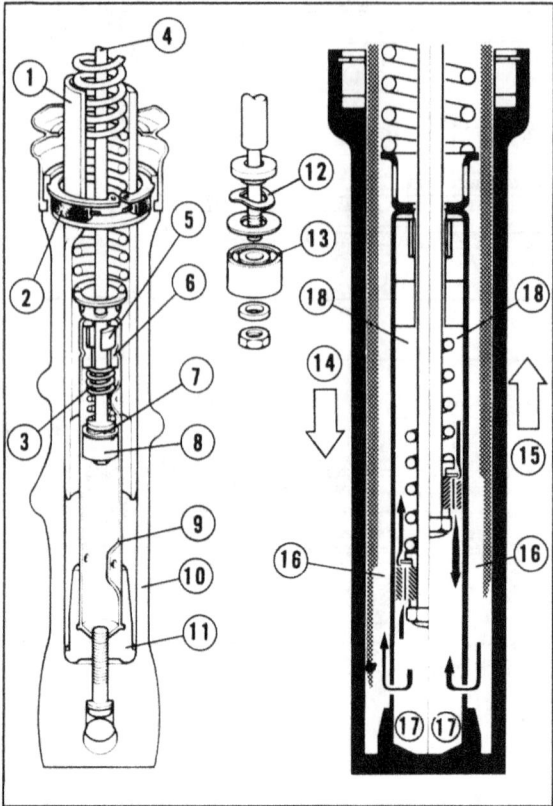

① Fork pipe
② Oil seal
③ Rebound stopper spring
④ Piston rod
⑤ Piston rod guide
⑥ Lock guide housing
⑦ Valve
⑧ Piston
⑨ Cylinder
⑩ Bottom case
⑪ Oil lock piece
⑫ Valve set spring
⑬ Second power hole
⑭ Compression
⑮ Extension
⑯ Chamber C
⑰ Chamber B
⑱ Chamber A

Fig. 5 17B.

Operation: Fig. 5-17B

- The piston, as it goes down, pushes a part of the fluid from the chamber "B" into "C". Most fluid can flow into the chamber "A" through the valve in the piston freely.
- As the piston travels up on its extension, the fluid is returned from the chamber "C" through the small opening into the chamber "A".

  This imposes a restraint on the spring and wheel action as noted in the previous section.

- Near the end of the compression, the fork pipe is placed over the oil lock piece. This holds the fork in place, thereby preventing it from crashing against the bottom.
- Damping increases as the piston reaches the end of the extension stroke. This feature plus a rebound stop spring combine to achieve exceptionally smooth cushioning.

  Rod type disassembly

- The models CB/CL250, 350K4 and K5 use front forks of the rod type.

  After pulling out the front fork assembly, set the fork as shown in Fig. 5-17B. Then remove the fork bottom pipe and damper unit using a hollow set wrench.

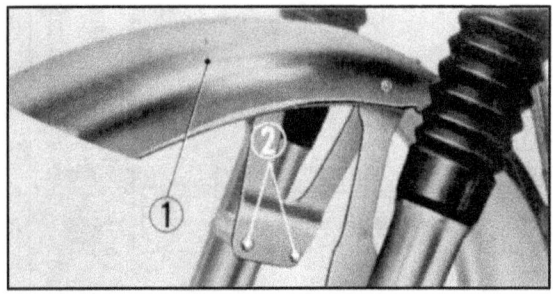

① Front fender ② 6 mm hex. bolt
Fig. 5-17. Removing the front fender

① Front fork bolt ② 8 mm hex. bolt
③ Front fork assembly
Fig. 5-18. Removing the front fork assembly

B. Disassembly (Piston type)

1. Separate the front wheel from the motorcycle in accordance with section on Page 84.

2. Remove the three 6 mm fender stay mounting bolts and one 8 mm bolt (fender stay and front brake arm attaching bolt) from the inside. The fender can be separated from the fork. (Fig. 5-17)

3. Unscrew the headlight case mounting bolts attaching the headlight assembly to the front fork.

   Remove the 8 mm bolts from the front side of the steering stem and slide the cushion assembly out from the bottom. (Fig. 5-18)

NOTE:

The front cushion removal can be facilitated by spreading the mounting ring of the bottom bridge by driving a wedge into the slot on the mounting ring.

4. Drain the oil in the cushion by removing the drain plug at the bottom or inverting the cushion and draining the oil out of the top mounting bolt hole before separating the front fork pipe from the front fork bottom case.

5. Remove the front fork boot, (CB250/350: front fork under cover), front cushion spring and then remove the 44 mm internal circlip using snap ring pliers.
   Pull out and disassemble the front fork bottom pipe and the front fork pipe assembly. (Fig. 5-19)

6. Disassemble the front fork pipe assembly by removing the fork piston snap ring, fork piston, stopper ring, damper valve, valve stopper ring, fork pipe stopper ring, and front fork pipe guide, in that order. (Fig. 5-20)

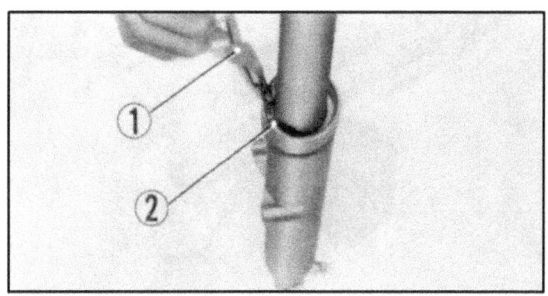

① Pliers (close) ② 44 mm internal circlip
Fig. 5-19. Removing 44 mm circlip

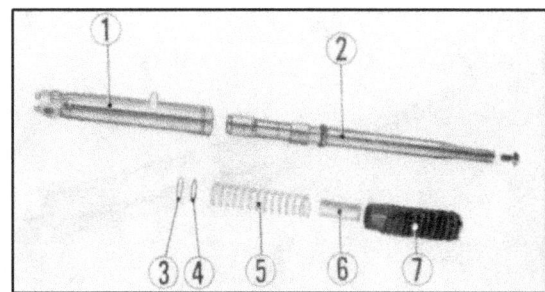

① Front fork bottom case ② Front fork pipe
③ 44 mm internal circlip ④ Spring under seat
⑤ Front cushion spring ⑥ Front fork under cover guide
⑦ Front fork boot
Fig. 5-20. Component parts of front fork

C. Inspection (Piston type)

1. Front fork oil change

   Changing the oil in the front fork should be performed at the initial 300 miles (500 km) and every 12,000 miles (20,000 km) thereafter.

   1) Remove the front fork bolt, drain plug and drain the oil from the front fork, allow sufficient time to drain the oil completely. (Fig. 5-21, 22)

   2) Clean inside with oil solvent. Do not use gasoline for cleaning.

   3) Reinstall the drain plug and pour **200 cc (12.2 cu-in)** of engine oil **SAE 10W** (AP1 service classification).

2. Inspect for oil leak

   Oil leaks are due to defective or an improperly installed oil seal, loose drain plug, damaged front fork bottom case etc. Perform an inspection of the respective areas and repair or replace the defects.

3. Inspect front cushion spring

   Measure the free length of the spring with a vernier caliper. (Fig. 5-23)

   mm (inch)

Standard Value	Serviceable Limit
210 (8.27)	Replace if under 196 (7.72)

4. Front cushion trueness

   Set the spring up on its end on the surface gauge and measure the amount of tilt with a square and vernier caliper.

   mm (inch)

Standard Value	Serviceable Limit
Within 5 (0.2)	Replace if over 8 (0.32)

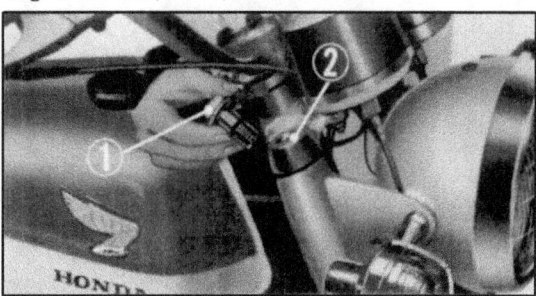

① Front fork bolt ② Oil filler opening
Fig. 5-21. Removing the front fork bolt

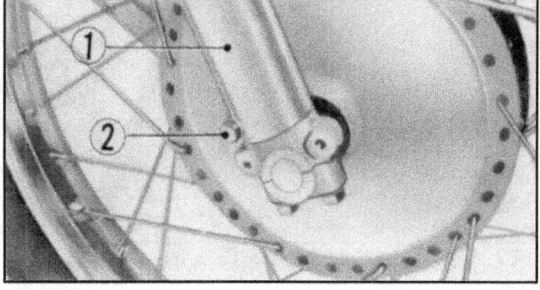

① Front fork bottom case ② Front fork drain plug
Fig. 5-22. Removing front fork drain plug

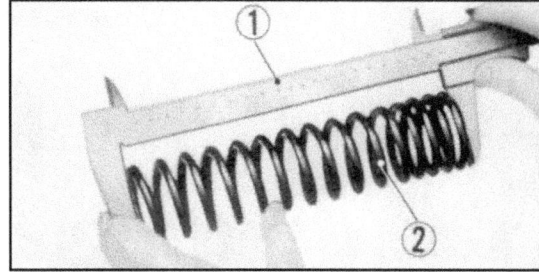

① Vernier caliper ② Front cushion spring
Fig. 5-23. Measuring free length of cushion spring

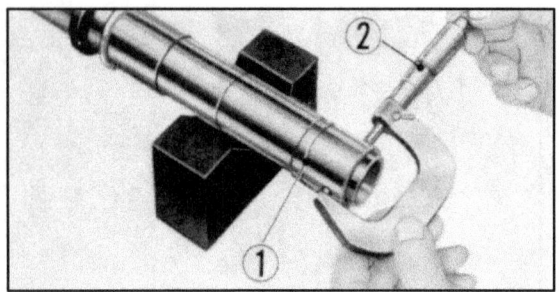

① Front fork piston　② Micrometer
Fig. 5-24. Measuring front fork piston diameter

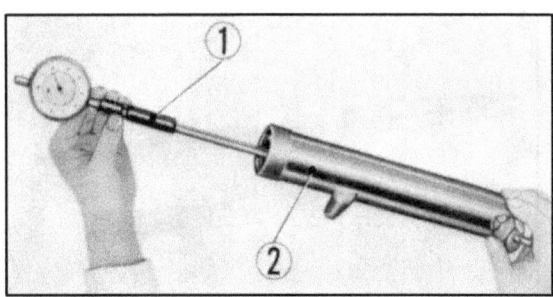

① Cylinder gauge　② Front fork bottom case
Fig. 5-25. Measuring front fork bottom case

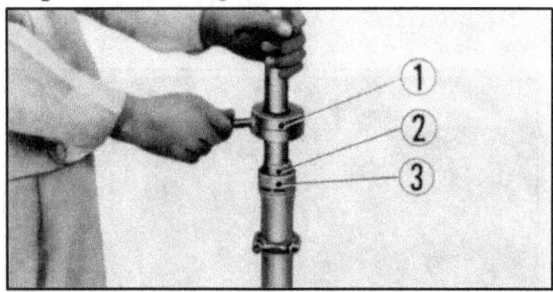

① Front fork oil seal driving weight
② Front fork oil seal driving guide　③ Oil seal
Fig. 5-26. Driving front fork oil seal

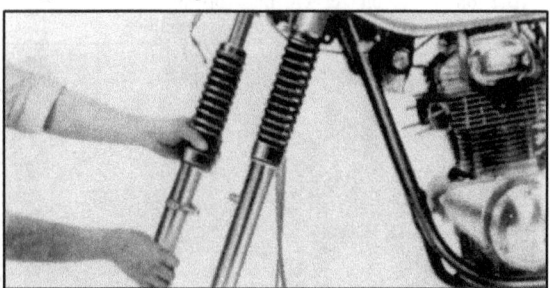

Fig. 5-27. Installing the front fork into the steering

5. Front fork piston diameter

Measure the diameter with a micrometer. (Fig. 5-24)

mm (inch)

Standard Value	Serviceable Limit
37.395～37.420 (1.472～1.473)	Replace if under 37.385 (1.472)

6. Front fork bottom case diameter

Measure the inside diameter of the bottom case with a cylinder gauge. (Fig. 5-25)

mm (inch)

Standard Value	Serviceable Limit
37.500～37.540 (1.476～1.478)	Replace if over 37.680 (1.484)

D. Reassembly (Piston type)

1. Clean the parts thoroughly before assembling.
2. Assemble the individual components into the front fork pipe assembly.

NOTE:

After completing the assembly of the front damper valve into the front fork pipe, make sure that the damper valve is operating smoothly.

3. Insert the front pipe assembly into the front fork bottom case using the following special tools, front fork oil seal driving guide, front fork oil seal driving weight. Exercise care not to damage the oil seal. (Fig. 5-26)

4. Assemble the front cushion spring and the boot (CB250/350: front fork under cover).

5. Install the front cushion assembly on the steering stem. Fill each cushion with the following amount of automatic transmission fluid (AFT) through the front fork bolt hole and install the front fork bolt upon completing filling. Lock the cushion in the bottom bridge by tightening the 8 mm hex. bolt. (Fig. 5-27)

MODEL	FORK OIL VOLUME, TO FILL AFTER DRAINING		FORK OIL CAPACITY TO FILL DRY ASSEMBLY	
	c.c.	oz.	c.c.	oz.
CB/CL-250, 350	175～185	5.9～6.3	195～205	6.6～6.9
CB/CL-250, 350K1	175～205	5.9～6.9	195～205	6.6～6.9
CB/CL-250, 350K2	175～205	5.9～6.9	195～205	6.6～6.9
CB/CL-250, 350K3	175～205	5.9～6.9	195～205	6.6～6.9
CB250, 350K4	105～110	3.6～3.7	125～130	4.2～4.4
CL350K4	105～110	3.6～3.7	125～150	4.2～4.4
CB350G	105～110	3.6～3.7	125～130	4.2～4.4
CL350K5	105～110	3.6～3.7	125～130	4.2～4.4
SL350, 350K1	160～170	5.4～5.8	180～190	6.1～6.4
SL 350K2	160～170	5.4～5.8	180～190	6.1～6.4

6. Install the front fender and the front wheel.
7. Upon completion of the front cushion assembly, check for proper operation and assure that there is no binding.

A. Description (Rod Type)

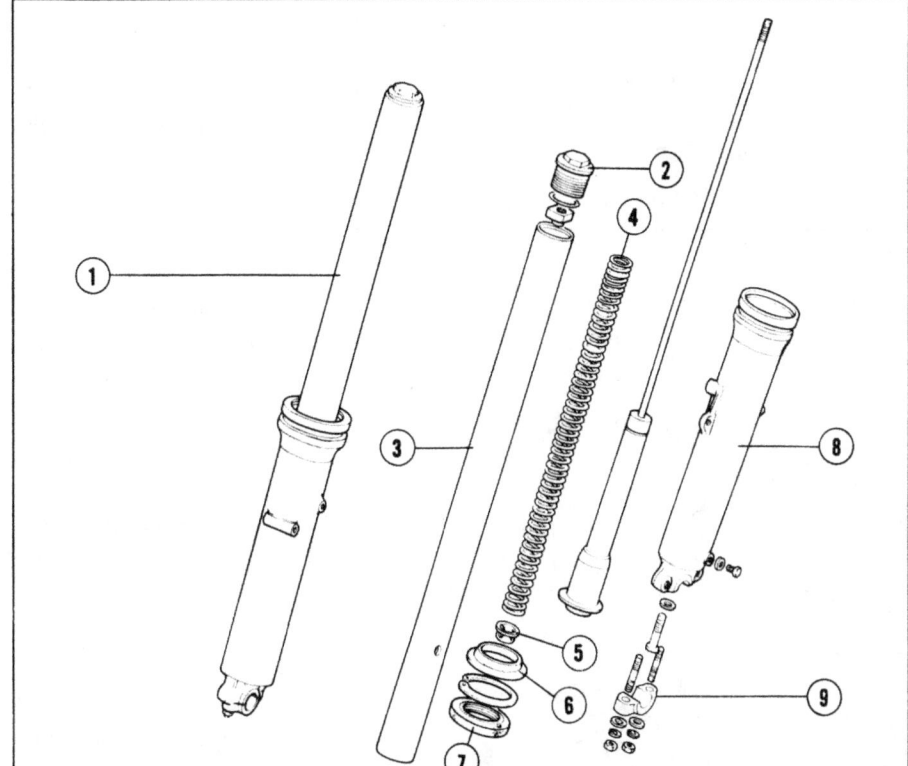

① Front fork assembly
② Front fork bolt
③ Front fork pipe
④ Front suspension spring
⑤ Cushion spring seat
⑥ Dust-seal, 33×47×10
⑦ Oil seal, 33-46-10.5
⑧ Front fork bottom case
⑨ Front axle holder

Fig. 5-28.

B. Disassembly

- The rod type front forks should be disassembled in the same manner as the piston type up to step 1~3 on page 66.

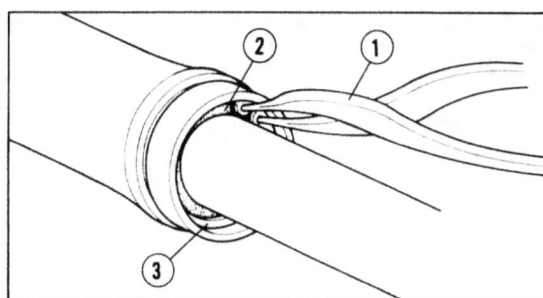

Fig. 5-29. ① Snap ring plier ② Oil seal
③ 47 mm internal circlip

6. Unscrew the 8 mm bottom case bolt using a hollow set wrench (Tool No. 07917-3230000) and remove the damper unit from the bottom case.

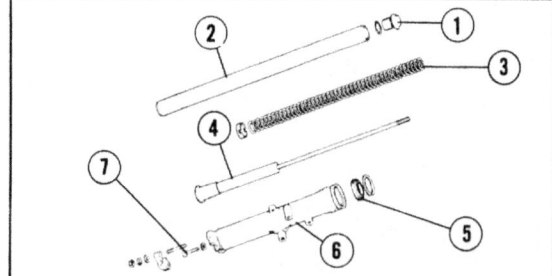

Fig. 5-30. ① Front fork bolt ⑦ 8 mm socket bolt
② Front fork pipe
③ Front cushion spring
④ Damper
⑤ Oil seal 33-46-10.5
⑥ Front fork bottom case

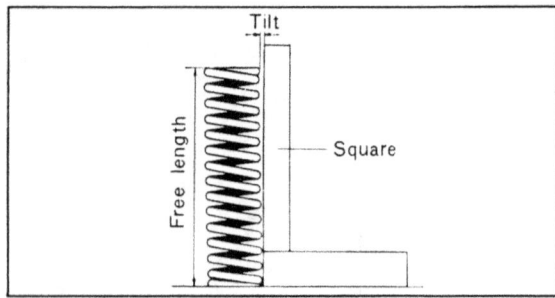

Fig. 5-31. Measuring the free length

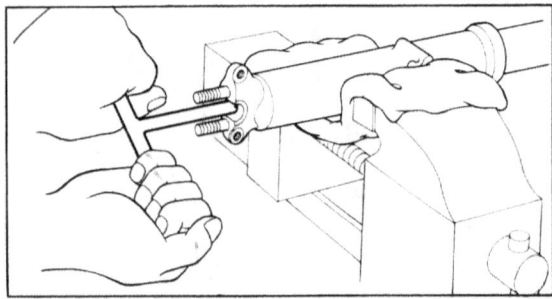

Fig. 5-32.

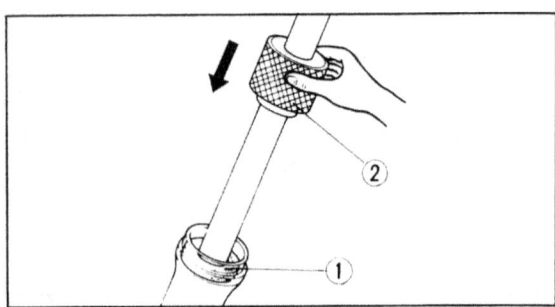

Fig. 5-33. ① Oil seal ② Oil seal driving guide

C. Inspection

1. Check the front suspension spring.
2. Check the fork pipe and bottom case for damage or excessive wear.
3. Check the oil seal for damage.
4. Check for excessive clearance between the shock absorber piston and the cylinder.

D. Reassembly

1. Reassemble in the reverse order of disassembly. Take care not to allow dust, dirt or other foreign matter to adhere to the component parts.
2. Install the fork pipe into the bottom case. Apply a coat of thread lock cement to the socket bolt and tighten it using a socket wrench.
3. Apply a coat of Honda ATF to both sides of the oil seal and install it using a front fork oil seal driving guide (Tool No. 07947-2730100, CB, CL250 · 350 models), (07949-2730100 SL350 model)

NOTE:
- Do not forget to install the snap ring.
- Replace the seal with a new one.

4. Apply a coat of thread lock cement to the threaded part of the damper.

   Making sure that the 8 mm lock nut is completely screwed onto the threaded part of the damper, tighten the fork bolt.
5. Remove the front fork bolt and pour a specified amount of Honda ATF into the front fork pipe, refer to page 68.
6. Install and tighten the front fork bolt.
7. Route the front forks through the holes in the fork top bridge and tighten them with the 8 mm setting bolt and 10 mm setting bolts.

NOTE:

Remove oil, if any, from around the front forks.

8. After reassembling, check the front forks for smooth movement. Also check if oil leaks from the oil seals.

5·4 STEERING STEM

A. Description

The steering stem is in a sense a "pivot joint" located between the front fork and the frame. It is supported by ball bearings at its upper and lower ends and pivots in the frame head. A steering damper is provided to adjust the stem for different riding or road conditions – the adjustment can be made by means of steering damper knob ①. Turning the knob clockwise will increase the friction between damper plates ⑦ to "tighten" the steering, and vice versa.

The handlebar lock is built into the steering stem.

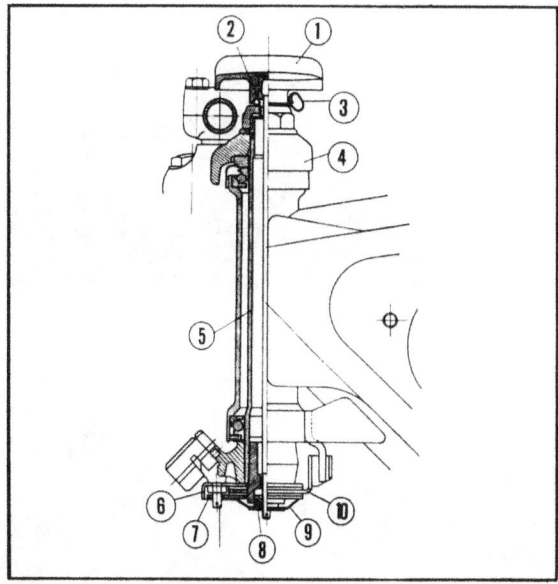

① Steering damper knob
② Damper lock spring setting bolt
③ Steering damper lock spring
④ Front fork top bridge   ⑤ Steering stem
⑥ Steering damper plate A   ⑦ Steering damper plate B
⑧ Steering damper spring nut   ⑨ Steering damper spring
⑩ Steering damper friction disk
Fig. 5-34. Sectional view of steering stem

B. Disassembly

1. Separate the handlebar in accordance with section 5·1B on page 61~62.
2. Remove the front wheel in accordance with section 5·13B on page 84.
3. Disassemble front cushion in accordance with section 5·3B on page 64.
4. Remove the top bridge plate in accordance with section 5·2B on page 63.
5. Remove the steering stem top thread and withdraw steering stem out of the head pipe, be careful not to drop the steel balls. (Fig. 5-35)

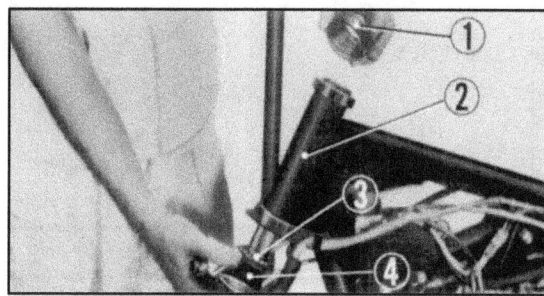

① Steering head top thread   ② Head pipe
③ #8 Steel balls   ④ Steering stem
Fig. 5-35. Removing the steering stem

C. Inspection

1. Inspect steel balls for wear and other damage.
2. Inspect both the top and bottom cone and ball races for any wear or damage.
3. Inspect the steering head dust seal for wear and damage.
4. Inspect the top end of steering stem for damaged threads.
5. Inspect steering handle lock for damage or defects.

D. Reassembly

1. Mount the steering handle lock on the steering stem.
2. Mix the 1/4″ steel balls (37) in grease, lay into the lower (19) and upper (18) ball races, and carefully insert the stem into the head pipe, exercising care not to drop the balls. The top thread should first be hand-tightened fully and then be backed off about 1/8 turn. Tightening it excessively will cause hard steering and backing it off excessively will cause loose steering. (Fig. 5-36)

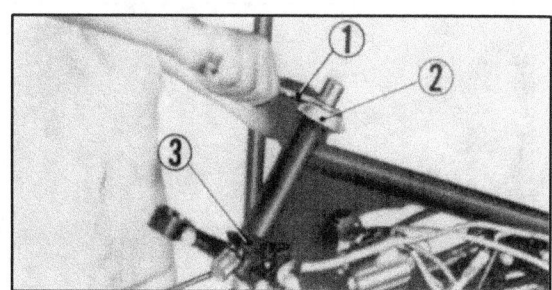

① 48 mm pin spanner   ② Steering head top thread
③ Steering stem
Fig. 5-36. Reassembling the steering stem

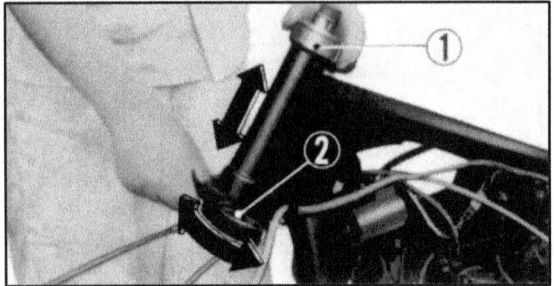

① Steering head top thread ② Steering stem
Fig. 5-37. Check of stem operation

Fig. 5-38. Fuel tank

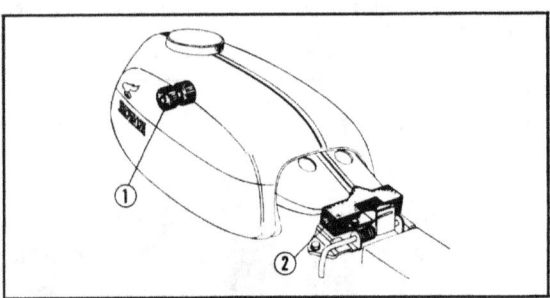

① Fuel tank front cushion ② Fuel tank rear cushion
Fig. 5-39. Schematic view of tank rubber cushion

Fig. 5-40. Removing the fuel tank

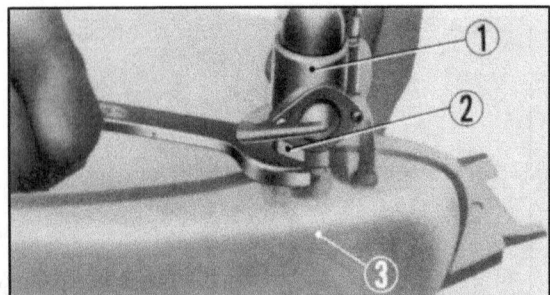

① Fuel cock assembly ② Joint nut ③ Fuel tank
Fig. 5-41. Removing the fuel cock assembly

NOTE:

Special attention is required to tighten the top thread. It must be tightened in conjunction with the steering stem nut and the front fork bolt. If the stem nut is properly tightened, the steering assembly will turn to either lock under its own weight assisted only by a slight initial force. Further there should not be any looseness of the stem in either the vertical or the horizontal directions. (Fig. 5-37)

3. Assemble the top bridge front cushion and front wheel.
4. Install the handlebar and damper knob.
5. Adjust the play of the clutch, brake and throttle cables.

5·5 FUEL TANK

A. Description

The fuel tank is made by press-working and is mounted on the half frame (upper member of frame body) with rubber cushions as shown in the figure at left. The models CB250/350K1 thru K5 are provided with no knee grip rubbers. Knee grip rubbers are attached to the tank mounted on the CB250/350 machines.

B. Disassembly

1. Unlock the seat latch located on the left front of the seat side.
2. Position the fuel cock lever to STOP position and remove the fuel tube from the fuel cock.

3. Remove one end of the fuel level tube and apply a clip on the tube to close off the fuel tube. Install a rubber cap or a plug on the tank fitting to prevent the fuel from draining. Detach fuel tank from the fuel tank rear cushion and carefully remove to the rear. (Fig. 5-40)

4. The fuel cock assembly can be removed from the tank by loosening the joint nut and unscrewing the fuel cock assembly. (Fig. 5-41)

C. Inspection

1. Inspect the fuel tank for leaks.

NOTE:
> Normally an air pressure test is performed by immersing the tank in water. However, exercise precaution since excessive pressure will rupture the tank seam.

2. Inspect for clogging of the filler cap vent hole.
3. Inspect the front and rear cushion rubbers for deterioration, wear and other damage.
4. Inspect for damage to the valve cock packing and the screen. (Fig. 5-42)
5. Inspect the fuel line for defects.

D. Reassembly

1. Install the fuel cock assembly on the tank.
2. Fit the front and rear rubber cushions to the frame body. The front rubber cushion should be inserted by pushing the fuel tank from the rear. Install the fuel tank rear bracket on the rear cushion. (Fig. 5-43)

NOTE:
> When installing the tank, particular attention should be given to the condition of the wires and their routing.

3. Install the two fuel lines using fuel line clips, also connect the fuel level tube to the tank valve.
4. Install the seat and secure with the seat latch.

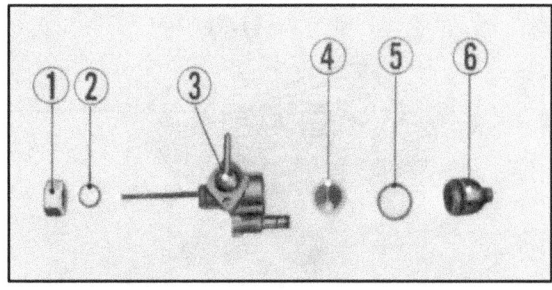

① Joint nut ② Joint nut packing ③ Fuel cock body
④ Screen ⑤ Cock packing ⑥ Fuel strainer cup
Fig. 5-42. Component parts of fuel strainer

① Fuel tank
Fig. 5-43.

5·6 FRAME BODY

A. Description

The frame body is of a semi-cradle, double-frame type. It is rigidly fabricated with high-strength steel tubing to carry the weight of the propelling machinery and the rider and also to provide free steering movement of the front wheel while maintaining the rear wheel in accurate alignment with the center plane of the machine. The major components of the frame body are as shown in the figure at left.

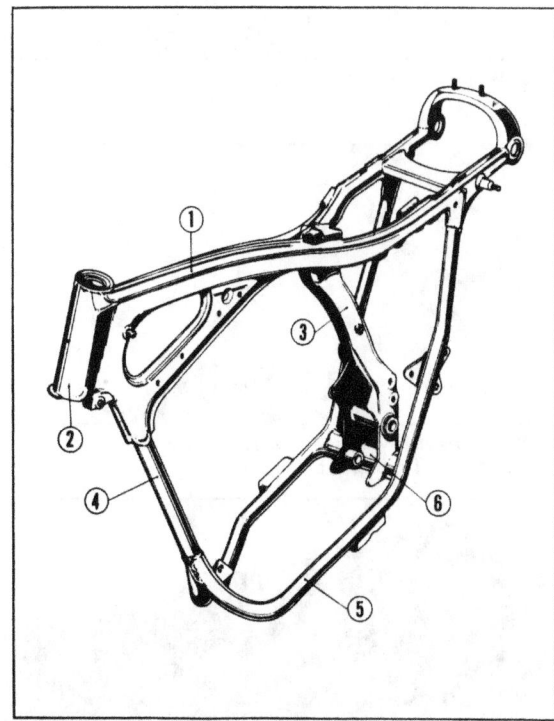

① Half frame ② Head pipe ③ Half pillar
④ Front down tube ⑤ Sub tube holder
⑥ Lower cross member
Fig. 5-44. Schematic view of frame body

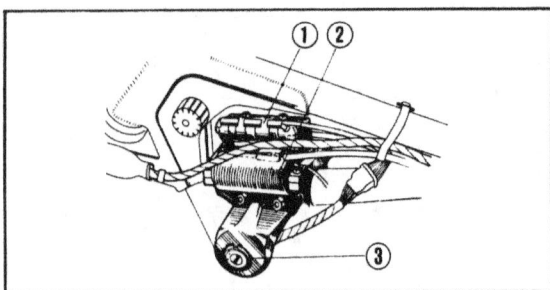

① Condenser ② Ignition coil ③ Ignition switch
Fig. 5-45. Mounting positions of electrical items

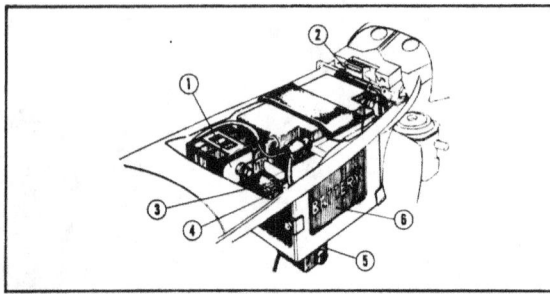

① Selenium rectifier ② Fuse ③ Magnetic starter switch
④ Winker relay ⑤ Pointless regulator ⑥ Battery
Fig. 5-46. Mounting positions of electrical items

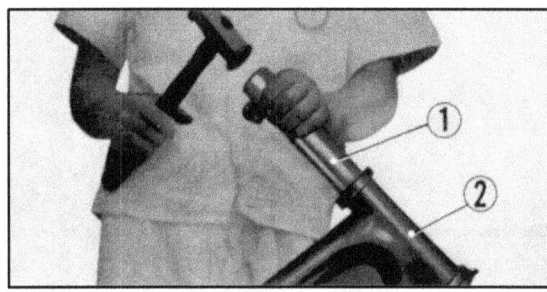

① Wooden drift ② Head pipe
Fig. 5-47. Removing the ball race

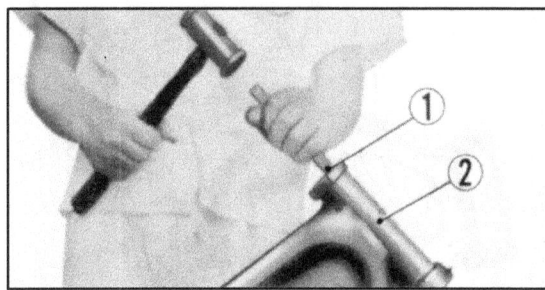

① Ball race driving tool ② Head pipe
Fig. 5-48. Driving the ball race

① Double seat
Fig. 5-49. Seat

B. Disassembly

1. Dismount the engine from the frame in accordance with section 4·3 on page 29.
2. Remove the seat and fuel tank in accordance with sections 5·5B and 5·7B on page 72.
3. Remove the air cleaner in accordance with section 5·10B on page 77.
4. Separate the handlebar in accordance with section 5·1B on page 61.
5. Disassemble the front wheel in accordance with section 5·13B on page 83.
6. Remove the top bridge in accordance with section 5·2B on page 63.
7. Disassemble the front cushion in accordance with section 5·3B on page 66, 69.
8. Remove the steering stem in accordance with section 5·4B on page 71.
9. Disassemble rear fork, rear fender and tool box in accordance with section 5·11B on page 78.
10. Remove the electric equipment from the frame. (Fig. 5-45, 46)
11. Detach the main stand in accordance with section 5·8B on page 66 and then the frame can be disassembled.
12. Knock out the ball races from the head pipe by using a wooden drift. (Fig. 5-47)

C. Inspection

1. Inspect the weld joints for any breaks or cracks.
2. Inspect the steering head pipe for twist, bends and misalignment.
3. Inspect the top and bottom steering head ball races for signs of wear.

NOTE:

The ball races should be fitted to the steering head pipe and must be bottomed securely. (Fig. 5-48)

4. Inspect the frame paint coating for any chips and rust spots.

D. Reassembly

Perform the assembly in the reverse order of disassembly.

5·7 SEAT

A. Description

A double seat is mounted. This seat is sponge rubber-padded to provide an optimum padding thickness under the average rider. Its center and rear sections are padded thicker to prevent the rider from sliding on the seat when rapidly starting or accelerating. The covering is easy-to-clean, high-strength vinyl material. The seat is hinged at the rear end so that it can be raised by unlatching at the front left side for servicing of the battery or other electrical parts.

B. Disassembly

1. Raise the seat and remove the two 8 mm hex. nuts at the seat hinge and separate seat from the frame. (Fig. 5-51)
2. The seat stay can be separated from the seat by unscrewing the two 6 mm nuts.

C. Inspection

1. Inspect the seat covering for wear, cracks and tears.
2. Inspect the hinge and the rubber seal to insure that they are not damaged or cracked.

D. Reassembly

1. Bolt the seat stay to the seat with the two 6 mm nuts.
2. Mount the seat hinge to the frame.
3. Assure that the seat front end is properly hooked by the latch.

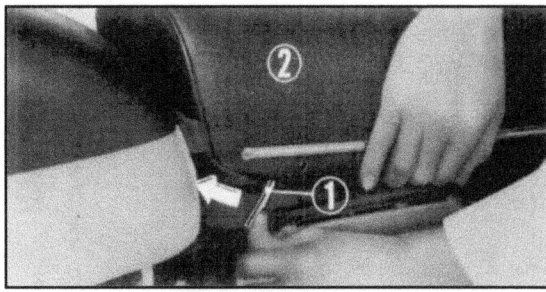
① Seat latch lever ② Seat
Fig. 5-50. Unlatching the seat latch lever

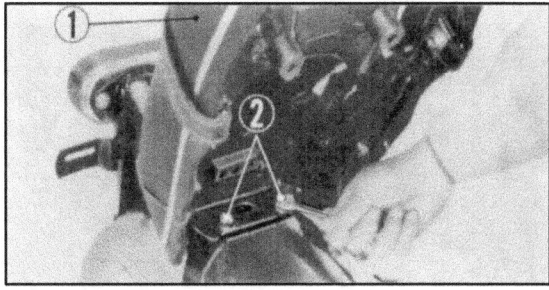
① Seat ② 8 mm hex. nuts
Fig. 5-51. Removing the seat

5·8 STANDS AND BRAKE PEDAL

A. Description

A main stand ⑮ and a side stand ⑲ fabricated with steel tubing are used. The former stand is mounted on pivot shaft ⑫ fitted to the lower cross member of the frame and is spring-loaded to provide an "over-dead center" action when erected or folded. The foot plates welded to the bottom ends of the stand provide a better "footing" for stable machine support. The latter stand is mounted on the pivot screw ⑱. The brake pedal ① is mounted on pivot bolt ③ located just in front of the main stand pivot shaft.

① Brake pedal ② Brake pedal spring
③ Rear brake pivot bolt ④ 14 mm washer
⑤ Brake rod joint pin ⑥ 1.6×2 cotter pin
⑦ Rear brake rod ⑧ Rear brake rod spring
⑨ Rear brake arm joint ⑩ Rear brake adjusting nut
⑪ Main stand spring ⑫ Main stand pivot pipe
⑬ Main stand stopper rubber (CL250/350)
⑭ 2.5×30 cotter pin ⑮ Main stand
⑯ Side stand spring ⑰ 10 mm hex. nut
⑱ Side stand pivot screw ⑲ Side stand

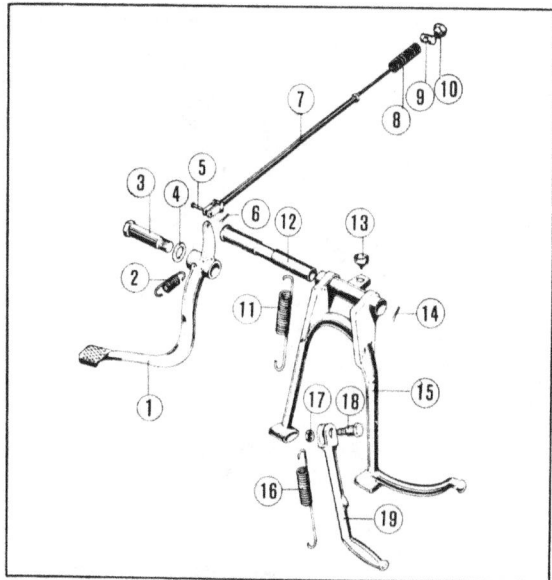
Fig. 5-52. Exploded view of stand and brake pedal

B. Disassembly

(Main Stand)

1. Raise the front wheel off the ground by placing a block underneath the engine.
2. Remove the stand spring from the right side.
3. After loosening the two 6 mm hex. nuts, remove the cotter pin from the left side, slide off the main stand pivot pipe and remove the main stand. (Fig. 5-53)

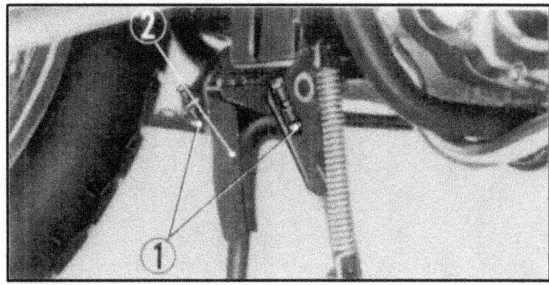
① 6 mm hex. nut ② Main stand
Fig. 5-53. Removing the main stand

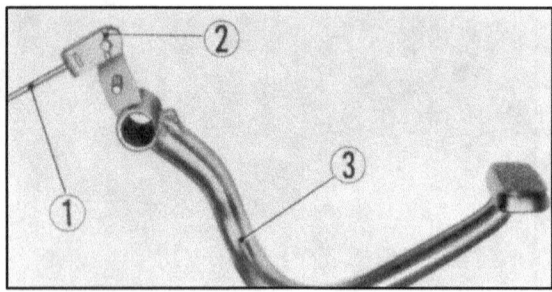

① Rear brake rod ② 1.6×12 cotter pin
③ Rear brake pedal
Fig. 5-54. Rear brake pedal

① Step bar ② 8 mm bolts ③ Side stand
Fig. 5-55. Removing the step bar

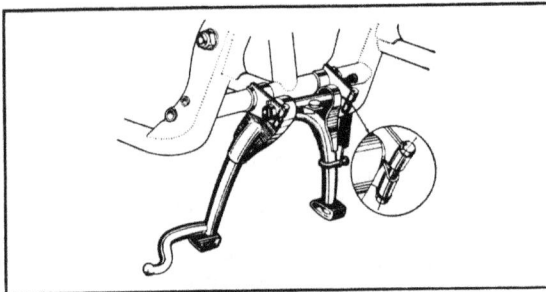

Fig. 5-56. Fixing the main stand with 6 mm bolts

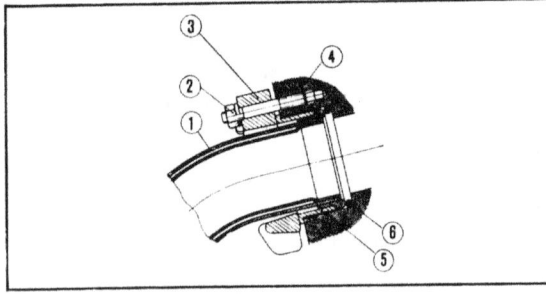

① Exhaust pipe ② 6 mm hex. nut
③ Exhaust pipe joint ④ Cylinder head
⑤ Exhaust pipe joint collar ⑥ Exhaust pipe gasket
Fig. 5-57. Cross-section of exhaust pipe and nut

(Rear Brake Pedal)

1. Remove the rear brake adjusting nut.
2. Unhook the brake pedal and stop switch springs.
3. Rear brake pedal can be removed by unscrewing the rear brake pivot bolt.
4. Rear brake rod can be separated from the brake pedal by removing the brake rod joint pin. (Fig. 5-54)

(Step Bar)

1. Unscrew the four 8 mm bolts and remove the step bar. (Fig. 5-55)
2. The side stand is mounted on the left side of the step bar and is removed by disassembling the side stand spring and side stand pivot screw.

C. Inspection

1. Main stand pivot pipe

   Measure the main stand pivot pipe diameter with a vernier caliper.

   mm (inch)

Standard Value	Serviceable Limit
17.2~17.3 (0.677~0.681)	Replace if under 17.15 (0.6751)

2. Rear brake pivot collar

   Measure the brake pedal pivot collar with a vernier caliper.

   mm (inch)

Standard Value	Serviceable Limit
14.1~14.2 (0.555~0.559)	Replace if over 14.3 (0.565)

3. Inspect the stand, step and brake pedal to insure that they are not bent or deformed.
4. Inspect all springs for breakage or loss of tension.

D. Reassembly

1. Clean all parts and grease all shaft areas. Fill the inside of the pivot pipe with grease.
2. Perform reassembly in the reverse order of disassembly.

NOTE:

Do not over-torque the 6 mm bolts. (Fig. 5-56)

Tightening torque: **80~100 kg-cm (6~8 ft-lb)**

5·9 EXHAUST PIPES AND MUFFLERS

A. Description

Two exhaust lines, one for each cylinder, are employed. Each line is made up of a dual-wall type exhaust pipe and a muffler. Piping layout for the exhaust lines and design of the mufflers are specially made to dampen the exhaust pressure waves and the resulting noise more effectively.

B. Disassembly

Unscrew the four 6 mm (K1:6 mm, K2~K5:8 mm) exhaust pipe flange joint nuts and the two 8 mm muffler flange bolts on the left side and remove the exhaust muffler.
(Fig. 5-59)

(On the CB250/350, unscrew the four 8 mm muffler flange nuts on the inside of both right and left side to remove the exhaust muffler.)

C. Inspection

1. Inspect the muffler gasket for damage.
2. Inspect the muffler for cracks, dents and other defects.

D. Reassembly

1. Install the exhaust pipe gasket on the cylinder head and temporarily tighten the pipe joint with the collar and 6 mm nuts.
2. After completing the muffler installation, tighten the exhaust pipe flange nuts. (Fig. 5-59)

NOTE:

If the exhaust pipe flange joint nuts are tightened first, it will be difficult to install the muffler.

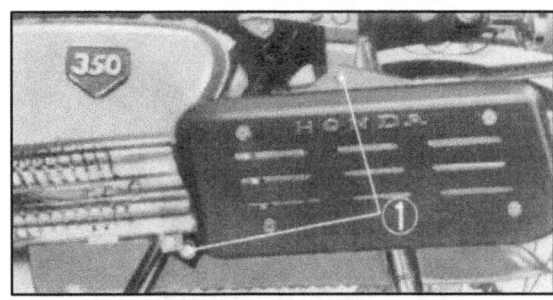
① 8×16 hex. bolt
Fig. 5-58. Removing the muffler

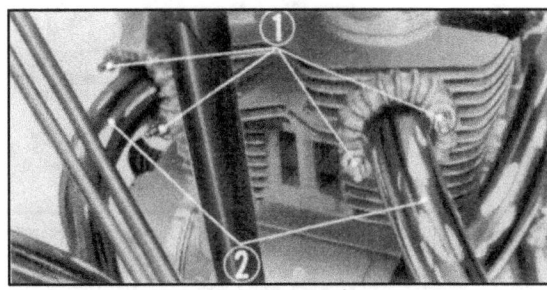
① 6 mm hex. nut   ② Exhaust pipe
Fig. 5-59. Installing the exhaust pipe

5·10 AIR CLEANERS

A. Description

Two air cleaners, one for each carburetor (cylinder), are arranged in "side-by-side" fashion and are located at the center of the frame. Each cleaner uses a replaceable paper filtering element to "clean" incomimg air. As shown in the figure at left, both cleaners are interconnected with each other by a central air passage. This design and a large capacity of the filtering elements assure constant supply of clean air to the engine even if any one of the elements is clogged.

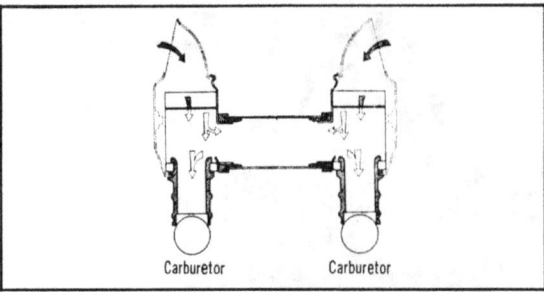
Fig. 5-60. Air flow in dual type air cleaner

B. Disassembly

1. Remove the air cleaner cover. When removing the air cleaner case from the left side of the CL250/350, the muffler must be removed first.
2. Remove the air cleaner case by removing cleaner element setting nut. (Fig. 5-61)
3. The air cleaner element can be separated from the frame by removing the air cleaner connecting tube clamp and the 6 mm bolt.

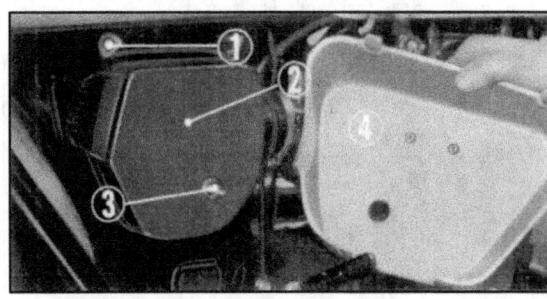
① 6×16 hex. bolt   ② Air cleaner case
③ Cleaner element setting nut   ④ Air cleaner cover
Fig. 5-61. Removing the air cleaner case

C. Inspection

1. Dust on the air cleaner element can be removed by tapping lightly and blowing off the loose dust particles with compressed air.
2. Inspect the air cleaner element to make sure that it is not damaged or clogged.
3. Also inspect the bonded section to make sure that the joints are not cracked or damaged.

D. Reassembly

Mount the air cleaner with the 6 mm bolts, install the air cleaner connecting tube on the carburetor with the clamp.

NOTE:
- After completing the installation of the air cleaner, check to make sure that the right and left air cleaners are interconnected. If there are any leaks in the system, unfiltered air will be drawned into the cylinder and cause rapid wear to the cylinder walls.
- Install the air cleaner case and the air cleaner cover.

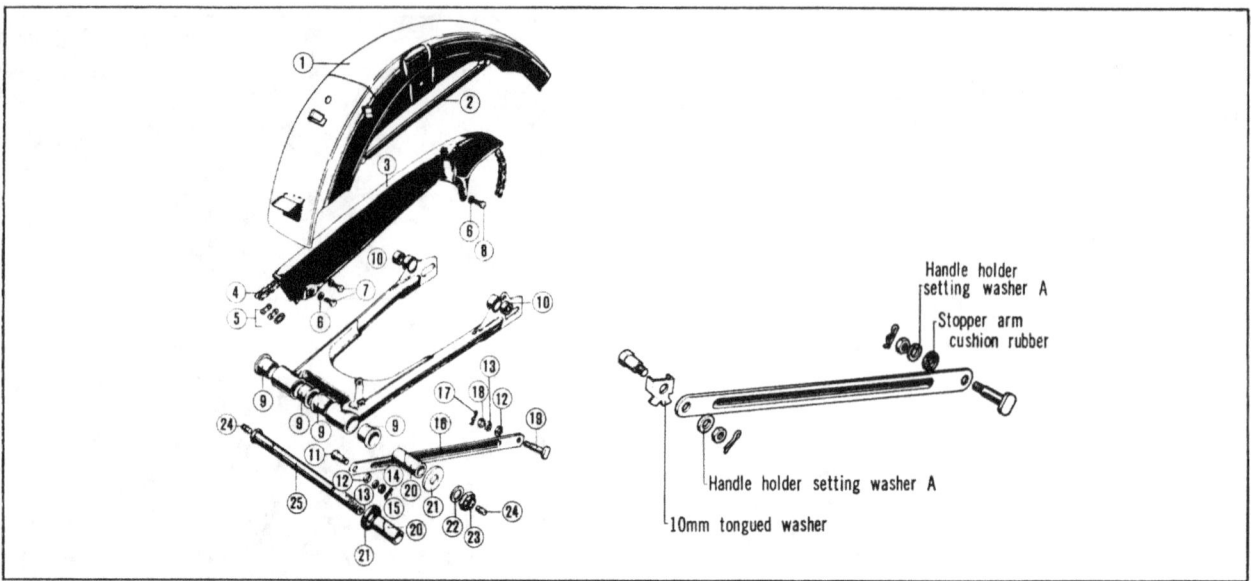

① Rear fender ② Rear bumper ③ Drive chain case ④ Drive chain ⑤ Drive chain joint ⑥ 6 mm flat washer
⑦ 6×8 hex. bolt ⑧ 8 mm flat washer ⑨ Rear fork pivot bush ⑩ Rear cushion under bush
⑪ Rear brake stopper arm bolt ⑫ 10 mm spring washer ⑬ 8 mm flat washer ⑭ 8 mm thin nut ⑮ 2×18 cotter pin
⑯ Rear brake stopper arm ⑰ 8 mm lock pin ⑱ 8 mm hex. nut ⑲ Rear brake stopper bolt ⑳ Rear fork center collar
㉑ Rear fork dust-seal cap ㉒ 14×26 washer ㉓ 14 mm self lock nut ㉔ Grease nipple ㉕ Rear fork pivot bolt
Fig. 5-62. Exploded view of rear fork and rear fender

5·11 REAR FORK AND REAR FENDER

A. Description

The rear fork is constructed as illustrated in the figure above. The front end of the fork is pivotally mounted on the boss provided on the half pillar of the frame body with pivot bushings and the rear ends are similarly joined to the bottom ends of the rear cushions with bushings. This pivoting-fork design permits free out-of-the-horizontal-plane movement of the rear axle (rear wheel). The rear fender is a press-worked part and is bolted to the frame body.

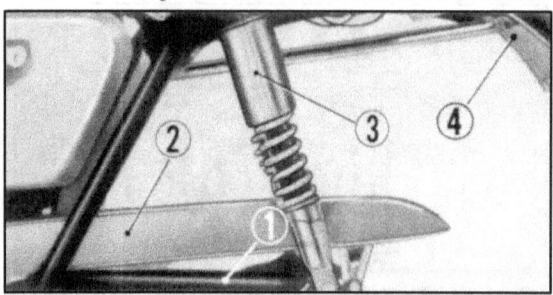

① Rear fork complete ② Drive chain case
③ Rear cushion assembly ④ Rear fender
Fig. 5-63. Rear fork and rear fender

B. Disassembly

[REAR FORK]

1. Remove the rear wheel in accordance with section 4·14B on page 58.
2. Disassemble the rear cushion in accordance with section 4·12A on page 55.
3. Remove the 14 mm self locking nut from the rear fork pivot bolt and extract the pivot bolt; the rear fork can be separated from the frame. (Fig. 5-64)
4. A light tap will remove the rear fork center collar from the rear fork.
5. Separate the drive chain case cover and the rear brake stopper arm from the rear fork.

① 14 mm self locking nut ② Rear fork
Fig. 5-64. Removing the rear fork

[REAR FENDER]

1. Raise the seat and disconnect the wiring for both the rear winker and taillights.
2. Unscrew the two rear winker setting bolts and pull off the fender from the rear fender setting rubber. (Fig. 5-65)
3. Tool box can be separated from the frame by unscrewing the four 6 mm mounting bolts.

① Lead connector ② Rear winker setting bolt
③ Rear fender
Fig. 5-65. Removing the rear fender

C. Inspection

1. Rear fork pivot bushing

   Measure the inside diameter of the bushing with a cylinder gauge or inside micrometer.

   mm (inch)

Standard Value	Serviceable Limit
20.000~20.033 (0.787~789)	Replace if over 20.18 (0.795)

2. Rear fork pivot bolt

   Place the pivot bolt on a V-block, rotate the bolt and measure the amount of bend with a dial gauge.

   mm (inch)

Standard Value	Serviceable Limit
Within 0.02 (0.0008) TIR	Replace if over 0.05 (0.002) TIR

D. Reassembly

[REAR FORK]

1. Drive in the pivot bushing and the center collar. Insert the rear fork dust seal cap. (Fig. 5-66)
2. Insert the pivot bolt through the side bracket and assemble the rear fork to the frame.
3. Install the rear wheel.
4. Install the drive chain.
5. When the assembly is completed, adjust the rear brake pedal and the drive chain tension.
6. Install the drive chain case.
7. Install the torque link.

[REAR FENDER]

1. Perform the reassembly in the reverse order of disassembly.

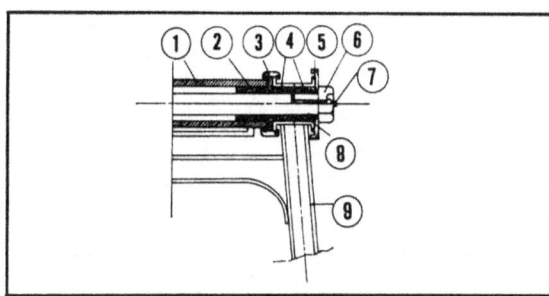

① Frame body ② Center pipe bush
③ Rear fork dust-seal cap rubber ④ Rear fork pivot bush
⑤ Rear fork dust-seal cap ⑥ Rear fork pivot bolt
⑦ Grease nipple ⑧ Rear fork center collar ⑨ Rear fork
Fig. 5-66. Cross-section of the rear fork pivot portion

5·12 REAR CUSHION

A. Description (De Carbon type)

The rear cushion features a "De Carbon" type damper. This damper is, as shown in the figure below, a double-acting type single cylinder in which nitrogen gas and oil are used to produce optimum damping performance under all bump and rebounding conditions. Over the damper is installed a dual-pitch spring which absorbs a wide range of vibrations or shocks and maintains the unit in accurate alignment. Another design feature is that the cushion is adjustable for different riding, loading and road conditions.

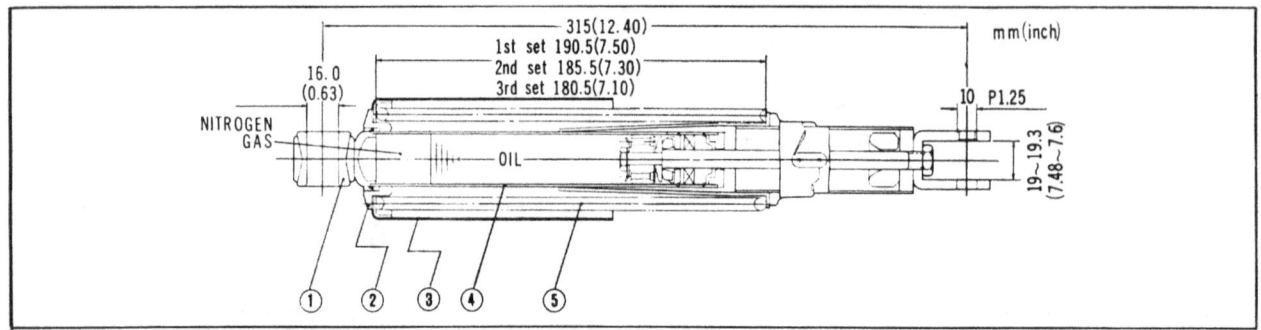

① Joint rubber ② Spring seat stopper ③ Rear cushion upper case ④ Rear damper assembly ⑤ Rear cushion spring
Fig. 5-67. Sectional view of rear cushion

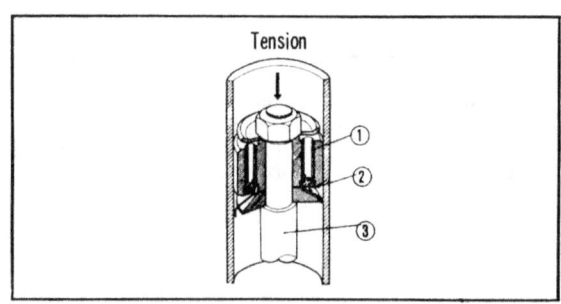

① Piston ② Valve ③ Rod
Fig. 5-68A.

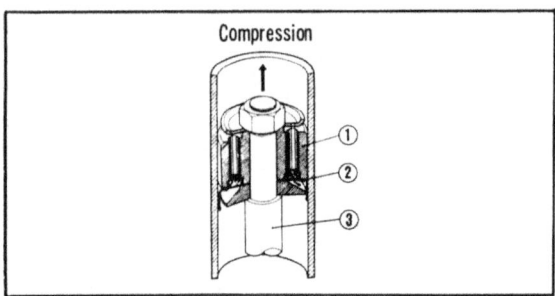

① Piston ② Valve ③ Rod
Fig. 5-68B.

B. Operation

This type of construction ensures good performance, being especially good at low speed. Further, vibrations stabilize very quickly.

Air and oil mixture will not occur and function will not deteriorate even when operated for extended periods over adverse road conditions.

The difference in pressure between the front and rear of the valve is small; noise is minimized; deterioration of the damping force is prevented. (Fig. 5-67)

The rear cushion employs a dual pitch spring, the section with the larger pitch absorbs the large vibrations while the section with the smaller pitch absorbs the smaller vibrations. This provides for exceptionally smooth riding. Further, there are three ranges of adjustment incorporated in the rear cushion, making it possible to adjust the cushion to the different riding, loading and road conditions.

Rear suspension adjustment

The rear cushion ① has three-ranges of adjustment in spring tension and can be adjusted to meet the different type of road or riding conditions. I position is for normal riding. The damper spring strength increasing progressively from II to III, and is to be used for heavily loaded conditions or when operating on bad roads. (Fig. 5-69)

① Rear cushion assembly
Fig. 5-69. Rear cushion adjustment

A. Description (Double-Tube two-way Valve) CB350G/CL350K5

The rear shock absorber assemblies feature the telescopic type oil dampers with bottom valve to give an optimum damping performance under all bumping and rebounding conditions. The damping performance on the extension side is well matched with that on the compression side, providing maximum damping.

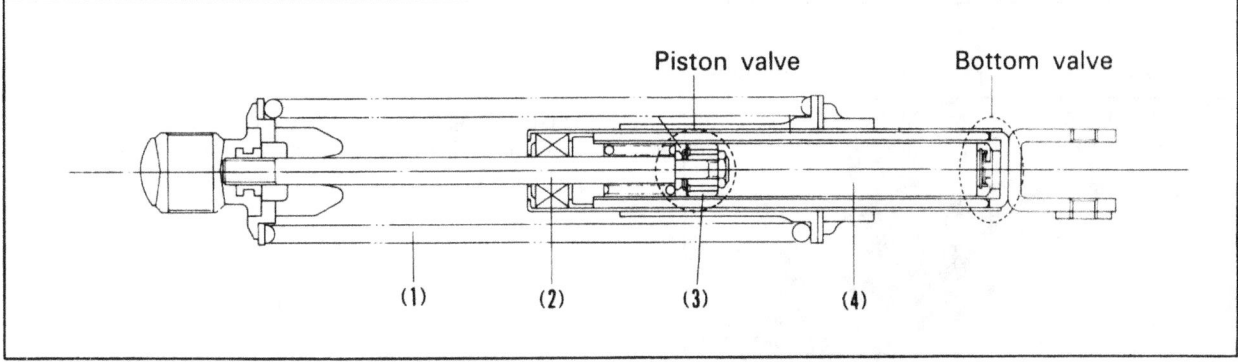

① Rear shock absorber spring
② Damper rod
③ Damper piston
④ Damper cylinder

Fig. 5-70.

B. Operation

Each oil damper is equipped with the piston valves A and B and bottom valve. On the extension side, the damping action is provided by means of the piston valves. While, on the compression side, the damping action is provided by means of the bottom valve.

On extension side:

The oil in the chamber [a] flows into the chamber [b] through the orifice (I) in the valve A (sheet metal). By the resisting force of this oil, the damping action is provided. The valve A is overlapped with the valve B (leaf spring) which covers the half of the orifice. The damping action is regulated by the deflection of the valve B. Under such a condition, the bottom valve is opened and the oil in the chamber [c] flows into the chamber [b] smoothly to prevent air bubbles from being produced.

On compression side:

The oil in the chamber [b] flows by amount of oil equivalent to the volume of damper rod into the chamber [c] through the orifice in the bottom valve. By the resisting force of this oil, the damping action is provided. At this time the piston valves are opened and the oil flows from the chamber [b] into the chamber [a] smoothly.

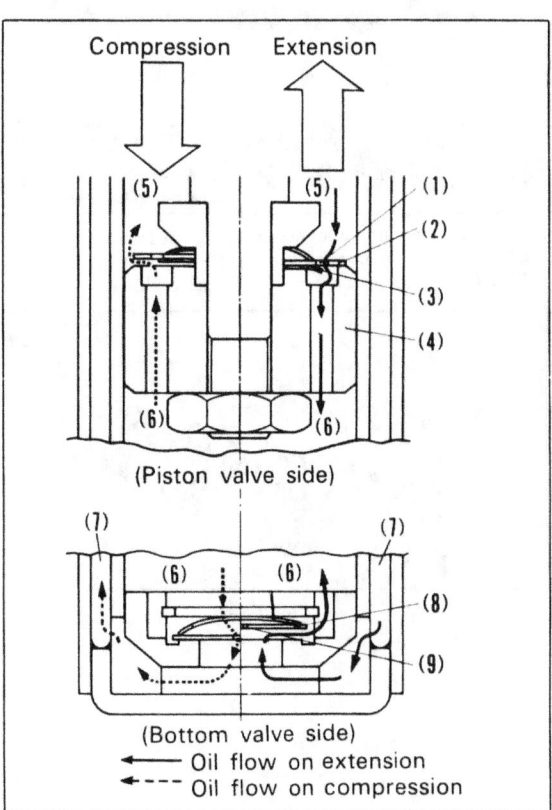

① Orifice (I)
② Valve "A"
③ Valve "B"
④ Piston
⑤ Chamber "a"
⑥ Chamber "b"
⑦ Chamber "c"
⑧ Bottom valve
⑨ Orifice (II)

Fig. 5-71.

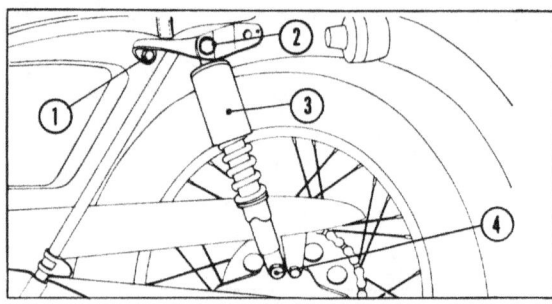

① 6 mm hex. bolt ② 10 mm hex. cap nut
③ Rear cushion assembly ④ 10 mm hex. bolt
Fig. 5-72. Removing the rear cushion assembly

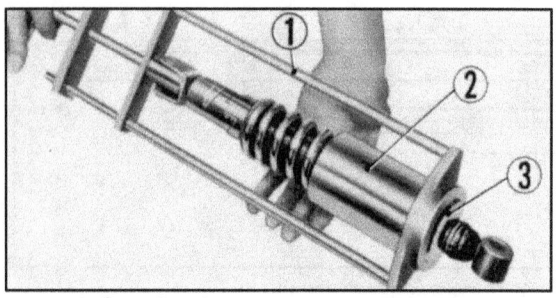

① Special tool ② Rear cushion assembly
③ Spring seat stopper
Fig. 5-73. Disassembling rear cushion

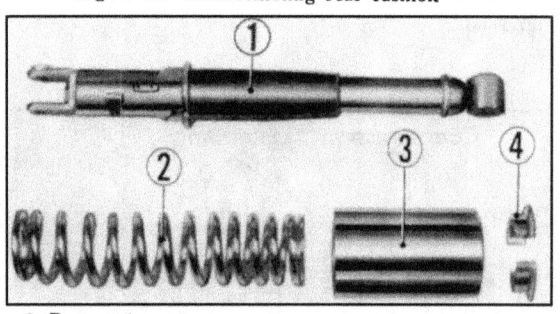

① Rear cushion damper assembly ② Rear cushion spring
③ Rear cushion upper case ④ Spring seat stopper
Fig. 5-74. Component parts of rear cushion

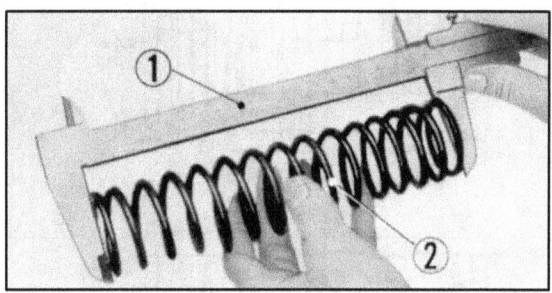

① Vernier caliper ② Rear cushion spring
Fig. 5-75. Measuring rear cushion spring

B. Disassembly

1. Remove the 6 mm bolt from the forward end of the side grip, loosen the 10 mm cap nut, 10 mm bolt and remove the rear cushion assembly. (Fig. 5-72)

2. Compress the rear cushion upper case by using a special tool and remove the rear cushion seat, lift off the upper case and then remove the cushion spring. (Fig. 5-73)

NOTE:

DO NOT DISASSEMBLE THE REAR CUSHION DAMPER ASSEMBLY, IT POSES A HAZARD SINCE IT CONTAINS COMPRESSED GAS.

C. Inspection

1. Rear cushion spring

   Measure the free length of the spring with a vernier caliper. (Fig. 5-75)

   mm (inch)

Standard Value	Serviceable Limit
201.3 (7.925)	Replace if under 175.3 (6.902)

2. Rear cushion spring trueness

   Set the spring up on its end on the surface gauge and measure the amount of tilt with a square and vernier caliper.

   mm (inch)

Standard Value	Serviceable Limit
Within 5 (0.2)	Replace if over 8.0 (0.32)

3. Inspect the cushion damper to insure that there is no fluid leakage.

4. Inspect the damper case and rod to insure that they are not damaged or deformed.

5. Inspect the rear cushion stopper to insure that it is not damaged or deformed.

D. Reassembly

1. Assemble the under seat, spring and upper case to the damper. Compress the assembly using a special tool and lock the assembly with the spring seat stopper. (Fig. 5-76)

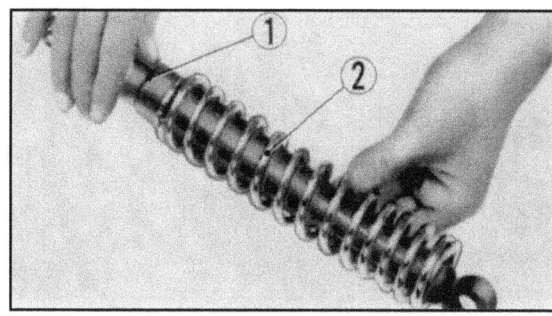

① Rear cushion damper assembly
② Rear cushion spring
Fig. 5-76. Assembling rear cushion

NOTE:

- Upon completing the assembly, actuate the cushion assembly by hand to make sure that there is no binding. (Fig. 5-77)

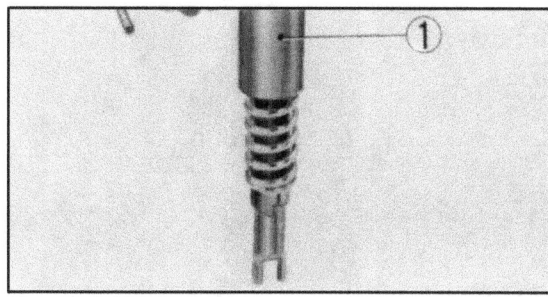

① Rear cushion assembly
Fig. 5-77. Checking operation of cushion

2. Install the cushion in the reverse order of disassembly. (Fig. 5-78)

NOTE:

After installing the cushion, check the alignment of the right and left cushion and also the alignment of the cushion mounting bolt for both right and left sides.

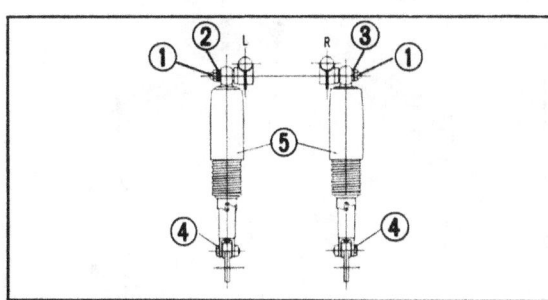

① 10 mm cap nut ② Side grip ③ Special washer
④ 10×32 hex. bolt ④ Rear cushion
Fig. 5-78. Mounting bolts and nuts of rear cushion

5·13 FRONT WHEEL

A. Description

The front wheel is constructed as shown in the figure at left. Referring to the figure, the wheel hub and brake panel are aluminum-alloy casting and contain the front brake components and speedometer drive gearing. The internal surface of the hub serves as a friction surface with which the brake shoes come in contact when expanded by the action of the cam. The front axle is supported at its both ends by ball bearings which are held in place by axle distance collar. The speedometer drive gear which is in mesh with the pinion is mounted on the axle, just outside of the bearing.

① Front wheel axle ② Front wheel side collar ③ Oil-seal
④ 6302R ball bearing ⑤ Front axle distance collar
⑥ Oil-seal ⑦ Speedometer gear ⑧ Speedometer pinion
⑨ Front wheel axle sleeve ⑩ Front brake shoe
⑪ Front brake cam B ⑫ Front brake cam ⑬ Front wheel hub
⑭ Brake arm spring ⑮ Front brake arm A

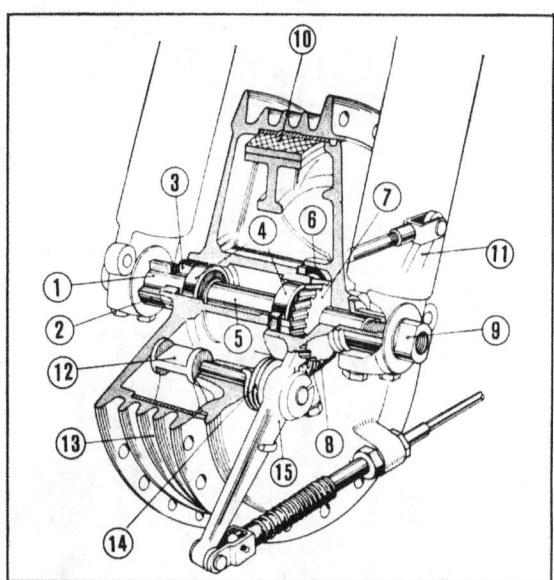

Fig. 5-79. Cross-section of front wheel

84

① Front brake stopper arm bolt
② 8.2 mm tongued washer   ③ Front brake stopper arm
Fig. 5-80. Removing the brake stopper arm

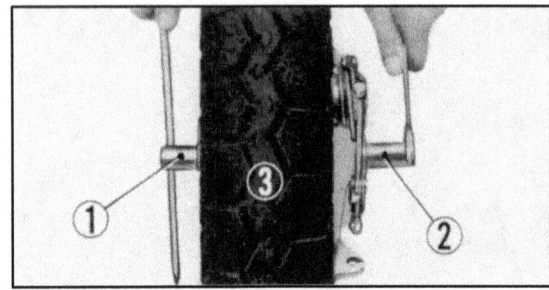

① Front wheel axle   ② Front wheel axle sleeve
③ Front wheel tire
Fig. 5-81. Removing the front wheel axle

① Front wheel tire   ② Oil-seal
Fig. 5-82. Removing the oil-seal

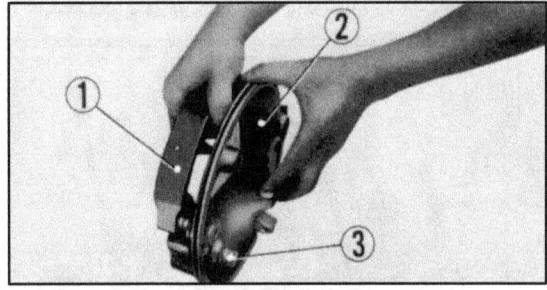

① Front brake shoe   ② Front brake panel
③ Front brake cam
Fig. 5-83. Removing the front brake shoe

① Dial gauge   ② Front wheel rim
Fig. 5-84. Measuring rim runout

B. Disassembly

1. Place a suitable support block under the engine to raise front wheel off the ground.
2. Disconnect the front brake cable, the speedometer cable from the speedometer gear and the brake stopper arm. (Fig. 5-80)
3. Remove the 8 mm nuts which support the lower axle holder on both the right and left sides. The wheel will then drop away from the fork.

4. Insert a bar into the hole on the right side of the front wheel axle and remove the shaft on the left side with a 17 mm wrench.

   Brake panel can be separated from the front wheel.
   (Fig. 5-81)

5. Remove the panel, oil seal, two 6302R ball bearings, and front axle distance collar. (Fig. 5-82)

6. Remove the front brake arm and pull out the front brake cam; the brake shoes can be removed from the panel by spreading the shoes apart by hand. (Fig. 5-83)
7. Separate the tire and tube from the rim.

C. Inspection

1. Front fork rim runout

   Insert the axle through the wheel hub and support it on two V-blocks. Set the dial gauge against the side of the rim and rotate the wheel. (Fig. 5-84)

   mm (inch)

Standard Value	Serviceable Limit
0.5 (0.02) TIR	Repair or replace if over 2.0 (0.080) TIR

2. Front axle bend
   Place the axle on a V-block, rotate the axle and measure the amount of bend with a dial gauge. (Fig. 5-85)

   mm (inch)

Standard Value	Serviceable Limit
Within 0.05 (0.002) TIR	Replace if over 0.2 (0.008)

3. Radial clearance of 6302R ball bearing
   Place a dial gauge against the bearing outer and measure the clearance.

   mm (inch)

Standard Value	Serviceable Limit
0.003~0.016 (0.0001~0.0007)	Replace if over 0.05 (0.002)

4. Front brake drum inside diameter
   Measure the diameter with a vernier caliper. (Fig. 5-86)

   mm (inch)

Standard Value	Serviceable Limit
180~180.3 mm (7.087~7.099 in)	Replace if over 182 (7.17)

5. Thickness of brake lining
   Measure the lining thickness with a vernier caliper.

   mm (inch)

Standard Value	Serviceable Limit
5.5~5.7 (0.217~0.224)	Replace if under 3.0 (0.118)

6. Check thickness of front brake cam
   Replace if excessively worn or worn in "steps".
7. Inspect anchor pin for wear or damage.
8. Inspect and tighten any loose spokes.
   Tightening torque : **20~25 kg-cm (1.4~1.8 ft-lb)**
9. Check for air leak by submerging the tube in water.
10. Check the tire for damage to casing, both inside and outside.
11. Balance wheel assembly.

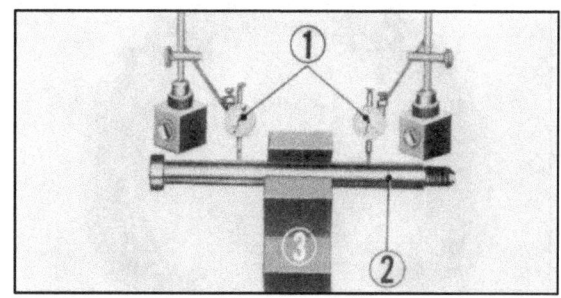

① Dial gauge ② Front wheel axle ③ V-block
Fig. 5-85. Checking the front axle for bend

① Vernier caliper ② Front wheel hub
Fig. 5-86. Measuring front brake drum inside diameter

D. Reassembly

1. The tube can be easily mounted by inflating with small amount of air to make the tube firm. (Fig. 5-87)

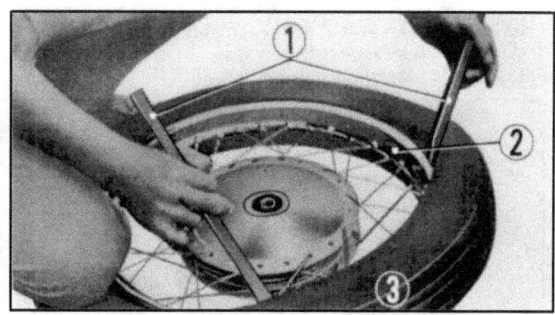

① Tire lever ② Front wheel rim ③ Front wheel tire
Fig. 5-87. Installing the tire

NOTE :

- After the tire is mounted, inflate with approximately 1/3 the designated pressure and lightly tap around the tire with a wooden hammer to eliminate any pinching of the tube. (Fig. 5-88)

① Wooden hammer ② Front wheel tire
Fig. 5-88. Tapping around the tire

① Valve stem
Fig. 5-89. Valve angle

- The valve stem should be positioned pointing toward the axle to prevent damage to the tube. (Fig. 5-89)
- Inflate the tire to the specified pressure.

  For normal riding: 1.8 kg/sq. cm (25.6 lbs/sq. in)
  For high speed riding: 2.0 kg/sq. cm (28.4 lbs/sq. in)

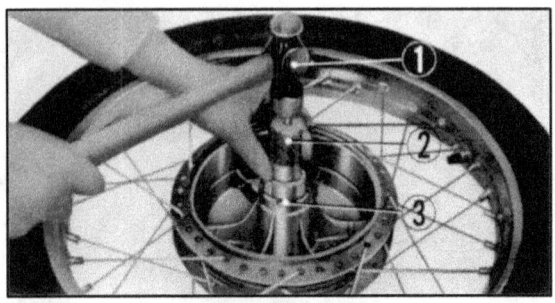

① Hammer   ② Bearing driver   ③ 6302R ball bearing
Fig. 5-90. Driving the bearing

2. Grease the 6302R ball bearing and pack the inside of the front wheel hub with grease, and insert the distance collar. Drive the ball bearing in using the front wheel bearing driver (Tool No. 07946-2860100 and 07946-2860200). (Fig. 5-90)

NOTE:

The 6302R ball bearing incorporates a seal on the outside, make sure that the bearing is installed correctly.

① Front brake arm A   ② Front brake arm B
③ Front brake panel
Fig. 5-91. Installing the brake arm

3. Hook the spring on the front brake shoe and then install the anchor pin and brake cam. Assemble the unit to the front brake panel.

NOTE:

Punch marks on the brake arms and brake cams must be aligned. (Fig. 5-91)

Ⓐ Decrease   Ⓑ Increase
Fig. 5-92. Front brake cable adjustment

4. Assemble the panel together with the side collar to the front wheel.
5. After tightening the front axle, mount the front wheel on the fork, connect the front brake stopper arm and assemble the front axle holder with 8 mm nuts.
6. Connect the speedometer cable to the speedometer gear.
7. Connect the front brake cable to the brake stopper arm and adjust the free travel. The specified free travel is **15~30 mm (0.6~1.2 in)**. Loosen the nut ⓑ and make the adjustment with nuts ⓐ. (Fig. 5-92)

FRONT WHEEL (disc brake system)

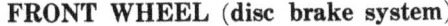

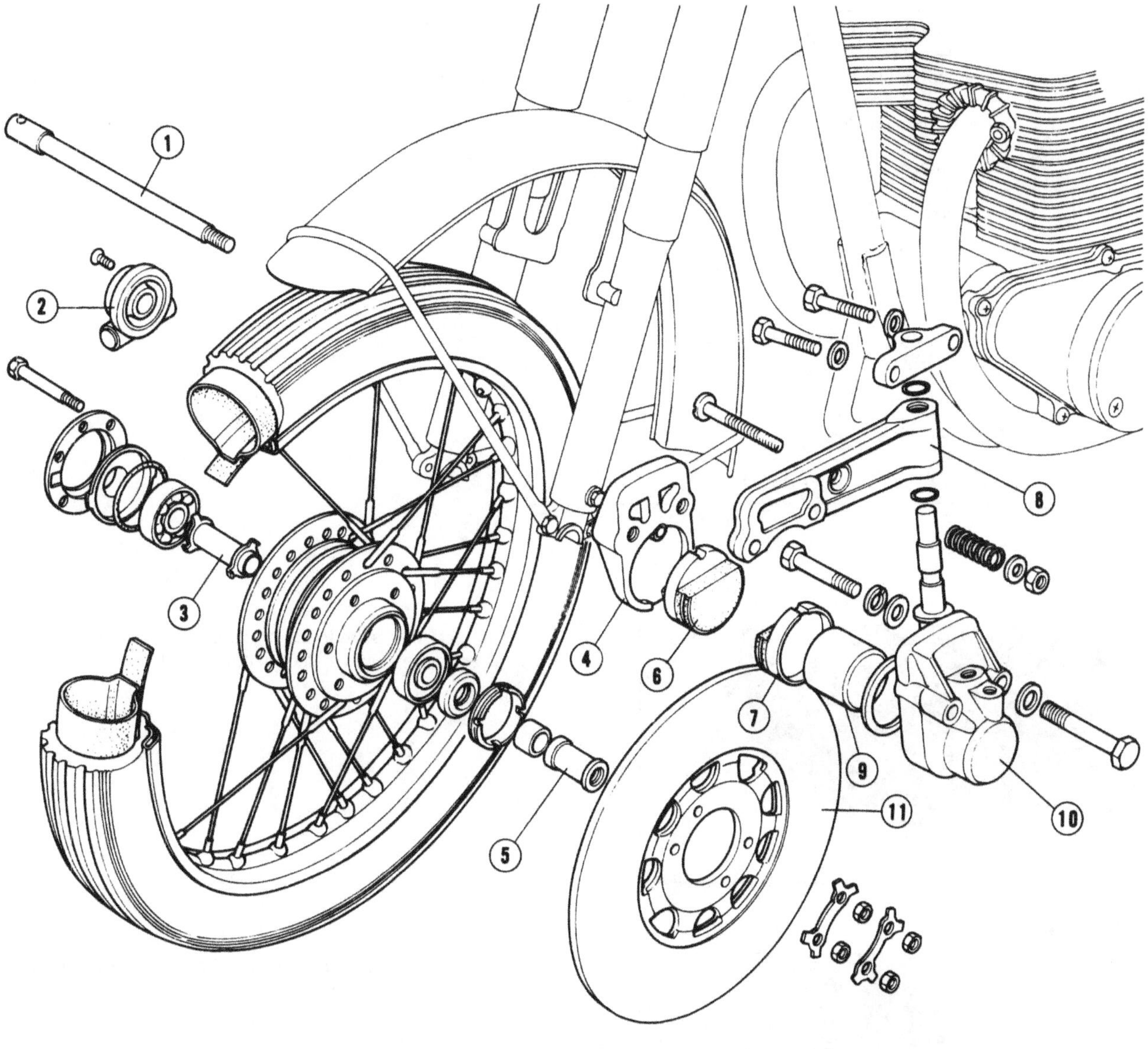

① Front wheel axle　② Speedometer gear box　③ Front axle shaft spacer
④ Caliper B　⑤ Front wheel axle nut　⑥ Pad B
⑦ Pad A　⑧ Caliper holder　⑨ Piston
⑩ Caliper A　⑪ Front brake disc

Fig. 5-93: Front wheel disassembled (CB250/350)

To service front wheel

Standard tools:

10 mm wrench	12 mm box wrench
14 mm wrench	Standard type screwdriver No. 3
12 mm wrench	Pliers

Torque specifications

Unit: kg-cm (lb-ft)

Part	Thread dia. (mm)	Torque
Front brake disc	6	180~230 (13~17)
Caliper bolt	8	300~400 (22~29)
Holder joint	6	120~200 (9~14)

A. Disassembly

No.	Disassembly procedure	Note
1	Place wood block(s) under engine	
2	Speedometer cable	*1
3	Axle holder attaching nut	*2
4	Front axle shaft	
5	Front wheel bearing retainer	*3
6	Hold engine with jack and remove front wheel	
7	Remove dust seal from front wheel bearing retainer	
8	Remove nuts and lock plate and remove brake disc	*4
9	Front wheel bearings	
10	Gear box and retainer cover	

① Speedometer cable
Fig. 5-94.

*1 Disconnect the speedometer cable by removing 5 mm oval head screw and disconnecting cable.

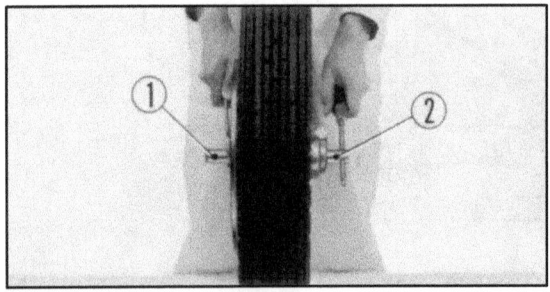

① Axle nut ② Axle shaft
Fig. 5-95.

*2 Using the two screwdrivers as shown, remove the axle nut and remove the axle shaft.

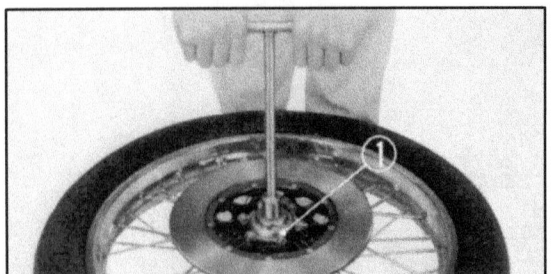

① Bearing retainer
Fig. 5-96.

*3 Remove the front wheel bearing retainer from the wheel hub and the dust seal from the bearing retainer.

*4 Straighten tabs of washers remove the nuts and lock plate and remove the front brake disc from the wheel. Remove the gear box and retainer cover from the other side.

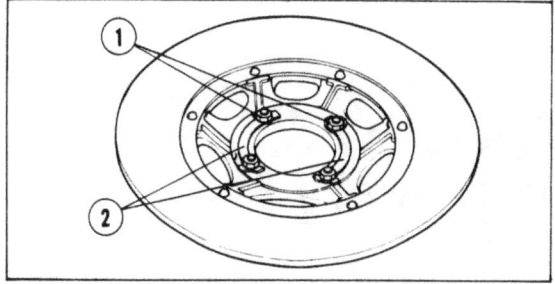

① Nuts ② Lock plate
Fig. 5-97.

B. Inspection

• Measure the brake disc

Place the brake disc on a level stand. Using a dial gauge, measure the brake disc at several points as shown.

If the face runout exceeds 0.3 mm (0.0118 in.), replace the disc.

Measure the disc thickness. If the thickness is below 6 mm (0.2362 in.), replace the disc.

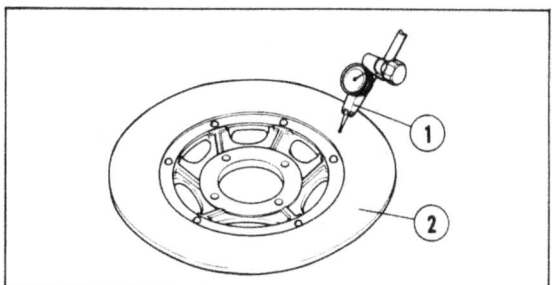

① Dial gauge ② Brake disc
Fig. 5-98.

• Check the wheel rim for lateral runout and radial clearance

Rotate the wheel and check the wheel rim for lateral runout and radial clearance using a dial gauge.

Unit : mm (in)

	Standard	Repair limit
Lateral runout	0.5 (0.0197), max.	2.0 (0.0787), min.
Radial clearance	0.5 (0.0197), max.	2.0 (0.0787), min.

• Measure the front wheel ball bearings

Unit : mm (in)

	Standard	Repair limit
Axial clearance	0.07 (0.0028)	0.1 (0.0039)
Radial clearance	0.003 (0.0001)	0.05 (0.0020)

Check the spokes for looseness.

Check the tire tube for leaks.

Check the tire for entry of foreign material or damage.

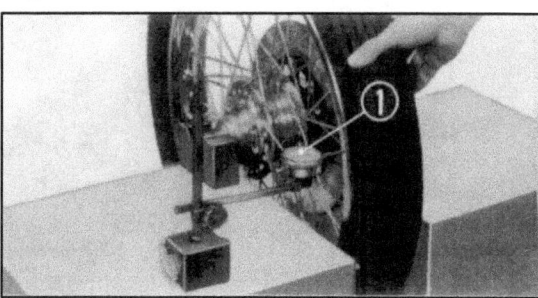

① Dial gauge
Fig. 5-99.

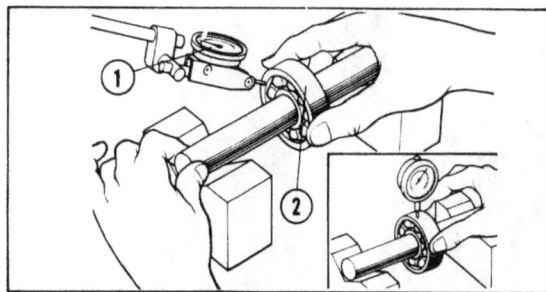

① Dial gauge ② Ball bearing
Fig. 5-100.

C. Assembly

• Install the 6302Z ball bearings to the wheel hub.
• Install the dust seal to the bearing retainer and then install the bearing retainer in place. Install the o-ring to the wheel hub.

① Bearing driver
Fig. 5-101.

① Gear box retainer ② O-ring
Fig. 5-102.

- Fit the tab of gear box retainer to the recess in gear box retainer cover and install them to the wheel hub.

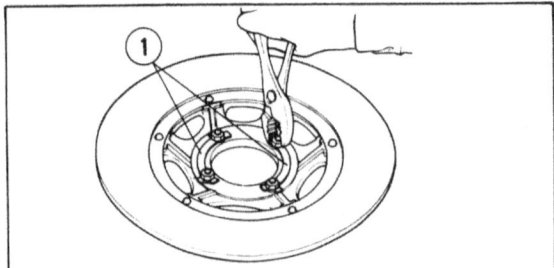

① Lock plate
Fig. 5-103.

- Install the brake disc to the wheel.
  NOTE:
  After tightening the nuts, lock them by bending the tabs of the lock plate.

① Gear box retainer ② Speedometer gear box
Fig. 5-104.

- Install the speedometer gear box from the right side and install the front axle.
- Install the front wheel to the front forks and tighten the axle holder bolts and nuts.
  NOTE:
  Be sure the speedometer gear box is installed correctly. To tighten the axle holder bolts and nuts, begin with the left side (disc plate side) first.
- Connect the speedometer cable to the gear box.

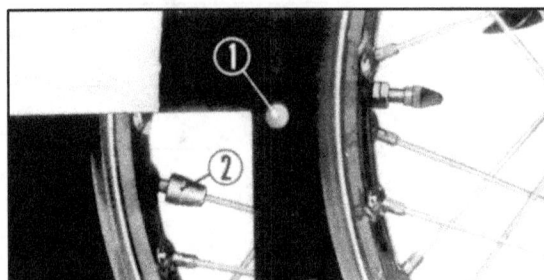

① Balance mark ② Balance weight
Fig. 5-105.

- Check the wheel for balance.
  a. Make chalk marks on the circumference of the wheel and slowly rotate the wheel two or three turns.
  b. If the wheel is unbalanced, it always stops rotating when the heaviest part comes to the bottom.
  c. To rebalance the wheel, install a balance weight opposite to the heaviest part.

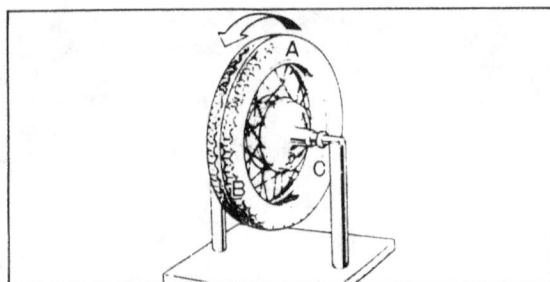

Fig. 5-106.

  d. Install the balance weight on a spoke. Rotate the wheel two or three turns to check for balance. If the wheel stops rotating when different parts come to the bottom, it is balanced. The balance weights are available in four different weights, 5 g (0.176 oz.), 10 g (0.353 oz.), 15 g (0.529 oz.) and 20 g (0.705 oz.).
  e. The front wheel balance should be checked with the brake disc installed.

Front disc brake
- The disc brake system mainly consists of the brake lever, master cylinder, calipers and brake disc.

A. Disassembly of calipers and master cylinder

> **Disassembly precautions**
> 1. Clean dirt and dust off the parts. Take care not to allow foreign material to enter the parts.
> 2. Set aside the disassembled component parts in groups to facilitate assembly.

No.	Disassembly procedure	Note
1	Front wheel	
2	Drain brake fluid from master cylinder	
3	Oil joint bolt and brake hose	*1
4	Calipers A and B	*2
5	Holder setting bolts	*3
6	Joint bolt	*4
7	18 mm snap ring	*5
8	Primary cup	*6

*1 Remove the oil joint bolt and disconnect the brake hose.

① Joint ② Oil joint bolt
③ Brake hose
Fig. 5-107.

*2 Remove the three caliper attaching bolts and one adjusting bolt and remove the calipers A and B as an assembly.

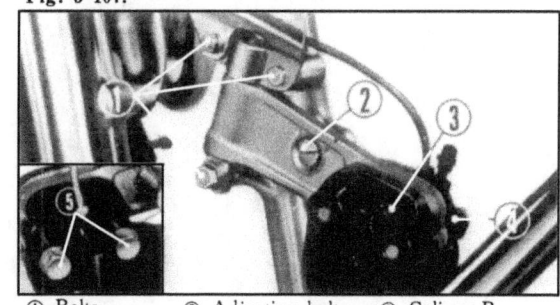

① Bolts ② Adjusting bolt ③ Caliper B
④ Caliper A ⑤ Caliper bolts
Fig. 5-108.

*3 Remove the two caliper setting bolts and separate the caliper assembly into two parts A and B.
  • Remove the pad A and piston from the caliper A.
  • Remove the pad B from the caliper B.

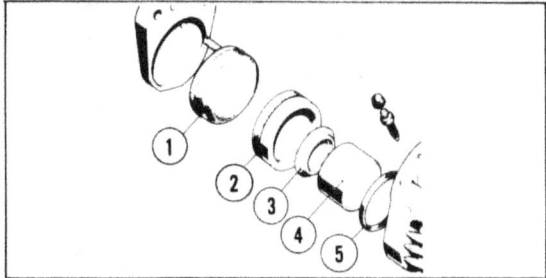

① Pad B ② Pad A ③ Pad seat
④ Piston ⑤ Piston seal
Fig. 5-109.

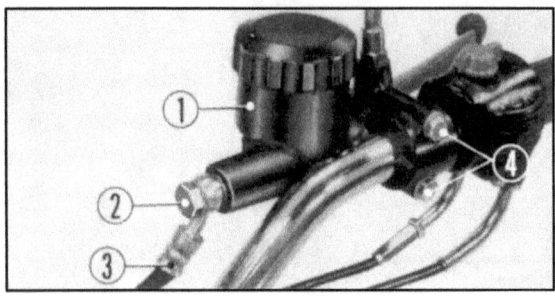

① Master cylinder body   ② Joint bolt
③ Brake hose   ④ Setting bolts
Fig. 5-110.

*4 Loosen the master cylinder joint bolt and disconnect the brake hose.
- Loosen the master cylinder bolts and remove the master cylinder from the handlebar.
- Disassemble the master cylinder.

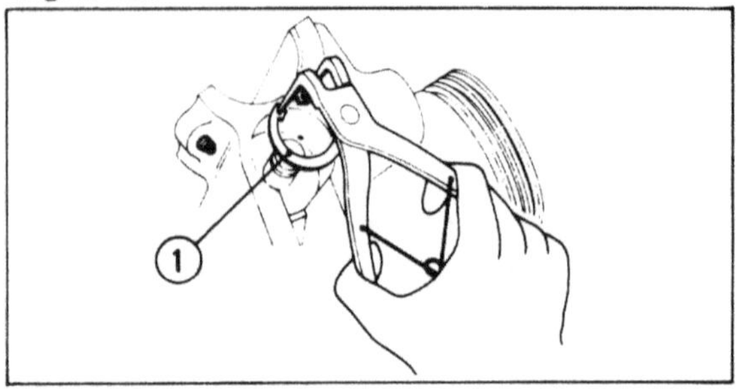

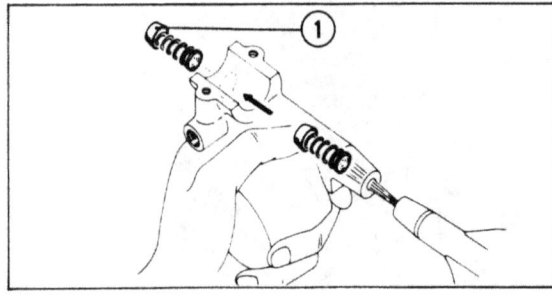

① 18 mm snap ring
Fig. 5-111.

*5 Remove the 18 mm internal snap ring using the special tool.

① Primary cup
Fig. 5-112.

*6 Remove the 10.5 mm washer, piston, primary cup, spring and check valve in this order.

To remove the primary cup, direct compressed air of $2\sim3$ kg/cm² ($28\sim43$ lb/in²) in pressure to the cylinder union (brake hose joint). If the check valve is damaged, any other tool may be used to remove the primary cup.

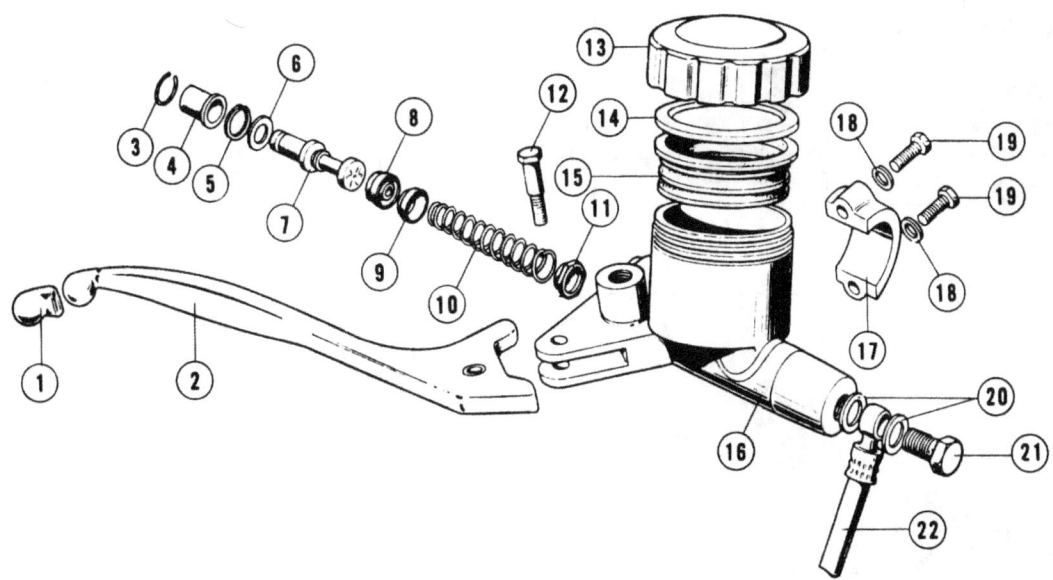

① Lever cap ② Braker lever ③ Stopper washer
④ Boot ⑤ 18 mm internal snap ring ⑥ 10.5 mm washer
⑦ Piston ⑧ Secondary cup ⑨ Primary cup
⑩ Spring ⑪ Check valve ⑫ Handlebar lever joint bolt
⑬ Cap ⑭ Master cylinder plate ⑮ Diaphragm
⑯ Master cylinder body ⑰ Master cylinder holder ⑱ Spring washers
⑲ 6 mm bolts ⑳ Oil bolt washers ㉑ Oil bolt
㉒ Brake hose

Fig. 5-113. Master cylinder disassembled

NOTES:

1. Wash all disassembled metal parts in trichloro-ethylene or equivalent fluid and dry them thoroughly.
2. The check valve must be washed in brake fluid.
3. Never wash the brake parts in mineral oils such as gasoline or cleaning fluid.

B. Inspection of caliper and master cylinder

NOTES:

1. Check the piston for wear or damage and replace if necessary.
2. Check the inside surface of the master cylinder for scores and replace if necessary.
3. Check the spring for damage and replace if necessary.

1. Check the brake disc pads for wear

   Red lines are scribed in the pads A and B. If the pads wear down to the lines, replace them with new ones. Install new pads so that the brake disc to pad clearance is 0.15 mm (0.0059 in.). To adjust the clearance, turn the caliper adjusting bolt counterclockwise until the pad bears on the disc. Then back off the adjusting bolt 1/2 turn and tighten the lock nut.

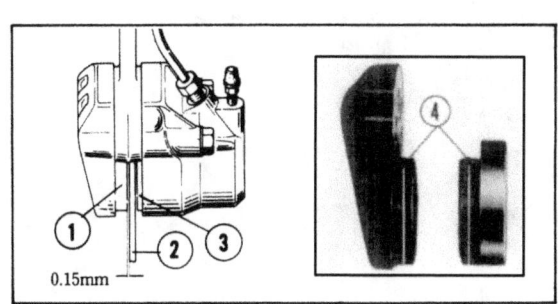

① Pad B ② Pad A
③ Brake disc ④ Service limit lines
Fig. 5-114.

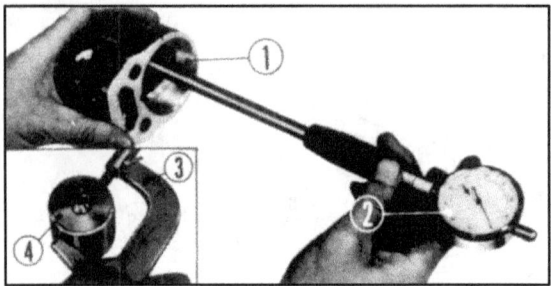

① Caliper cylinder　② Cylinder gauge
③ Micrometer　④ Piston
Fig. 5-115.

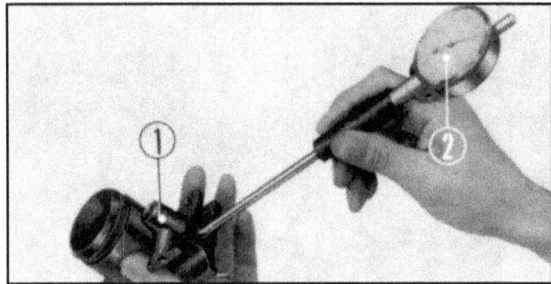

① Master cylinder　② Cylinder gauge
Fig. 5-116.

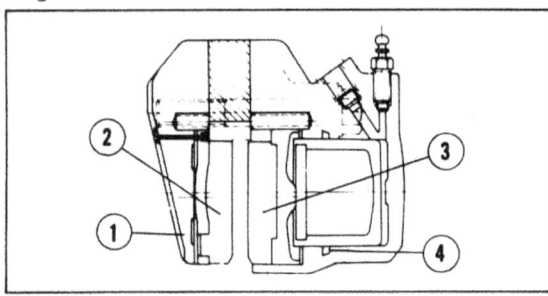

① Caliper B　② Pad B　③ Pad A
④ Caliper A
Fig. 5-117.

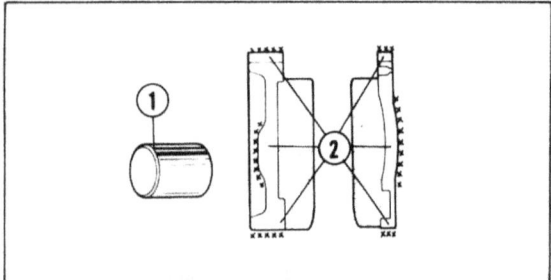

① 11×15 dowel pin, full-sized
② Apply grease to areas marked (×).
　Quantity of grease:
　　About 1 g (0.0353 oz.)/unit (equivalent to 11×15 dowel pin)
Fig. 5-118.

2. Measure the caliper cylinder and piston

Using a cylinder gauge, measure the cylinder bore and piston O.D. If the clearance between the two exceeds 0.11 mm (0.0043 in.), replace.

Unit: mm (in)

	Standard	Repair limit
Cylinder bore	38.18~38.20 (1.5031~1.5039)	38.215 (1.5045)
Piston O.D.	38.115~38.48 (1.5006~1.5150)	38.105 (1.5002)

3. Measure the master cylinder and piston

Using a cylinder gauge, measure the cylinder bore and piston O.D. If the clearance between the two exceeds 0.11 mm (0.0043 in.), replace.

Unit: mm (in)

	Standard	Repair limit
Cylinder bore	14.0~14.043 (0.5512~0.5529)	14.055 (0.5533)
Piston O.D.	13.957~13.984 (0.5495~0.5506)	13.940 (0.5488)

C. Assembly of caliper and master cylinder

To assemble, reverse the disassembly procedures.

Calipers

- Install the pads A and B.

  NOTE:

  When installing the pads, apply a coat of grease to the calipers to prevent entry of dirt or water. When repairing, apply a coat of grease to the sliding surfaces and rear faces of the calipers and pads and to the dowel pin as shown.

- Install the caliper assembly to the front forks.

Master cylinder

> **Assembly precaution**
>
> The brake system is most important for safe riding, especially rubber parts as they play a critical role. Whenever any damage or deterioration to the rubber parts is noted, they must be replaced immediately. Take care not to allow foreign material to enter the brake parts when assembling.

- Wash the component parts and thoroughly dry them using compressed air.
- Apply a coat of brake fluid to the inside of the cylinder.
- Install the check valve to the return spring and install them in the cylinder as a unit. When installing, be sure to install the spring with a end having a larger dia, inward. Take care not to allow the check valve to come out of the spring.

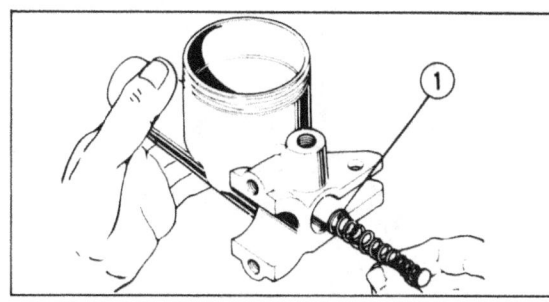

① Check valve
Fig. 5-119.

- Applying a thin coat of brake fluid to the outer surface of the primary cup and install it, taking care not to damage it. Be sure that the cup is correctly positioned in the cylinder.

  Install the secondary cup to the piston.
- Install the 18 mm snap ring and rotate the snap ring to check for proper fit.
- Install the boot.

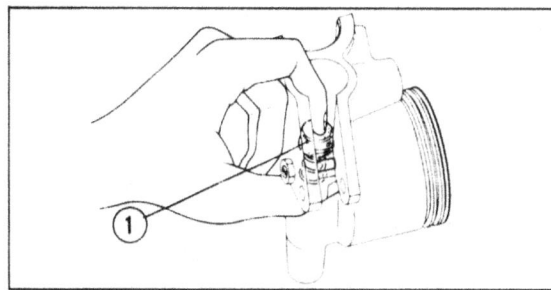

① Primary cup
Fig. 5-120.

NOTES:
1. Connect the brake pipe.
2. Install the cylinder to the handlebar.
3. Bleed the brake lines.
4. Road-test the motorcycle to check for air or oil leaks and for operation.
5. Check the brake fluid level.

D. Adjustment of disc brake

When the brake is disassembled, it must be adjusted and bled completely.

1. Check the brake lever free play

   The lever free play is specified to be 2~5 mm (0.0787~0.1969 in.) at the tip of the lever. If the free play is out of specification, check and replace if necessary.

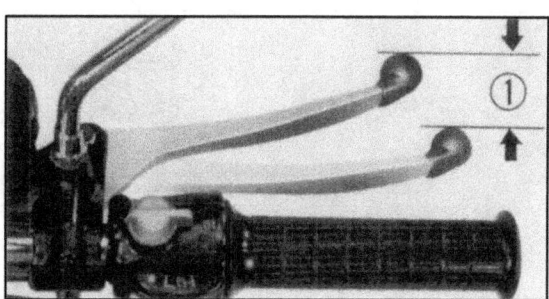

① 2~5 mm
Fig. 5-121.

2. Check the brake fluid level

   Fill the master cylinder oil reservoir up to the level line.
   CAUTION:

   Do not allow the brake fluid to come in contact with the painted surfaces, rubber parts and instruments.

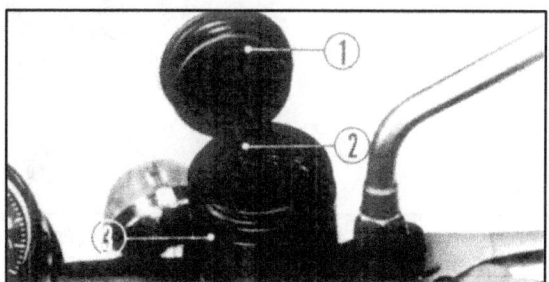

① Diaphragm   ② Brake fluid
③ Master cylinder
Fig. 5-122.

96

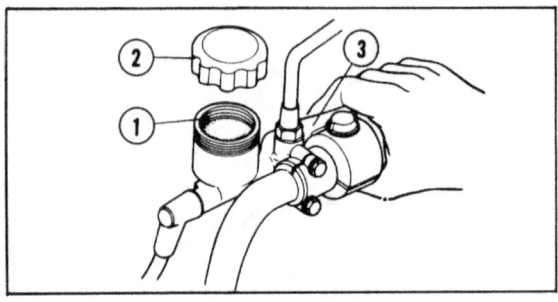

① Diaphragm ② Cap ③ Brake lever
Fig. 5-123.

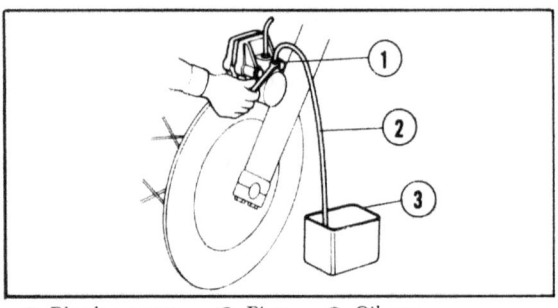

① Bleeder screw ② Pipe ③ Oil can
Fig. 5-124.

3. Bleed the brake lines

Air trapped in the brake lines will reduce the braking effect and result in dangerous riding.

If the brake lever feels spongy when it is squeezed or if the brake fluid level drops excessively, bleed the brake lines. To bleed, proceed as follows:

a. Fill the master cylinder oil reservoir up to the level line.

b. Install the diaphragm to prevent the fluid from splashing.

c. Put a pipe on the bleeder screw located to the caliper. Prepare an oil can.

d. Squeeze the brake lever and operate it several times until a resistance is felt. With the lever squeezed, loosen the bleeder screw about 1/2 turn. As soon as the lever bears on the handlebar pipe, tighten the bleeder screw. Continue the bleeding operation until air bubbles are no longer noted in the fluid flowing out of the bleeder hole.

NOTE:

While bleeding, add brake fluid.

5·14 REAR WHEEL

A. Description

The rear wheel is of a similar construction to the front wheel described in the previous section, the difference being that the drive sprocket is bolted to the left side of the hub and that the axle is movably mounted for drive chain tension adjustment. The installation or arrangement of the major components is illustrated in the figure below, to which reference can be made in studying the construction of the wheel.

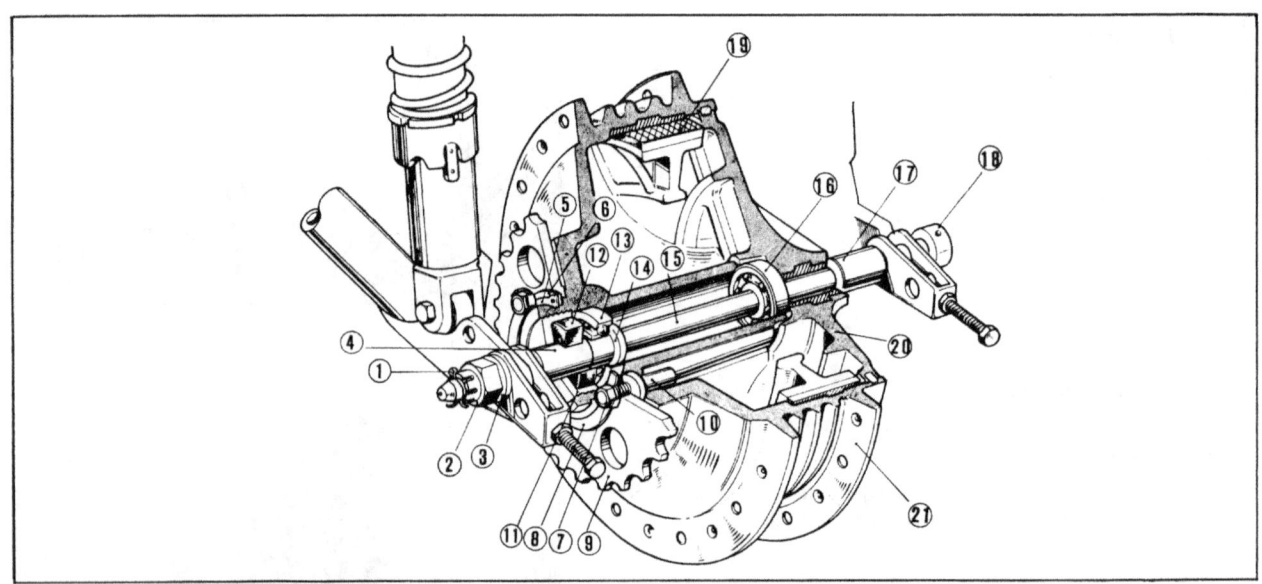

① 4×30 cotter pin ② 10 mm castle nut ③ 16.5×30 washer ④ Rear wheel side collar ⑤ 69 mm external circlip
⑥ 70 mm washer ⑦ 10 mm thin nut ⑧ 10 mm tongued washer ⑨ Final driven sprocket ⑩ Driven sprocket fixing bolt
⑪ Rear wheel bearing retainer ⑫ Dust-seal ⑬ 6304Z ball bearing ⑭ Rear axle distance collar B
⑮ Rear axle distance collar A ⑯ 6303Z ball bearing ⑰ Rear wheel collar ⑱ Rear wheel axle ⑲ Rear brake shoe
⑳ Rear wheel brake panel ㉑ Rear wheel hub
Fig. 5-125. Cross-section of rear wheel

B. Disassembly

1. Remove the drive chain joint, and disconnect the chain. (Fig. 5-126)
2. Remove the rear brake adjusting nut; separate the brake rod from the brake arm; remove the rear brake stopper bolt and separate the stopper arm from the panel.
3. Extract the cotter pin from the axle.

① Drive chain joint clip ② Drive chain
Fig. 5-126. Removing the drive chain joint

4. Remove the rear axle nut and extract the rear wheel axle. Tilt the motorcycle and remove the rear wheel. (Fig. 5-127)

① Rear wheel
Fig. 5-127. Removing the rear wheel from the frame

5. Remove 69 mm external circlip, and 70 mm washer, straighten the 10 mm tongued washer, and remove 10 mm thin nuts. The final driven sprocket can then be separated from the rear wheel hub. (Fig. 5-128)

① 10 mm thin nuts ② 10 mm tongued washer
③ Final driven sprocket ④ 69 mm external circlip
Fig. 5-128. Removing the final driven sprocket

6. Remove the rear wheel bearing retainer by using bearing retainer tightening wrench. (Tool No. 07910-3290000). Pull out the 6303Z and 6304Z ball bearings, and rear axle distance collar. (Fig. 5-129)

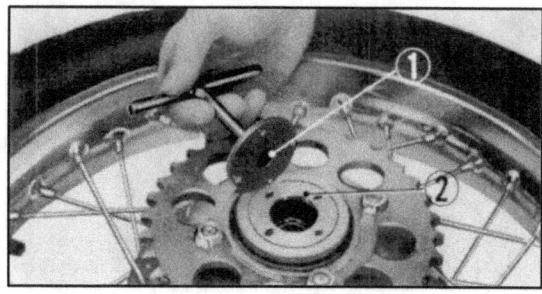

① Bearing retainer tightening wrench
② Bearing retainer
Fig. 5-129. Removing the bearing retainer

7. Remove 2×15 mm cotter pin and anchor pin washer. Separate the brake arm from the panel in order to extract the rear brake shoe. (Fig. 5-130)

① 2×15 cotter pin ② Brake shoe setting washer
③ Rear brake shoe ④ Rear brake panel
Fig. 5-130. Removing the rear brake shoe

① Tire lever ② Rear wheel rim ③ Rear wheel tire
Fig. 5-131. Removing the rear wheel tire

① Dial gauge ② Front wheel rim
Fig. 5-84. Measuring rim runout

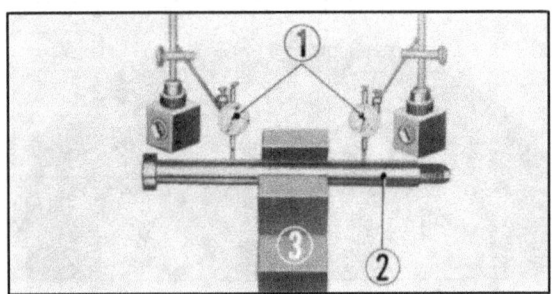

① Dial gauge ② Rear wheel axle ③ V-block
Fig. 5-132. Checking the rear axle for bend

① Vernier caliper ② Rear wheel hub
Fig. 5-133. Measuring rear brake drum inside diameter

① Rear wheel tire ② Wood spacer piece
③ Rear wheel rim
Fig. 5-134. Inspecting the inside of tire

8. Using tire levers, remove tire and remove tube as illustrated in Fig. 5-131.

C. Inspection

1. Rim runout. (Fig. 5-84 Same as front wheel)
   Insert the axle through the wheel hub and support it on the two V-blocks. Set the dial gauge against the side of the rim and rotate it.

   mm (inch)

Standard Value	Serviceable Limit
Dial runout within 0.5 (0.020)	Replace or repair if over 2.0 (0.079)

2. Rear axle bend
   Place the axle on the V-block, rotate the axle and measure the amount of bend with a dial gauge. (Fig. 5-132)

   mm (inch)

Standard Value	Serviceable Limit
Within 0.05 (0.002) TIR	Replace if over 0.2 (0.008) TIR

3. Radial clearance of the 6303Z and 6204Z ball bearing.
   Place a dial gauge against the bearing outer and measure the clearance.

   mm (inch)

	Standard Value	Serviceable Limit
6303Z	0.003~0.018 (0.0001~0.0007)	Replace if over 0.05 (0.002)
6304Z	0.0005~0.0020 (0.0002~0.0008)	Replace if over 0.06 (0.0023)

4. Rear brake drum inside diameter
   Measure the diameter with a vernier caliper. (Fig. 5-133)

   mm (inch)

Standard Value	Serviceable Limit
160.0~160.3 (6.300~6.312)	Replace if over 162 (6.38)

5. Thickness of brake lining
   Measure the lining thickness with a vernier caliper.

   mm (inch)

Standard Value	Serviceable Limit
5.5~5.7 (0.217~0.224)	Replace if under 3.0 (0.118)

6. Inspect anchor pin for wear or damage.
7. Inspect and tighten all loose spokes.
   Tightening torque: 20~25 kg-cm (1.4~1.8 ft-lb)
8. Inspect tube for air leak by inflating and immersing it in water.
9. Inspect the tire and tube for any damage on the inside and outside. (Fig. 5-134)

D. Reassembly

1. The tube can be easily mounted by inflating with enough air to make the tube firm.

   NOTE:
   - After the tire is mounted, inflate with approximately 1/3 the designated pressure; lightly tap around the tire with a wooden hammer to eliminate any pinching of the tube.
   - The valve stem should be pointed toward the axle.
   - Inflate the tire to the specified pressure.

     For normal riding: 2.0 kg/cm^2 (28.4 lbs/in^2)
     For high speed riding: 2.2 kg/cm^2 (31.3 lbs/in^2)

2. Grease the 6304Z ball bearing and pack the rear wheel hub with grease. Insert the spacer and drive the bearing into place using the rear wheel bearing driver (Tool No. 07946-2860200 and 07949-2860000). (Fig. 5-135)

   NOTE:
   The 6303Z and 6304Z ball bearings incorporate a seal on the outside, therefore, make sure that the bearing is installed correctly.

3. Mount the final drive sprocket on the drive flange with the sprocket retaining bolts, nut and tongued washer. (Fig. 5-136)

4. Assemble the rear brake shoe to the brake panel and install the spring to hold the shoe in place.

   Install the rear brake cam and brake arm on the panel. Assemble the brake shoe setting washer and lock with the cotter pin. (Fig. 5-137)

   NOTE:
   When installing the brake arm on the panel, align the punch marks on the brake arm to the brake cam.

5. The chain joint clip setting should be carefully made by paying attention to the chain driving direction. (Fig. 5-138)

6. Assemble the panel on the rear wheel and mount the wheel assembly on the frame. Install the drive chain and make the proper adjustment before final torquing of the rear wheel axle.

   NOTE:
   Adjust the chain so that there is **1 to 2 cm (0.4 to 0.8 in)** of slack and make sure that the chain adjusters on both sides are in the same relative position. (Fig. 5-139)

① Hammer ② Bearing driver
Fig. 5-135. Installing the bearing

① Final driven sprocket ② 69 mm external circlip
③ 10 mm tongued washer ④ 10 mm thin nut
Fig. 5-136. Assembling the final driven sprocket

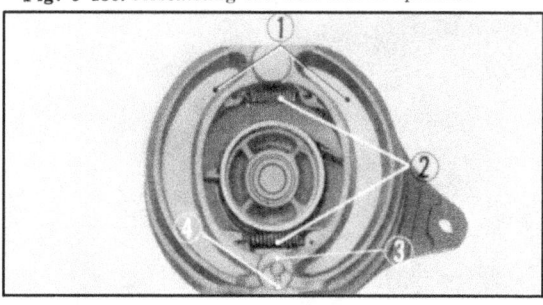

① Rear brake shoe ② Rear brake shoe spring
③ Brake shoe setting washer ④ 2×15 cotter pin
Fig. 5-137. Installing the brake shoe

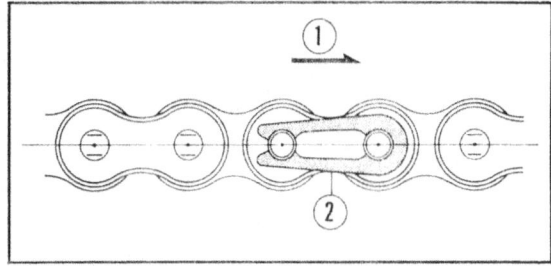

① Chain driving direction ② Chain joint clip
Fig. 5-138. Setting the chain joint clip

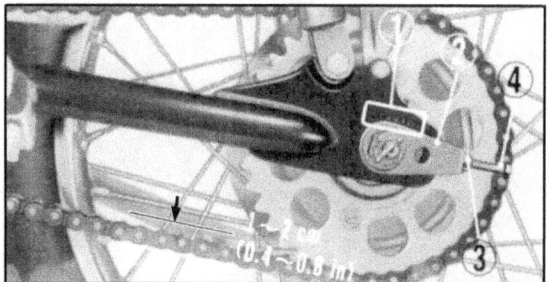

① Reference mark ② Drive chain adjuster ③ Lock nut
④ Drive chain adjusting bolt
Fig. 5-139. Adjusting slack of drive chain

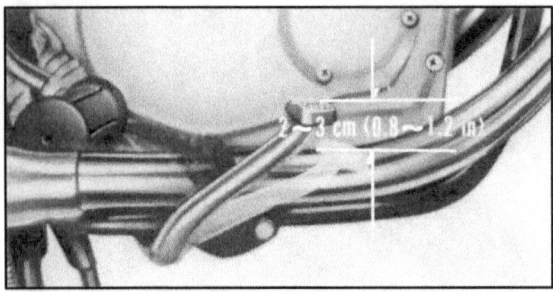

① Rear brake pedal
Fig. 5-140. Rear brake pedal play

① Rear brake arm ② Rear brake adjusting nut
Ⓐ Decrease Ⓑ Increase
Fig. 5-141. Adjusting the rear brake

7. Install the rear brake arm to the rear brake panel.
8. Install the rear brake rod to the brake arm. Adjust rear brake arm to set rear brake pedal free play.

NOTE:

The free play of the rear brake pedal should be from **2 to 3 cm (0.8 to 1.2 in.)** (Fig. 5-140, 141)

9. Install the chain case.

6. ELECTRICAL PARTS

6·1 IGNITION SYSTEM

A "battery-coil" type ignition system is employed. A schematic layout of the components of this system is shown in the figure at right.

The ignition coil ③ which is simply a transformer has its primary circuit opened at regular intervals by a set of contact points (breaker points) ④ operated by a cam. Opening and closing this circuit causes the magnetic field to expand and collapse, inducing an a-c voltage in the secondary winding. This high voltage is fed to the spark plugs ⑥ and causes them to arc and ignite the fuel-air mixture.

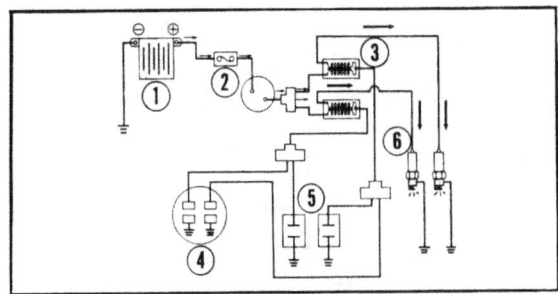

① Battery ② Fuse ③ Ignition coil ④ Breaker point
⑤ Condenser ⑥ Spark plug
Fig. 6-1. Ignition system

1. Ignition Coil

A. Description

Two independent ignition coils, one for each spark plug, are used. Each coil has the primary and secondary windings wound on an iron core. The former winding has 200 to 300 turns of **0.6 mm (0.024 in)** dia. enameled copper wire and the latter winding 10,000 to 20,000 turns of **0.08 mm (0.003 in)** dia. wire of the same type. These windings are inductively coupled together and are synthetic resin-molded in one and the same case with two terminals extended.

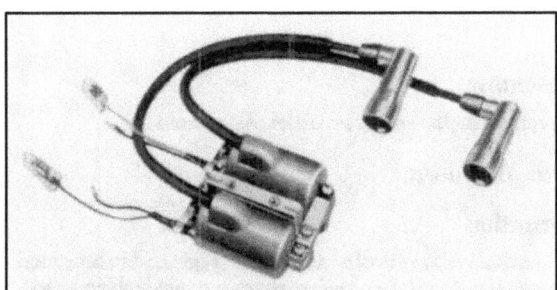

Fig. 6-2. Ignition coil

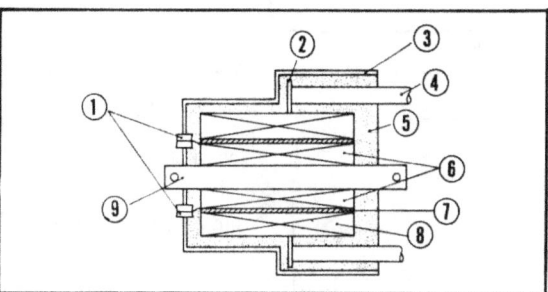

① Primary terminal ② High tension terminal ③ Case
④ High tension cord ⑤ Synthetic resin ⑥ Primary coil
⑦ Bobbin ⑧ Secondary coil ⑨ Iron core
Fig. 6-3. Sectional view of ignition coil

B. Removal

1. Raise the seat and remove the fuel tank.
2. Disconnect both the right and left high tension cords from the spark plugs.
3. Unfasten the wire harness clamp.
4. Disconnect the right and left ignition coil wiring at the connectors.
   Left coil: Yellow and black cords
   Right coil: Blue and black cords
5. Disconnect the condenser (mounted on the ignition coil base) wiring (yellow and blue cords) at the connector.
6. Unscrew the two ignition coil mounting bolts to remove the coil from the frame. (Ignition switch and horn are also mounted by these bolts.)

C. Inspection

1. Bench testing ignition coil

   Check the ignition coil using the service tester by following the procedure on the next page. (Fig. 6-4)

   Connect the power cord to the 17V battery and ground the black ground cord. Connect the ignition primary cord plug to the tester and connect the opposite terminal end to the primary terminal of the coil. Connect red test lead to the black terminal of the ignition coil, and the white lead to the yellow cord of the left coil (right coil to the blue cord).

   Connect the high tension cable (red) to the secondary coil terminal.

   Position the selector knob to COIL TEST. Adjust the three point spark tester to the maximum distance spark is maintained and then note this distance. The coil is satisfactory if the distance is greater than **7 mm (0.28 in)**.

NOTE:
Spark condition as shown in Fig. 6-5A is normal. Fig. 6-5B shows the spark condition when the test leads are connected in reverse at the ignition coil.

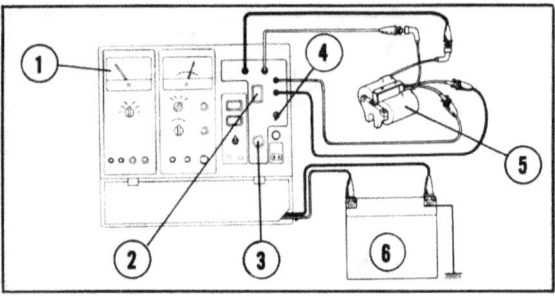

① Service tester ④ Coil test switch
② Spark gap finder ⑤ Ignition coil
③ Spark gap check dial ⑥ Battery
Fig. 6-4.

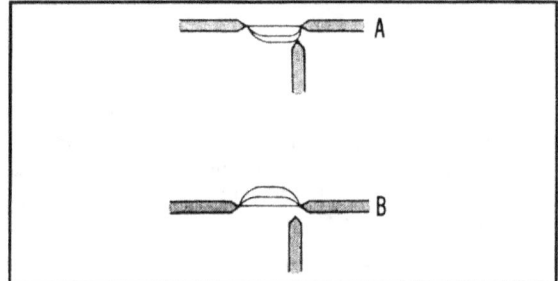

Fig. 6-5.

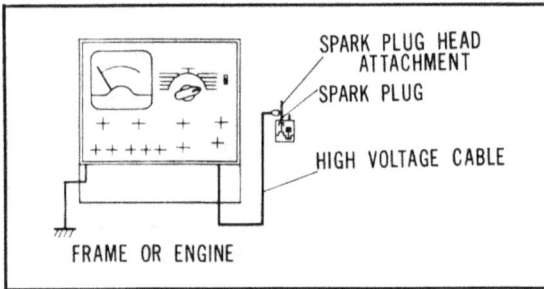

Fig. 6-6. Ignition coil test

Fig. 6-7. Spark advancer

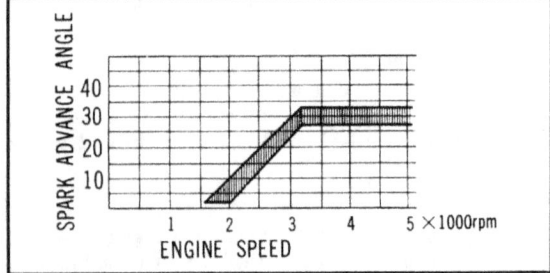

Fig. 6-8. Spark advancer characteristics

Inspection with a service tester (Tool No. 07308-0010000)

1. Ignition coil
   This test is conducted to check the coil performance. If the engine fails to start, check the spark plug, points and condenser for condition.
   1) Connect as shown in Fig. 6-4.
   2) Turn the service tester coil test switch to COIL TEST.
   3) Observing the spark jumping across a 3-point spark gap, turn the check dial and measure the jumping distance. If the spark jumps more than 6 mm (0.236 in) in air, the coil is in good condition.

NOTE:
If the spark appears in the form Ⓑ in Fig. 6-5, connect the high tension cable to the tester in the reverse direction and measure the jumping distance with the spark in the form Ⓐ.

D. Reassembly
1. Reassemble in the reverse order of removal.

2. Spark Advancer

A. Description
The spark advancer is of a centrifugal type and is mounted on the camshaft. As the engine reaches a considerable speed, the flyweights expand out, opposing the force of the springs. This radial movement of the flyweights due to centrifugal force causes the point cam to move in the direction of rotation, that is, in the direction of advancing the ignition timing to obtain satisfactory burning of the mixture under all speed and load conditions.

B. Removal
1. Remove the point cover.
2. Unscrew the two cross screws and remove the contact breaker point assembly.
3. Unscrew the spark advancer mounting bolt and remove the spark advancer.

C. Inspection
1. Check to make sure that the governor weights are operating smoothly. Repair or replace if they are not operating properly.
2. Spark advancer specification.
   - Crankshaft speed at start of spark advance, 1600~2000 RPM.
   - Crankshaft speed at full spark advance, 3200~3800 RPM.
   - Range of spark advance, 27~33°.

D. Reassembly
Perform the reassembly in the reverse order of removal.

3. Breaker Point

A. Description

The breaker point is one of the major functional parts of the ignition system. It is located in the cam case and consists essentially of a base plate, breaker arms and two sets of contacts points, stationary and moving as will be seen in the figure at right.

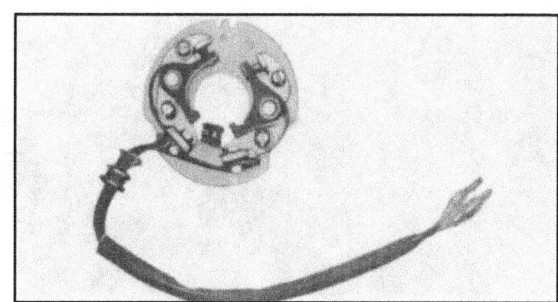

Fig. 6-9. Contact breaker

B. Disassembly

1. Remove the contact breaker.
2. Unscrew the two mounting screws to remove the contact breaker arm from the base plate.

C. Inspection

1. Contact breaker point gap and ignition timing adjustment

   Adjustment of the point gap and ignition timing should be made for both R/H and L/H cylinder at the same time. To adjust, proceed as follows:

   Contact breaker point gap:

   Turn the generator rotor counterclockwise and check the point gap when it is maximum. The correct gap is **0.012~0.016 in. (0.3~0.4 mm)** for the L/H and R/H points. Then loosen the contact breaker plate locking screws ⑤ when the point cam ① is at maximum lift and move the contact breaker plate ④. Tighten the locking screws when the correct gap is obtained. Adjust both L/H and R/H points in the same manner. Recheck the gap after tightening the locking screws.

NOTE:

Wipe the contact breaker point surfaces with clean rag if dirty.

① Point cam
② L/H contact breaker point
③ R/H contact breaker point
④ Contact breaker plate
⑤ Contact breaker plate locking screws
Fig. 6-10.

Ignition timing:

Adjust the ignition timing upon completing the adjustment of the contact breaker point gap.

L/H

1. Turn the generator rotor ⑥ counterclockwise and align "LF" mark ⑧ (on L/H cylinder) to timing mark ⑦. The ignition timing is correct if the L/H contact breaker points ② start opening.

To check the ignition timing, connect a 12V-3W bulb as shown in the figure and observe the moment the bulb comes on.

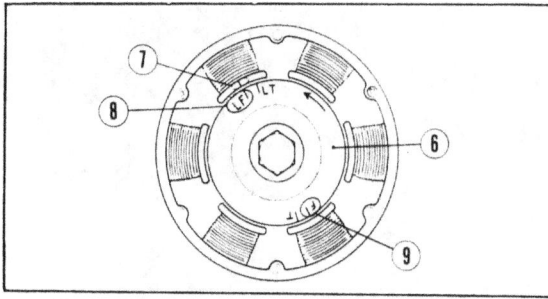

⑥ Generator rotor ⑦ Timing mark
⑧ "LF" mark   ⑨ "F" mark
Fig. 6-11.

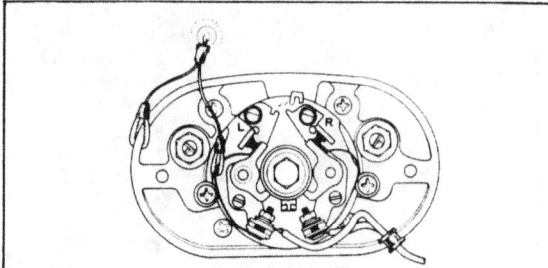

Fig. 6-12.

⑩ Base plate locking screws　⑪ Base plate
⑫ L/H contact breaker plate locking screws
⑬ R/H contact breaker plate locking screws
Fig. 6-13.

2. If the ignition timing is incorrect (either advanced or retarded), align "LF" mark to the timing mark, loosen base plate locking screws ⑩ and slowly turn base plate ⑪ until the bulb comes on.

NOTE:

The ignition timing will be advanced if the base plate is turned clockwise; it will be retarded if the base plate is turned counterclockwise.

Tighten the base plate locking screws upon completion of the adjustment. Turn the generator rotor again and check if the contact breaker point gap of 0.012~0.016 in. (0.3~0.4 mm) is maintained for the L/H breaker point.

R/H side

3. Then connect the bulb to the R/H contact breaker point. Turn the generator rotor counterclockwise 180 degrees (1/2 turn) and align "F" mark ⑨ with timing mark ⑦. If the bulb comes on when the marks are aligned, the ignition timing is correct. If the ignition timing is incorrect, loosen contact breaker plate locking screws ⑬ and vary the R/H point gap within the range of correct gap to adjust the ignition timing.

NOTE:

- Ignition point gap must remain within limits of (0.012~0.016 in) 0.3~0.4 mm after ignition timing has been set. If correct timing results in a point gap which is outside these limits, increase or decrease both point gaps equally to bring gaps within limits, then retime by rotating base plate.

  e.g. If left point gap is set at **0.35 mm (0.014 in.)** and right point gap produces correct timing at **0.42 mm (0.017in.)**, decrease both gaps by **0.02 mm (0.001 in.)**, and rotate base plate to time ignition.

  If both point gaps cannot be adjusted within limits, replace point assemblies.

- Make sure to turn the rotor counterclockwise. Never reverse the rotor direction.

- **0.1 mm** error of contact point gap will result in **10 degree** of ignition timing.

- It is advisable that L/H and R/H contact point gaps be identical in setting.

○ Checking ignition timing with a timing light.

An accurate timing check and adjustment can be made by using a timing light. Follow the procedure below for performing timing with the service tester.

1. Connect the power cord to the battery and ground the black ground cord.
b. Set the selector knob to TIMING.
c. Plug in the timing light cord and attach the high voltage cord to the spark plug head attachment.
d. Start the engine and with the engine idling, point the timing light on the rotor mark, the left cylinder to the "LF" mark and to the "F" mark for the right cylinder. The timing is correct if the respective marks on rotor are aligned to the index mark on the stator. If it is necessary to make readjustment, perform the adjustment in accordance with the procedure described on the previous page.

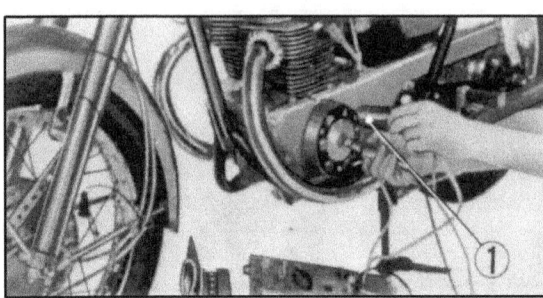

① Timing light
Fig. 6-14A. Start of spark advance

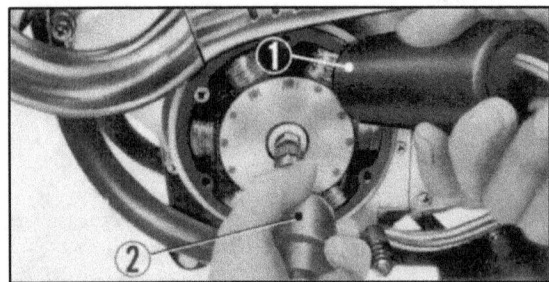

① Timing light　② Tachometer
Fig. 6-14B. End of spark advance

Next, operate the engine at approximately 4000 rpm and at this speed, if the index mark is between the two marks located 27~33° before the "LF" or the "F" mark, the ignition timing at the full advance condition is satisfactory.

If there is malfunction with the ignition timing even though the RPM is constant, the fault is probably with the advancer spring or a defect in the breaker points, therefore, the unsatisfactory parts should be repaired or replaced.

e. The engine RPM is checked with a revolution counter, however, the service tester can also be used. Set the tachometer switch to the ON position, insert the tachometer cable, place the tachometer against the center of the A.C. generator rotor and then read off the engine speed by engine speed scale meter.

D. Reassembly

Perform the reassembly in the reverse order of the disassembly.

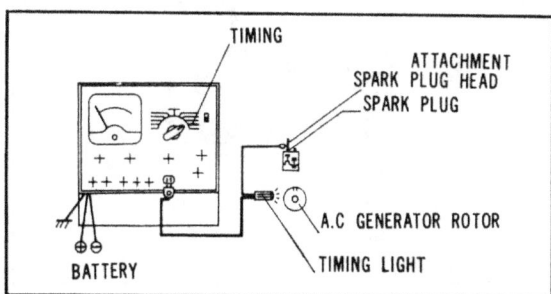
Fig. 6-15. Ignition timing test

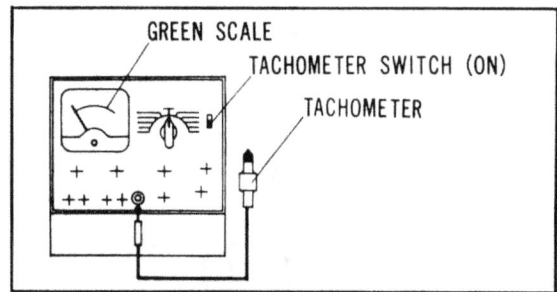
Fig. 6-16.

4. Condenser

A. Description

The condenser is a small electrical part mounted on the ignition coil base. It provides a means of preventing the spark plugs from flashing over abnormally. The condenser used on the present machines is rated to $0.22 \sim 0.26 \mu F$.

B. Removal

Perform the removal in the same procedure as for the ignition coil outlined on 6·1B (page 101).

C. Inspection

Condenser test
1. When using a battery and bulb, connect as shown in Fig. 6-17. If the bulb does not come on, the condenser is in good condition.
2. When using a multi-meter, connect as shown in Fig. 6-18. If the resistance is infinite in the XI range of Ω scale.
3. Inspection with service tester (Tool No. 07308-0010000).
   · Connect as shown in Fig. 6-19.
   · Turn the switch "II" to "CAPACITY" (condenser capacity measurement).
   · Push the "CAPACITY" button and read the scale on the tester. Specification: $0.22 \sim 0.33 \mu F$

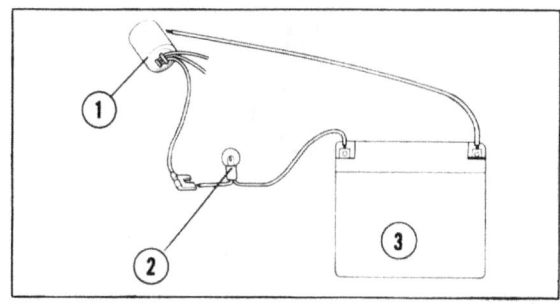
① Battery ② Bulb ③ Condenser
Fig. 6-17.

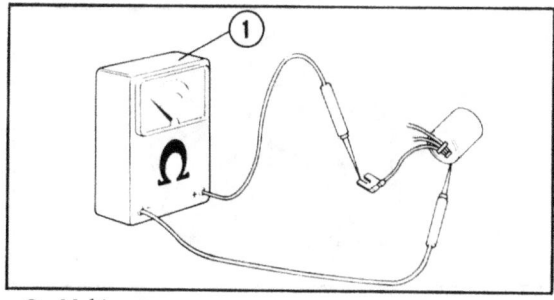
① Multi-meter
Fig. 6-18.

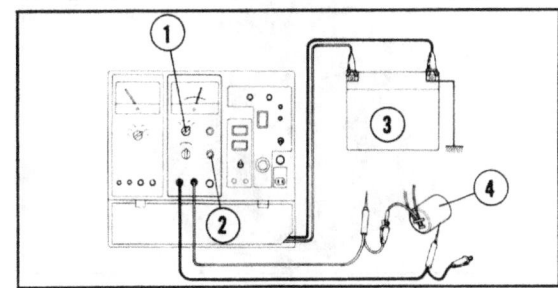
① Switch "II" ② "CAPACITY" button
③ Battery ④ Condenser
Fig. 6-19.

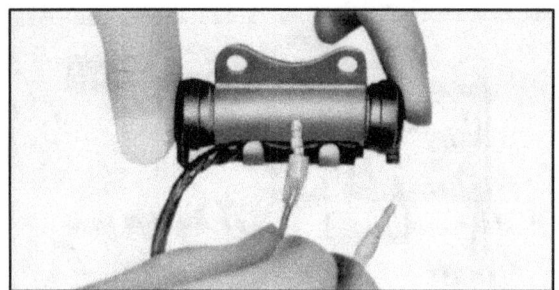

Fig. 6-20. Short-circuiting of the condenser

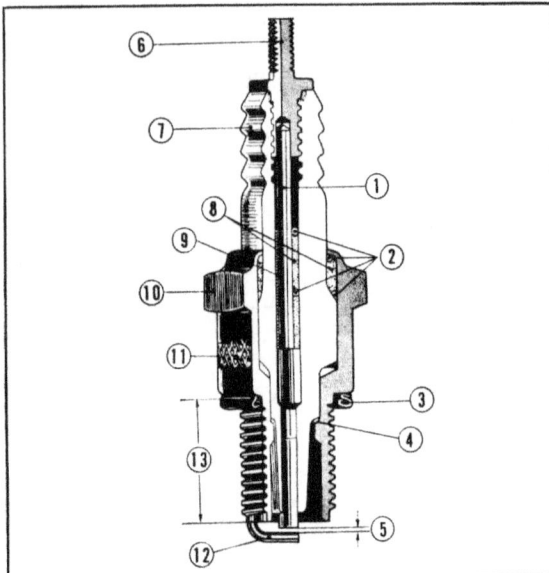

① Center electrode ② Wire packing ③ Gasket
④ Plate packing ⑤ Sparks gaps ⑥ Terminal
⑦ Insulation (with carrugation)⑧ Filled powder
⑨ Bonding ⑩ Hex. nut ⑪ Metallic main body
⑫ Side electrode ⑬ Length of thread (reach)
Fig. 6-21. Cross-section of spark plug

Fig. 6-22. Satisfactory condition

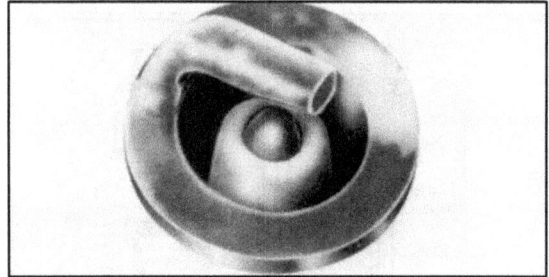

Fig. 6-23. Excessively burnt condition

NOTE:
- Upon completion of measurement, the condenser terminal should be short circuited to discharge the charge accumulated in the condenser. If not, a shock may be expected to the touch. (Fig. 6-20)
- The condensers function is to hold electricity temporarily. If the internal insulation is defective or the capacity is insufficient, the secondary voltage is lowered, the plug sparking is weakened. and the ignition becomes defective.

5. Spark Plug

A. Description

The standard spark plug used is the **NGK B-8ES**. The main parts of the spark plug are the electrodes, insulator and the plug body. (Fig. 6-21)

Also, the spark plug must be comparable with the heat characteristics of the engine, however, it is impossible to produce a plug which can be used universally.

During operation, if the temperature of the electrode is too low, carbon or oil will form on the electrode and will cause misfiring of the plug, therefore, the temperature of the electrode must be high enough to prevent the plug from fouling. This is called the self cleaning temperature and it is approximately 450~600°C (842~1112°F). However, if the temperature becomes too high the electrode will be heated to the point that it will cause the fuel mixture to ignite and result in pre-ignition. This temperature is called pre-ignition temperature and is about 750~850°C (1382~1562°F). Because of this, the spark plug should be selected so that the heat rating is higher than the self cleaning temperature but lower than the pre-ignition temperature.

To designate the heat characteristics, the term heat range refers to the operating temperature of the plug. The higher number (colder) designations are used for high speed driving. Conversely, plugs with a lower number indicate that it is a hotter type plug.

As an example, if there is a tendency for the engine to overheat caused by burning of the electrodes or pre-ignition, while using the NGK 7ES plugs, the spark plugs should be replaced with plugs of a higher heat range such as the B-8ES. On the other hand if the plugs appear to be sooty, replace the spark plugs with those of a lower heat range such as the B-6E.

The standard NGK B-8ES spark plug has a thread diameter of 14 mm and a reach of **19 mm (0.784 in)**.

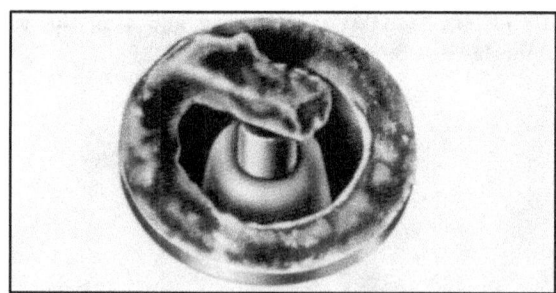

Fig. 6-24. Sooty condition (dry)

B. Removal

1. Remove the high tension lead from the spark plug.
2. Remove the spark plug using a spark plug wrench.

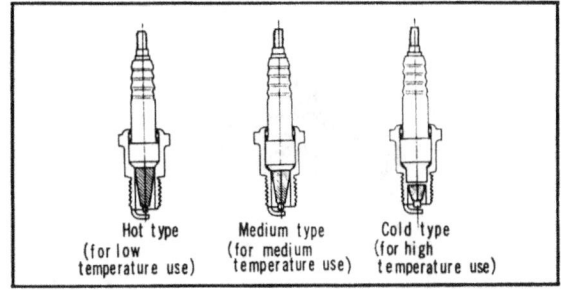

Fig. 6-25. Comparison of heat characteristics

C. Inspection

1. Spark plugs should be periodically inspected. If a spark plug is used for a long period of time, the electrode gradually burns and the sparking efficiency lowers.

   The spark plug efficiency can be detected with a spark plug tester. Inspect the sparking condition by changing the tester internal pressure, with the rated voltage applied.

2. It is best to use a spark plug cleaner for cleaning, however, when cleaner is not available, scrape with a piece of wire or needle, and wash with gasoline and wipe off with a dry rag. (Fig. 6-27)

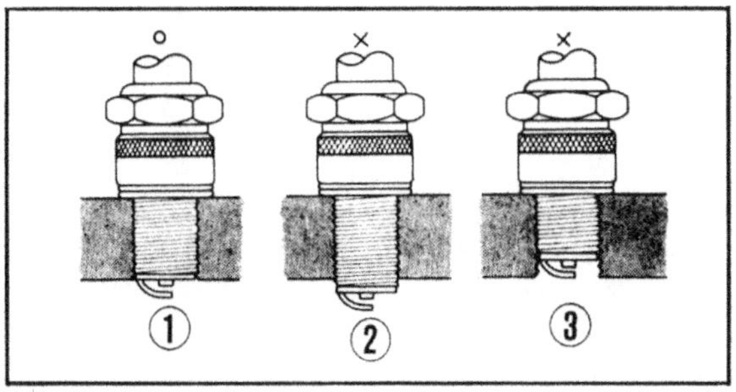

3. After cleaning, adjust the spark gap. Adjust with a thickness gauge so that the gap is between **0.7 mm~0.8 mm (0.028~0.032 in)**. (Fig. 6-28)

D. Installation

1. When reinstalling spark plug, wipe off oil and dust around the spark plug hole on the cylinder head.
2. The spark plug should first be screwed in finger tight and then torqued with the spark plug wrench until tight, about 1/2 to 3/4 turn.

① Reach is correct ② Reach is too long
③ Reach is too short
Fig. 6-26. Spark plug reach

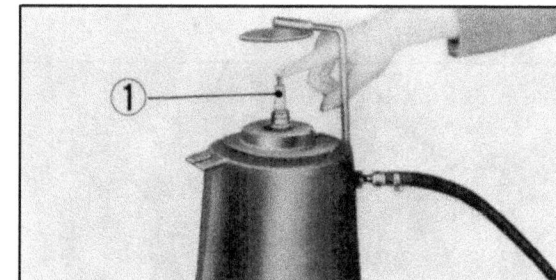

① Spark plug
Fig. 6-27. Spark plug cleaning

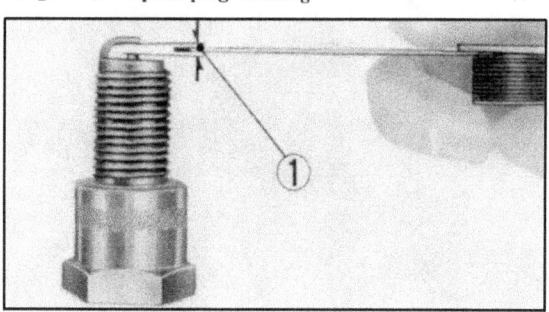

① 0.7~0.8 mm (0.028~0.32 in)
Fig. 6-28. Spark gap measuring

108

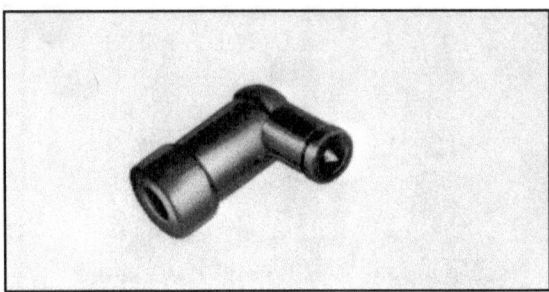

Fig. 6-29. Noise suppressor cap

6. Noise Suppressor

A. Description

To prevent the oscillating current which contains a high frequency radio wave produced by the high tension ignition circuit, the spark plug is fitted with a suppressor.

The suppressor consists of a resistor cap housed in a shielded cover.

B. Removal

1. Remove the noise suppressor cap from the spark plug.
2. Remove the cap from the high tension lead.

C. Inspection

Parts which are cracked will cause a short circuit when driving in inclement weather, therefore, it should be replaced.

D. Reinstallation

Perform the installation in the reverse order of removal.

NOTE:

The high tension lead carries the high voltage to the spark plug, therefore, it should be inserted securely into the cap. Further, do not put a sharp bend in the high tension lead or route it so that it is binding against the frame.

① A.C. generator rotor   ② A.C. generator stator
Fig. 6-30. A.C. generator

6·2 GENERATING SYSTEM

1. Alternator (A.C. generator)

A. Description

An alternator having six poles is used. The rotor of the generator is key-mounted on the left crankshaft and the stator is bolted to the crankcase cover. The arrangement of the poles is as shown in the figure at left.

B. Disassembly

1. Remove the left crankcase cover.
2. Remove the A.C. generator rotor with a rotor puller (Tool No. 07933-2160000).
3. Remove the stator from the left crankcase cover.

C. Inspection

1. Check the stator coil for open or short circuit.

   The check is performed with the service tester by measuring the resistance value of the coil. A good coil will have a resistance value shown in the table below, however, an unusually low resistance or an infinite resistance indicates that there is a short or an open circuit in the coil.

Testing Leads	Standard Resistance Values
Yellow ....Pink	1.1 Ω
White..................Pink	0.55 Ω

2. A.C. voltage measurement

   Rotate the selector knob on the tester to the A.C. VOLTAGE position and connect the (+) side of the tester lead to the yellow lead (day operation) or the white lead (night operation), and ground the (−) lead to the frame. Start the engine and perform the voltage measurement.

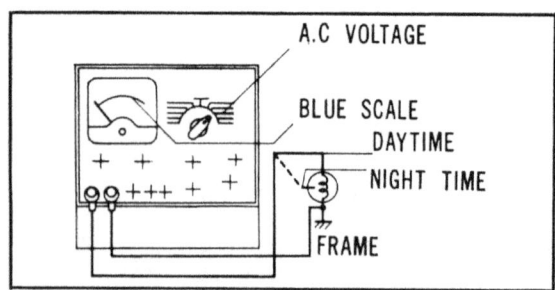

Fig. 6-31. A.C. voltage measurement

3. A.C. generator performance characteristics (reference)

Items		Specification
Engine speed (RPM)	Normal	300~11,500
	Maximum	15,000
Direction of rotation		Left hand rotation (Viewing from the left side)
Loads	Daytime	12V-12AH battery and two ignition coils
	Nighttime	One 35W lamp, three 3W lamps, one 7W lamps and the day time load
Charging characteristics Initial chargihg cut-in speed (battery, 12.6V)	Daytime	Under 1,400 RPM
	Nighttime	Under 2,000 RPM
Charging current at 5,000 RPM (battery, 14.8V)	Daytime	1.5~2.5A
	Nighttime	1.2~2.5A
Charging current at 10,000 RPM (battery, 15.5V)	Daytime	Under 4A
	Nighttime	Under 4A
Color of lead wires	Daytime	Yellow
	Nighttime	White
	Common	Orange

D. Reassembly

Perform the reassembly in the reverse order of disassembly.

NOTE:

Before installing the rotor on the crankshaft, clean both taper surfaces.

2. Silicon Current Regular

A. Description

To prevent the battery from becoming over-charged, a nonadjusting SCR (silicon current regulator) regulator is used. This will produce a very stable output voltage without any need for adjusting.

On the HONDA 250 and 350, a pointless type regulator, ZR906 (12V) is mounted on the bottom of the battery box. When the battery voltage is low, the regulator does not function and when fully charged or when approaching full charge, the regulator will function to ground the excess current. In this way, the battery is prevented from being over-charged.

B. Disassembly

Disconnect the wiring at the connectors and unscrew the two mounting bolts.

NOTE:

Do not remove the rubber caps on the bottom side of the regulator.

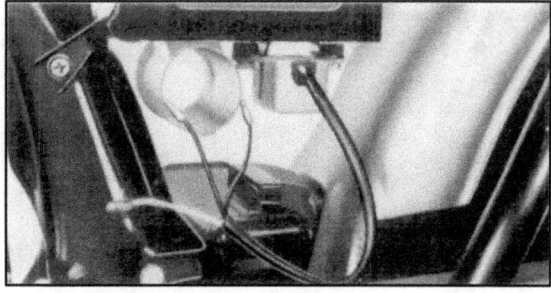

Fig. 6-32. Pointless regulator

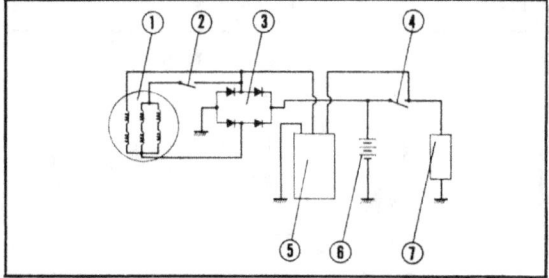

① A.C. generator ② Headlight switch
③ Selenium rectifier stack ④ Combination switch
⑤ Pointless regulator ⑥ Battery ⑦ Load
Fig. 6-33. Pointless regulator circuit diagram

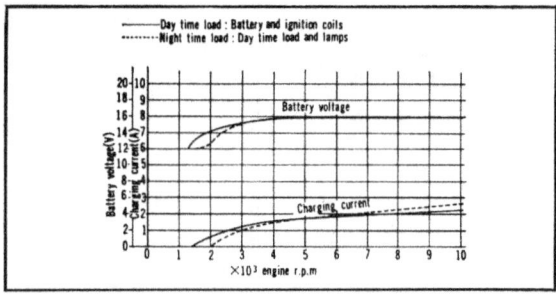

Fig. 6-34. A.C. generator battery charging characteristics (Without the pointless regulator)

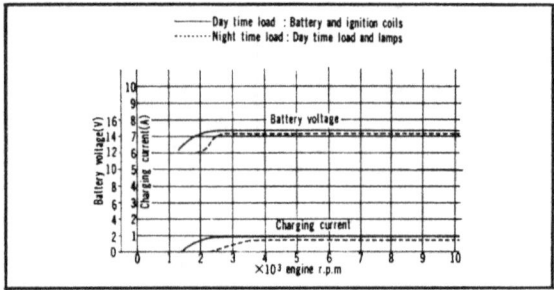

Fig. 6-35. A.C. generator battery charging characteristics (With the pointless regulator)

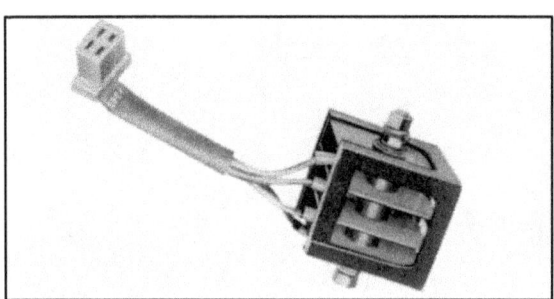

Fig. 6-36.

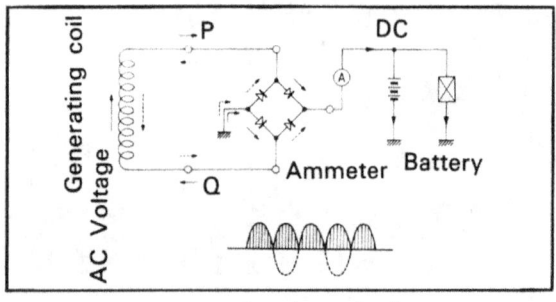

① Generating coil ② Battery ③ Load
Fig. 6-38.

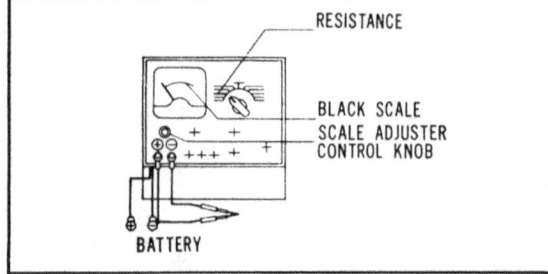

Fig. 6-39. Selenium rectifier stack

C. Inspection

1. Charging current measurement

   Connect an ammeter between the battery (+) terminal and the SCR, and check to see if the values obtained are in accordance with the standard specifications listed in the chart below.

   Fig. 6-34, 35 shows the battery charging performance with and without the regulator.

2. When the battery charge is low, the cause may be in the A.C. generator, selenium rectifier or defective wiring.

D. Reassembly

Perform the reassembly in the reverse order of disassembly.

NOTE:

- Exercise care not to make an error in the wiring when connecting the pointless regulator, as possible damage to the regulator, as well as to the battery may result.
- Use the ZR906 (12V) pointless regulator.

6·3 RECTIFYING SYSTEM

A. Description

It is often necessary to convert alternating current into direct current for specific needs such as battery charging. This process of current conversion is known as rectification and the device which performs this function is called a rectifier. The rectifiers used in the CB/CL250, 350 machines are of a selenium type. Fig. 6-36 shows a schematic layout of the full-wave rectifying circuit using four rectifiers, in which both sides of the A-C cycles are rectified.

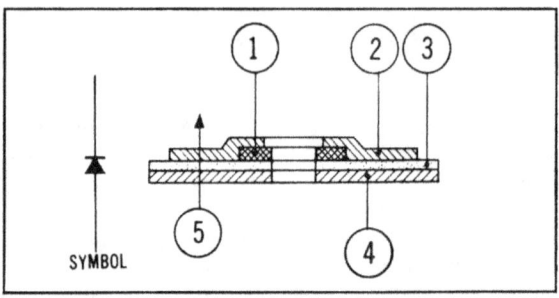

① Dielectric coating ② Anti-electrode ③ Selenium
④ Sheet ⑤ Positive direction
Fig. 6-37. Construction of selenium rectifier

B. Disassembly

Raise the seat, unscrew the mounts nuts and remove the rectifier.

C. Inspection

1. Measuring the current flow in both directions.

   Connect the battery to the tester and rotate the tester selector knob to the RESISTANCE position. Short the tester leads and adjust the gauge to "0".

The standard resistance values of the selenium rectifier in the normal direction are shown in the table below.

Connection		Resistance Value
Test leads	Rectifier terminal	
+ −	Yellow Red/white	Satisfactory if between 5~40 Ω
+ −	Pink Red/white	
+ −	Green Yellow	
+ −	Green Pink	

The resistance value in the reverse direction is measured by reversing the tester leads. Standard values are shown below.

Connection		Resistance Value
Test leads	Rectifier terminal	
+ −	Red/white Yellow	Satisfactory if over 600 Ω
+ −	Red/white Pink	
+ −	Yellow Green	
+ −	Pink Green	

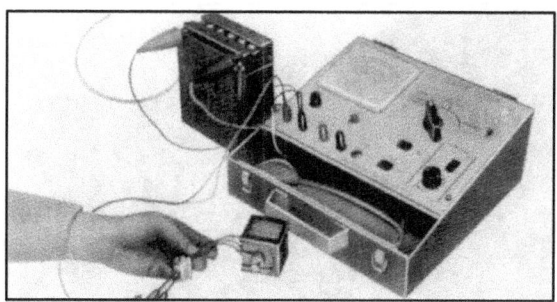

Fig. 6-40. Rectifier resistance measurement

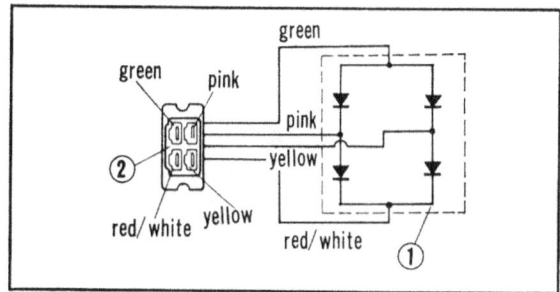

① Rectifier stack ② Rectifier female coupler
Fig. 6-41. Rectifier wiring diagram

A simple test can be performed without the use of a tester by following the diagram shown in Fig. 6-42. For testing in the normal direction, connect the (+) side of the battery to the yellow or the pink lead of the selenium rectifier and the (−) side to the red/white lead. If the bulb lights up, it indicates satisfactory condition. In this manner, perform the complete test in accordance with the test connections shown in the table above for the normal direction test.

For testing in the reverse direction, connect the (−) side of the battery to the yellow or the pink lead and the (+) side of the battery to the red/white lead of the rectifier. The selenium rectifier is satisfactory if the bulb does not light up.

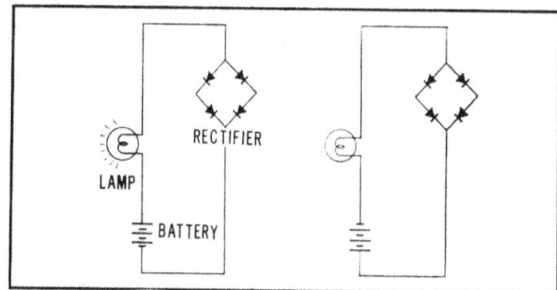

Fig. 6-42.

NOTE:
Applying a reverse current to the rectifier for a long period will weaken the rectifier, therefore, testing in the reverse direction should be kept to a minimum.
2. The service life of the selenium rectifier is affected by temperature, therefore, it should not be exposed to excessive current for a long period. Further, the wafers should not be bent or scratched.

D. Reassembly

Perform the reassembly in the reverse order of disassembly.

6·4 BATTERY

A. Description

A battery meeting the specifications shown below is used on all current models.

Item	Specification
Type	YUASA 12N12A-4A (Vaccum sealed dry charged battery)
Battery voltage	12V
Capacity rating	12AH
Electrolyte specific gravity	1.26~1.28 at 20°C (68°F)
Electrolyte capacity	0.72 lit. (0.19 US. gal. 0.16 Imp. gal.)

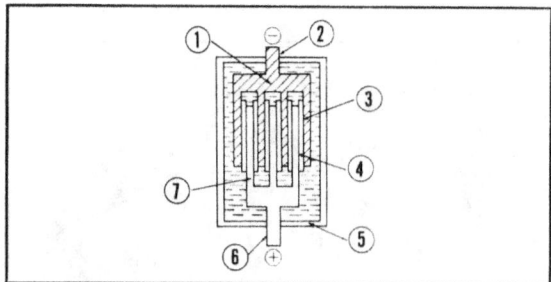

① Pole ② ⊖ Terminal ③ Negative plate
④ Separator and glass mat ⑤ Container
⑥ ⊕ Terminal ⑦ Positive plate
Fig. 6-43. Battery construction

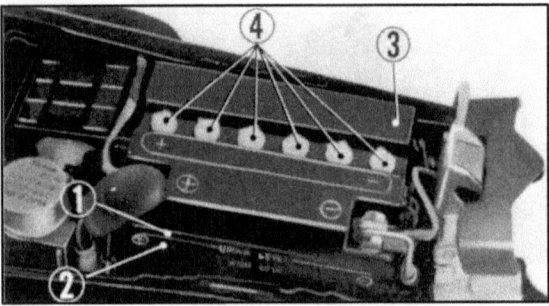

① Upper Level mark ② Lower level mark ③ Battery
④ Yellow filler caps
Fig. 6-44. Battery inspection

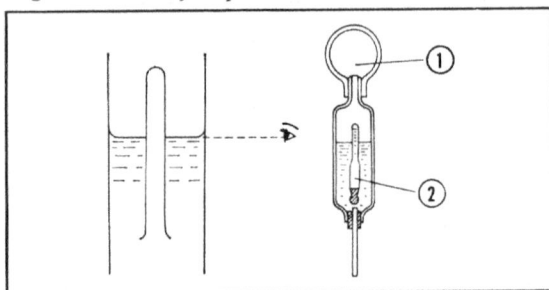

Fig. 6-45. Measuring the specific gravity

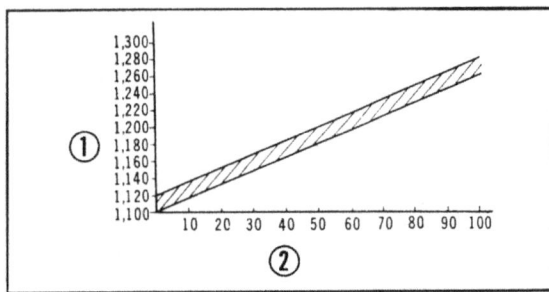

① Specific gravity (20°C) ② Residual capacity (%)
Fig. 6-46. Specific gravity and residual capacity chart

B. Removal

1. Raise the seat and disconnect the black ground cable and the green ground lead from the (−) terminal of the battery. From the (+) terminal, remove the red and the red/white leads.
2. Remove the battery from the battery case.

C. Inspection

1. Check the battery electrolyte level

   Raise the seat and observe the battery electrolyte level marking on the side of the battery to make sure that the electrolyte level is between the upper and lower marks. If the level is below the lower level marking, add distilled water to the battery.

   NOTE:

   When adding distilled water, do not fill above the upper level mark.

2. Check the specific gravity of the battery electrolyte

   The specific gravity is measured with a hydrometer, the type shown in Fig. 6-45. When making a reading of the measured value, the electrolyte level in the hydrometer should be held at eye level and the scale read at the fluid level. Temperature of the electrolyte can be measured by a rod thermometer.

   The relation between the battery capacity and the specific gravity (residual capacity) is shown in Fig. 6-46. When the specific gravity is 1,189 at 20°C (68°F) (less than 50%) the residual capacity is small and if continued to be used in such a condition, it will eventually lead to trouble as well as shortening the battery life, therefore, the battery should, under such a condition, be recharged as soon as possible. (Fig. 6-47)

   The electrolyte used in the battery must be comprised of pure sulfuric acid diluted to the designated specific gravity. The specific gravity will vary with the temperature, therefore, the specific gravity index is based on the electrolyte temperature of 20°C (68°F). The temperature correction formula should be used to derive the proper specific gravity for the temperature of the electrolyte.

   $$S_{20} = S_t + 0.0007(t - 20)$$

   Where:

   S_{20} = Specific gravity of the electrolyte corrected to 20°C (68°F)
   S_t = Specific gravity of the electrolyte measured temperature, t°C
   t = Temperature of the measured electrolyte

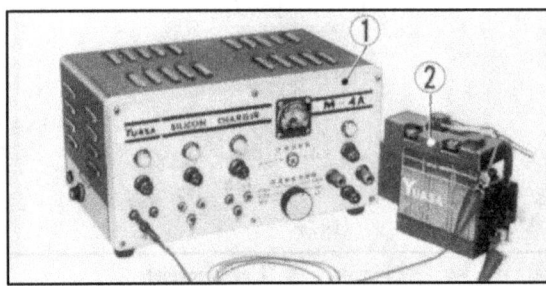

① Battery charger ② Battery
Fig. 6-47. Charging the battery

3. Battery charging procedure

   • There are two methods of charging of a battery, namely, the constant current method and the constant voltage method. In the constant current method, the battery is charged at a constant current throughout the charging period. This method is safe and is recommended for initial charging of the battery. In the constant voltage charging method, a constant voltage is applied during the charging period. In this method, the charging period can be shortened by applying a larger current, however, one drawback is that if too large a current is applied, the battery will overheat.

   ○ Charger hook-up

   Connect the positive terminal (+) and the negative battery terminal (−) to the respective terminal of the charger.
   (Fig. 6-47)

When more than one battery is to be charged at once, they should be connected in series, as shown in Fig. 6-48.

The charger voltages must be the sum of the battery voltages. For example, to charge three 12V batteries, the charger must have an output voltage in excess of 16 (16 (15)+16 (15)+16 (15) or 48 (or 45) volts.

4. Charging

A fully discharged battery will require a charging rate that is 1.25 higher than the normal charge rate of the battery. As an example, a 12AH battery will require 15AH charging rate (12AH×1.25=15AH). There is a definite relationship between the charging current and the charging time. This is shown in Fig. 6-49. The charging current should not be greater than three times the 10 hours current rate. (For a 12AH battery, 1.2A×3= 3.6A).

As the battery approaches the full charge condition, gas will be released from the electrolyte. At this time, check the battery electrolyte to see if the specific gravity is up to the standard value of 1.26~1.28, and the terminal voltage is up to the standard value of 15~16V. Perform the check again after 30 minutes and again in an hour, and if the three check values are constant, the battery is fully charged and the charging can be terminated. (Fig. 6-49)

NOTE:

If during the charging process the temperature of the electrolyte should raise above 45°C (113°F) or if the gas is being released from the electrolyte in abundance, the charging should be stopped temporarily or the charging current reduced to a lower rate.

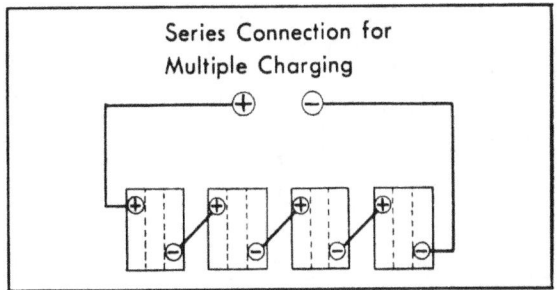

Fig. 6-48.

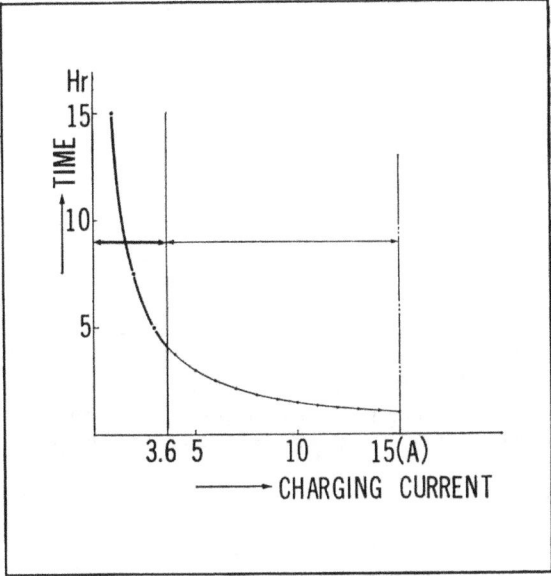

Fig. 6-49.

- Quick charger

    Quick charging should not be on battery which has been fully discharged. Further, quick charging method should not be frequently used. However, when it is inevitable and quick charging must be performed, the following items should be observed.

    For quick charging a 12AH battery, use the charging current rate of 12A. A battery which is 30% discharged, approximately 30 minutes should be adequate to charge the battery. However, if during the charging process the electrolyte temperature should rise above 50°C (122°F), the charging should be temporarily stopped or the charging current rate reduced.

- Other precaution
- If the electrolyte level falls during charging, refill with distilled water to the upper level mark.
- Inflammable hydrogen gas is discharged from the cells, therefore, do not charge batteries near any open flame.
- After charging, add distilled or battery water to the cells to bring the electrolyte to the upper mark.

    Tighten cell caps firmly and wash off with clean water if any acid spilled.

- The battery is now ready for installation. When installing a battery in the motorcycle, be sure not to pinch the battery vent tube. Explosion may result if the exhaust tube is blocked.

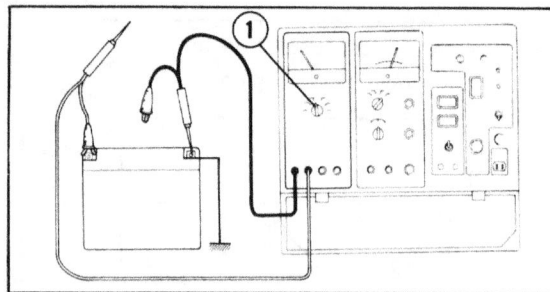

Fig. 6-50. D.C. voltage measurement

5. Check the terminal voltage (Tool No. 07308-0010000)

   The battery terminal voltage can be checked with a service tester. The standard battery voltage is 12V, however, immediately after charging, the voltage will be at 15~16V.

   Set the volt selector switch to the D.C. VOLTAGE position on the tester and clamp the (+) tester lead to the (+) terminal of the battery and then connect the other tester lead to the (−) terminal of the battery and read the voltage off the blue scale. When performing battery charging, refer to the battery charging section on page 112. (Fig. 6-50)

6. Other important items
   - On this model motorcycle a vacuum sealed dry charged battery is used. This battery does not require an initial charge. However, if the seal on the battery is found to be broken (the battery will be loose in the plastic envelope) the normal initial charging should be performed.
   - If the motorcycle is to be placed in storage for a long period, the leads to the battery should be disconnected and it is recommended that the battery be charged once a month to maintain it in good condition.

BATTERY TROUBLE SHOOTING AND CORRECTIVE ACTION

Trouble	Probable cause	Correct action
A. Sulfation The electrode plates are covered with white layer or in spots.	1. Charging rate is too low or else excessively high. 2. The specific gravity or the mixture of the electrolyte is improper. 3. Battery left in a discharged condition for a long period. (Left with the switch turned on). 4. Exposed to excessive vibration due to improper insulation. 5. Motorcycle stored during cold season with battery connected.	1. When motorcycle is in storage, the battery should be recharged once a month even though the motorcycle is not used. 2. Check the electrolyte periodically and always maintain the proper level. 3. In a lightly discharged condition, performiug recharging and discharging several times by starting the engine may be sufficient.
B. Self discharge Battery discharges in addition to that caused by the connected load.	1. Dirty contact areas and case. 2. Contaminated electrolyte or electrolyte excessively concentrated.	1. Always maintain a clean exterior. 2. Handle the replenishing electrolyte with care and use clean container.
C. Large discharge rate Specific gravity gradually lowers and around 1.100 (S.G), the winker and horn no longer function.	1. The fuse and the wiring is satisfactory, loads such as winker and horn does not function. In this condition the motorcycle will operate but with prolonged use, both ⊕ and ⊖ plates will react with the sulfuric acid and form lead sulfide deposits, (sulfation) making it impossible to recharge.	1. When the specific gravity falls below 1,200 (20°C:68°F), the battery should be recharged immediately. 2. When the battery frequently becomes discharged while operating at normal speed, check the generator for proper output. 3. If the battery discharges under normal charge output, it is an indication of overloaning, remove some of the excess load.
D. High charging rate The electrolyte level drops rapidly but the charge is always maintained at 100% and the condition appears satisfactory. A condition which is overlooked. (Specific gravity over 1.260)	1. The deposit will accumulate at the bottom and will cause an internal short and damage the battery.	1. Check to assure proper charging rate. 2. When overcharge conditions exist with the proper charging rate, place an appropriate resistor in the charging circuit.
E. Specific gravity drops Electrolyte evaporates.	1. Shorted 2. Insufficient charging 3. Distilled water overfilled 4. Contaminated electrolyte	1. Perform specific gravity measurement. 2. If the addition of distilled water causes a drop in specific gravity, add sulfuric acid and adjust to proper value.

6·5 STARTING SYSTEM

1. Starting Motor

A. Description

The starting motor complete with a planetary reduction gear is mounted on the front side of the crankcase.

When starter switch ① on the handlebar is pressed with ignition switch ② closed, current flows from the battery to the excitation coil (plunger-holding coil) ④ of the solenoid switch. This results in closure of the points and permits current to flow to the starting motor.

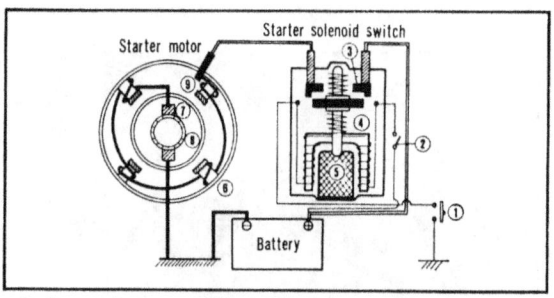

① Starter button switch ② Ignition switch
③ Contact unit ④ Excitation coil ⑤ Plunger
⑥ Pole ⑦ Brush ⑧ Armature ⑨ Field coil
Fig. 6-51. Starter circuit diagram

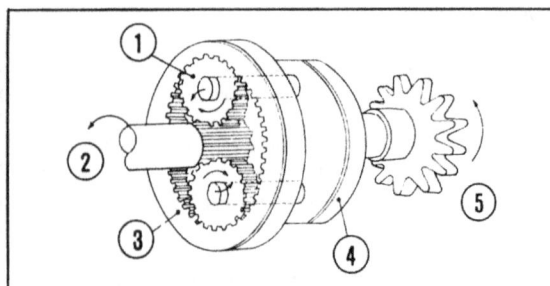

① Planetary gear ② Motor shaft ③ Internal gear
④ Sprocket shaft ⑤ Starting sprocket
Fig. 6-52.

The planetary reduction gear, constructed as shown in the figure at right, provides a means of the first-stage reduction; the second-stage reduction is accomplished by the sprocket and chain.

B. Disassembly

1. Remove the left crankcase rear cover and disconnect the neutral lead.
2. Remove the left crankcase cover.
3. Remove the generator rotor using a rotor puller (Tool No. 07933-2160000).
4. Remove the starting sprocket set plate and then remove the starting sprocket and the starting motor sprocket together as an unit.
5. Disconnect the starting motor.
6. Unscrew the two starting motor mounting bolts and remove the starting motor.
7. Unscrew the two 5 mm cross screws and remove both of the end brackets.
8. Unscrew the 3 mm brush lead mounting screws and the brushes from the brush holders. (Fig. 6-53)

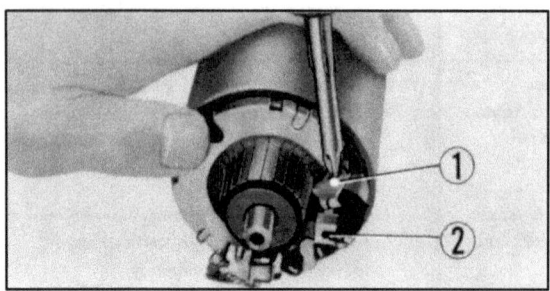

① 5 mm cross screw ② Carbon brush
Fig. 6-53. Removing carbon brush

C. Inspection

1. Check the wear of the brush by measuring the length of the brush with a vernier caliper.

mm (inch)

Standard Value	Serviceable Limit
12.5 (0.429)	Replace if under 7.5 (0.295)

Further, check to see that the brush is not stuck within the brush holder and preventing the brush from contacting the commutator.

2. Check the commutator mica undercut condition. Measure the amount of mica undercut. (Fig. 6-54)

mm (inch)

Standard Value	Serviceable Limit
0.6 (0.024)	Replace if under 0.3 (0.012)

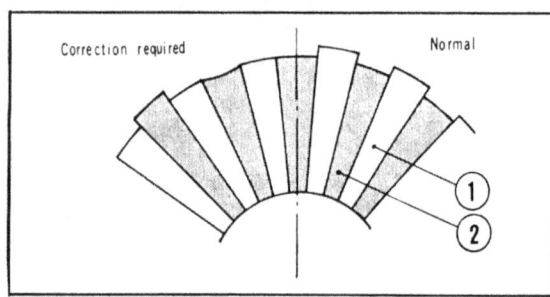

① Commutator ② Mica
Fig. 6-54. Commutator correction

It is difficult to repair the undercut of the commutator, therefore, this work should be performed by a specialist.

NOTE:
If the commutator has been repaired, the sharp edges and burrs should be removed.

3. Armature insulation test

   Perform a continuity check between the commutator and the shaft. If a short is indicated, the armature is defective and therefore, it should be replaced.

Fig. 6-55. Starting motor current measurement

4. Measure the starting current

   The starting current of the starting motor can be checked by mounting the external shunt on the tester and this will permit a maximum check up to 60A. Mount the external shunt box securely on the D.C. current output of the tester main unit; connect the two cords shown in Fig. 6-55.

   1) Tighten the shunt on the tester D.C. current output.
   2) Remove the primary starter cable, connect the red shunt cord to the starter terminal and connect the black shunt cord to the removed cable.
   3) Turn switch to the D.C. current (+), push the starter button, and note the stater current.

NOTE:
- When the shunt is installed on the tester, tighten firmly. When the meter deflection is reversed, the connection is reversed, therefore, the measurement should be performed by changing the switch to negative (−) position.
- Since the starter cranking current is greater than 60A, the starter chain should be disconnected when making this test. In this manner, the starter unloaded current is measured.

5. Starting motor specification (reference)

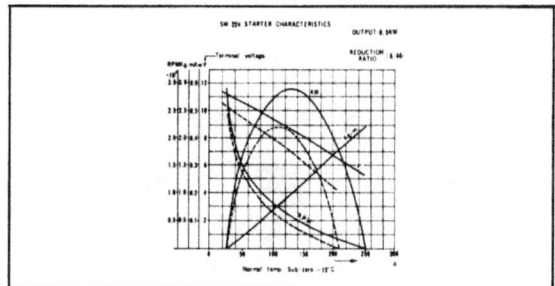

Fig. 6-56. Starting motor characteristics

Items	Specifications		
Rated voltage	12V		
Rated output	0.45 KW		
Rated operation	30 seconds		
Reduction ratio	6.44		
Direction of rotation	Clockwise (Viewing into the pinion)		
	Without load	With load	Stalling load
Voltage	11V	9V	5V
Amperage	35A Max.	120A	280A
RPM at sprocket torque	1,700 Min.	500 Min.	
		0.7 kg-m (5.06 ft. lbs)	1.8 kg-m (13.02 ft. lbs)
Primary reduction ratio	6.44 : 1		
Secondary reduction ratio	2.77 : 1		
Total reduction ratio	17.84 : 1		

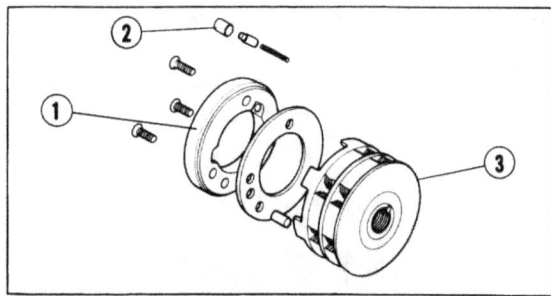

① Starting clutch outer ② 10.2 × 11.5 roller
③ A.C. generator rotor
Fig. 6-57. Starting clutch

D. Reassembly

Perform the reassembly in the reverse order of disassembly.

2. Starting Clutch

A. Description

The starting clutch is of a one-way type and is constructed in one piece with the generator rotor.

As drive is transmitted from the motor to sprocket ②, rollers ③ are moved within clutch outer ④ in such a manner as to provide a "wedge action" between the sprocket (now serving as a drive member) and the clutch outer. Now the clutch is engaged and the drive is transmitted through the clutch outer to the engine crankshaft. After the engine starts and it begins to "drive" the sprocket, the rollers are returned by centrifugal force and disengage the clutch wedges.

B. Disassembly

Perform the disassembly in accordance with section 6-5-B on page 115.

C. Inspection

1. Mount the starting sprocket on the generator rotor, rotate the sprocket and check the condition of operation. As shown in Fig. 6-60, the sprocket will lock when rotated in the A direction but it will be free to rotate in the B direction. If the above condition is unsatisfactory, check the rollers and the roller springs.

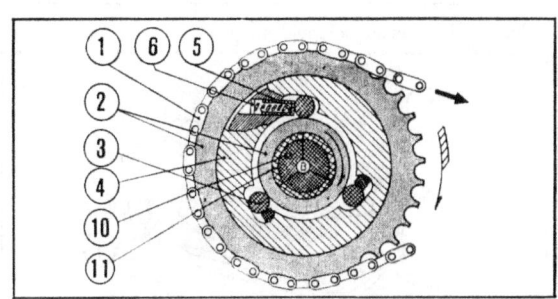

① Starting chain ② Starting sprocket ③ Roller
④ Clutch outer ⑤ Roller spring cap ⑥ Roller spring
⑩ Left crankshaft ⑪ 21 mm bushing
Fig. 6-58.

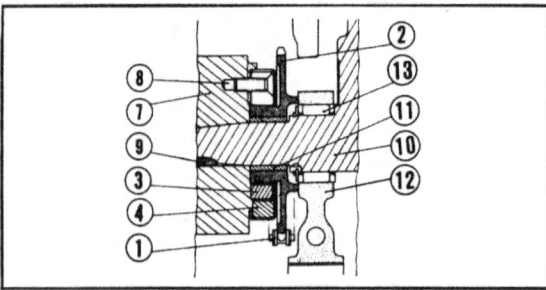

① Starting chain ② Starting sprocket ③ Roller
④ Clutch outer ⑦ A.C. generator rotor
⑧ Cross-point head screw ⑨ Woodruff key
⑩ Left crankshaft ⑪ 21 mm bushing ⑫ Bearing holder
Fig. 6-59.

① Starting sprocket ② Generator rotor
Fig. 6-60.

D. Reassembly

Perform the reassembly in the reverse order of disassembly.

NOTE:

When assembling the rollers and roller springs into the starting clutch assembly, all the parts should be completely cleaned.

3. Starter Magnetic Switch

A. Description

The starting motor, because of its characteristics, draws a large current that exceeds the capacity of a push-button starter switch of the type currently used when starting. This is the reason why the solenoid switch is placed in the starter circuit and the circuit is so designed that the switch is controlled by the push-button switch This switch is an electromagnetic switch having a capacity large enough to operate satisfactorily in the starter circuit and is constructed as shown in the figure below.

B. Removal

1. Open the seat and remove the air cleaner on the right side.
2. Disconnect the electrical leads from the starter magnetic switch.
3. Unscrew the two mounting bolts and remove the starter magnetic switch from the frame.

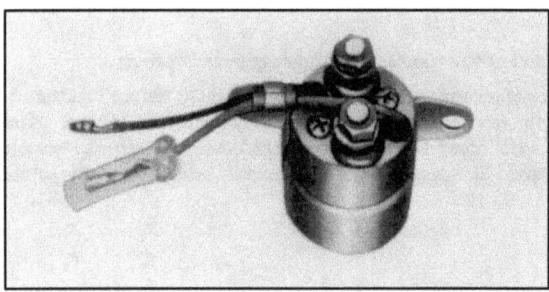

Fig. 6-61. Starter solenoid switch

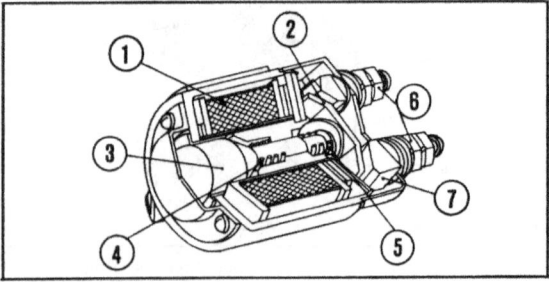

① Magnetic coil (primary coil)
② Contact (operating side) ③ Plunger ④ Return spring
⑤ Contact return spring ⑥ Terminals
⑦ Contact (fixed side)
Fig. 6-62.

C. Inspection

1. When the starter switch is depressed a "click" in the starter solenoid is heard; this indicates the movement of the plunger and closing of the terminal contacts.
2. After a long period of use, the contact points will become pitted and worn, and increasing the resistance to the current flow. When such condition develops, disassemble the solenoid switch and clean up the point contact areas with a file or emery paper.
3. Other causes which will result in the malfunction of the starter solenoid switch.
- Poor contact within the key switch.
- Defective magnetic coil.
- Improper action of the moving core.

D. Reassembly

Perform the reassembly in the reverse order of disassembly.

NOTE:

If the switch has been disassembled, adhesive cement should be applied to the mating surfaces to prevent moisture from entry into the switch.

6·6 SAFETY EQUIPMENT

The following equipment is installed on the motorcycle to insure safe riding. Also included are the controls to operate this equipment.

- Horn
- Speedometer/tachometer
- Various lighting equipment (such as the headlight, tail/stop light, turn signal lights, etc.)
- Kill switch

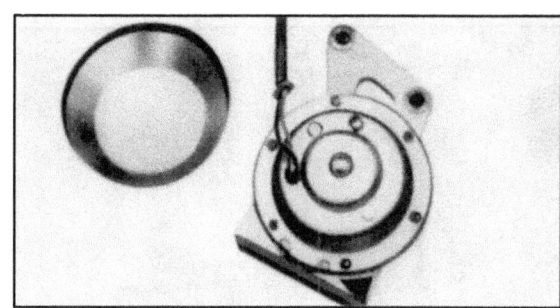

Fig. 6-63. Horn

1. Horn

A. Description

A curling type horn constructed as shown in the figure at left is used. Referring to the figure, it includes a metal diaphragm so mounted in a case that it vibrates back and forth as the magnetic field produced by the electromagnet (armature) varies in strength. This vibration takes place against the air to produce the sound waves.

B. Removal

1. Raise the seat and remove the fuel tank.
2. Disconnect the horn leads and unscrew the two horn mounting bolts.

NOTE:

The horn is accurately adjusted to produce the desired sound, therefore, the horn should not be disassembled if it is operating properly.

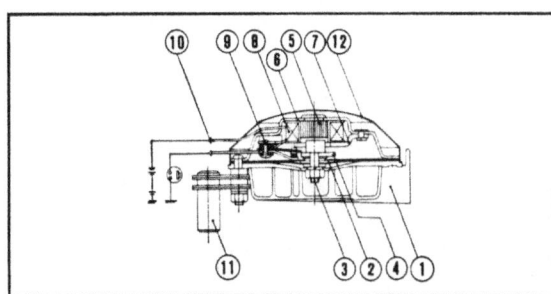

① Curling horn ② Diaphragm ③ Pole B
④ Armature ⑤ Pole A ⑥ Case ⑦ Core plate
⑧ Coil ⑨ Contact assembly ⑩ Coupler (black)
⑪ Horn clamp ⑫ Cover

Fig. 6-64. Horn construction

C. Inspection

If there is a change in pitch of the sound or if the loudness has decreased, check the horn by connecting it to a fully charged battery. If the quality of the sound is still poor, remove the horn cover and adjust by turning the adjusting screw. Tuning the screw to the right will increase the loudness.

D. Reassembly

Perform the reassembly in the reverse order of removal.

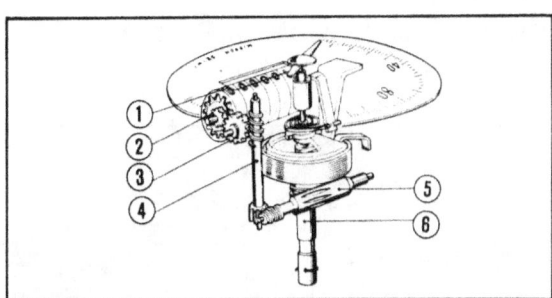

① Total ② 5th gear ③ 4th gear ④ 3rd gear
⑤ 2nd shaft ⑥ 1st shaft (magnet shaft)

Fig. 6-65.

2. Speedometer and Tachometer

A. Description

The speedometer incorporating the odometer is driven from the front wheel through a flexible shaft and the tachometer is similarly driven from the camshaft. These meters are constructed as shown in the figure at right.

B. Removal

Unscrew the flexible shaft coupling nut from the back of both units and then unscrew the mounting nuts to remove nut units.

C. Reassembly

Perform the reassembly in the reverse order of removal.

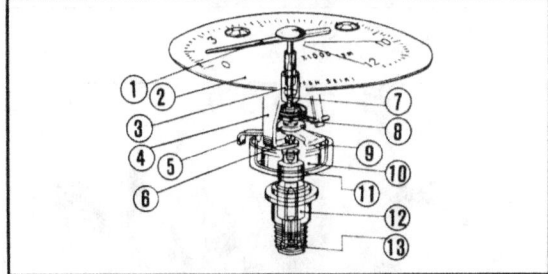

① Pointer ② Dial ③ Braking mechanism
④ Bearing bracket ⑤ Stopper ⑥ Pointer bearing
⑦ Pointer shaft ⑧ Braking spring ⑨ Induction disk
⑩ Magnet ⑪ Case ⑫ Magnet bearing
⑬ Magnet shaft

Fig. 6-66.

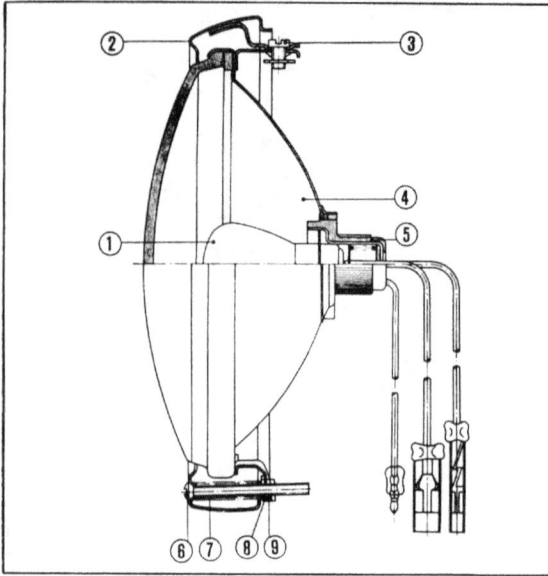

① Headlight bulb ② Headlight rim
③ Unit holder screw ④ Headlight unit
⑤ Headlight socket ⑥ Beam adjust screw
⑦ Beam adjust spring ⑧ Washer ⑨ Beam adjust nut
Fig. 6-67.

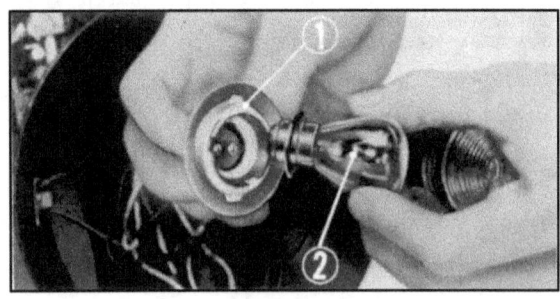

① Headlight socket ② Headlight bulb
Fig. 6-69.

① Adjusting screw ② Headlight mounting bolt
Fig. 6-70. Headlight (U.S.A. type)

① Adjusting screw
Fig. 6-71. Headlight (General export type)

3. Headlight

A. Description

The headlight is of a semi-sealed beam type. Its bulb can easily be removed from the socket for replacement or inspection. The types and ratings of the bulbs used in the headlights of the current models are as follows:

Country of Use	Headlight Bulb Rating
USA and general export	12V-35/25W
Britain and Germany	12V-35/35W
France	12V-36/36W

B. Removal

1. Remove the headlight rim from the case by removing the screws located at the bottom of the headlight rim.
2. The socket is twisted to the left and removed from the reflector.
3. Press the bulb inward and twist toward the left to disengage the socket pin and then remove the bulb.

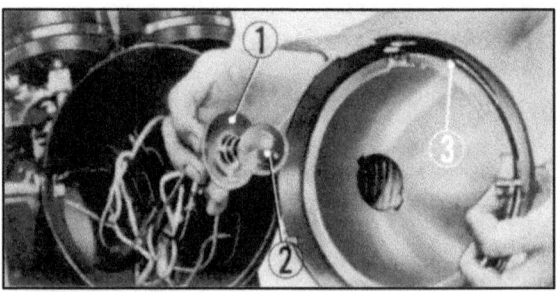

① Headlight socket ② Headlight bulb
③ Headlight rim
Fig. 6-68.

C. Inspection

1. Beam adjustment

   (U.S.A. type)

   Horizontal adjustment of the headlight is made by the adjusting screw at the front of the headlight. Turning this screw clockwise will move the beam toward the right of rider.

   The vertical adjustment is made by loosening the bolt which mounts the headlight assembly. Headlight is normally adjusted in the vertical direction so that the center of the beam intersects the ground at the point 50 mm (164 feet) in front of the motorcycle with the motorcycle in the riding attitude.

   (General export type)

   The general export type can be adjusted in the vertical direction; the adjustment being made with the adjusting screw.

2. Bulb replacement

   If the headlight bulb is inoperative, remove the bulb and check for broken filament either visually or with a tester. If the filament is broken, replace it with a bulb of the specified rating.

3. Also check the condition of the wiring and if they are damaged or frayed, repair or replace the wiring.

D. Reassembly

Perform the reassembly in the reverse order of removal.

NOTE:

When installing the socket assembly into the reflector, the "TOP" or the arrow marking should be at the top.

4. Tail/Stop Light

A. Description

The tail/stop light is a single light having a double filament and is constructed as shown in the figure at right. The types and ratings of the bulbs used in the tail/stop lights of the current models are as follows:

Country of Use	Tail/Stop Light Bulb Rating
USA, Britain, France, Belgium and general export	12V-23/7W
Germany	12V-5W (tail) 12V-18W (stop)

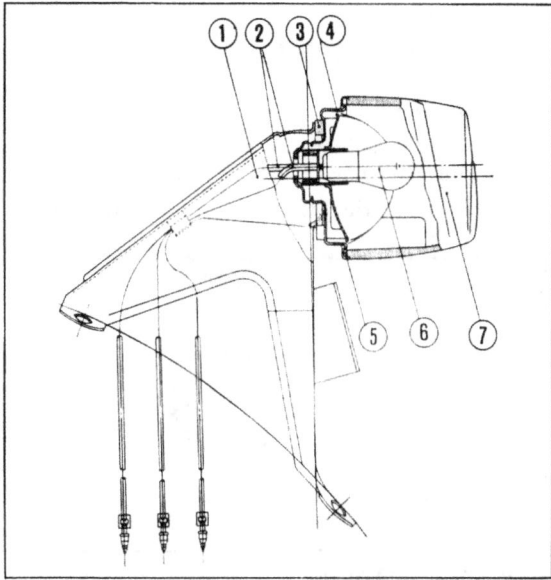

① Number plate bracket ② Cord
③ Taillight base packing ④ Taillight base
⑤ Taillight lens packing ⑥ Tail/stoplight bulb
⑦ Taillight lens
Fig. 6-72. Cross-section of tail/stop light

B. Removal

1. Remove the two screws retaining the tail/stop light lens.
2. Press the bulb inward Ⓐ and twist to the left Ⓑ, and the bulb can be removed Ⓒ. (Fig. 6-73)

C. Inspection

1. When the bulb does not operate, remove the bulb and check for broken filament visually or with a tester and if found defective, replace the bulb with one that is of a specified rating.

D. Reassembly

Perform the reassembly in the reverse order of removal.

NOTE:

When installing the taillight lens, do not overtighten the screws, as this may damage the lens.

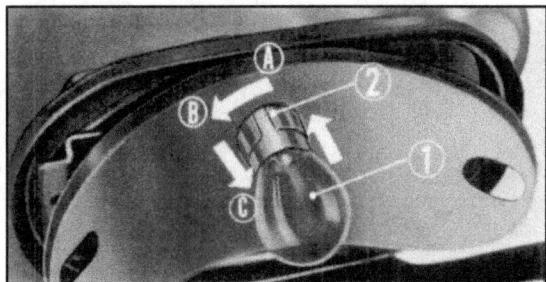

① Tail/stoplight bulb ② Tail light bulb socket
Fig. 6-73.

5. Winker Lights

A. Description

The turn signal lights are constructed as shown in the figure at right. The bulb is contained in a housing with reddish-yellow lens. The types and ratings of the bulbs used in the turn signal lights of the current models are as follows:

Country of Use	Turn Signal Light Rating
USA	12V-25W
France and general export	12V-10W
Germany	12V-18W

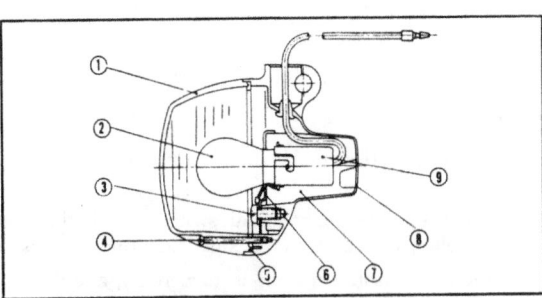

① Turn signal light lens ② Turn signal light bulb
③ Pan screw ④ Oval screw ⑤ Lens packing
⑥ Socket holder ⑦ Socket cushion
⑧ Turn signal light base ⑨ Turn signal light socket
Fig. 6-74. Cross-section of turn signal light

B. Removal

The removal procedure is identical with that of the tail/stop light described in 121-4-B.

C. Inspection

1. If the bulb is inoperative, remove the bulb and check for broken filament and if found to be defective, replace the bulb with one of specified rating.
2. Check the wiring for loose connectors or break in the wires and if found defective, repair or replace.

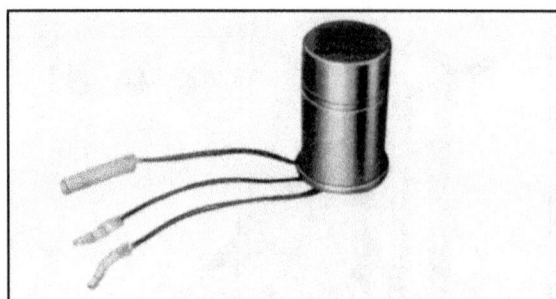

Fig. 6-75. Flasher relay

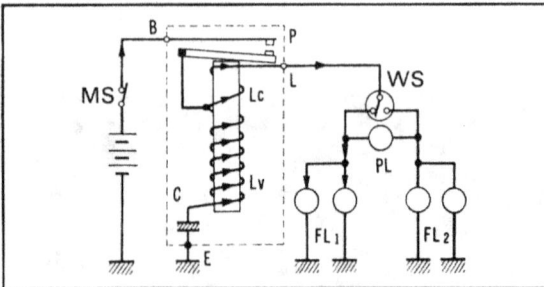

Fig. 6-77. Ignition switch (CS) closed

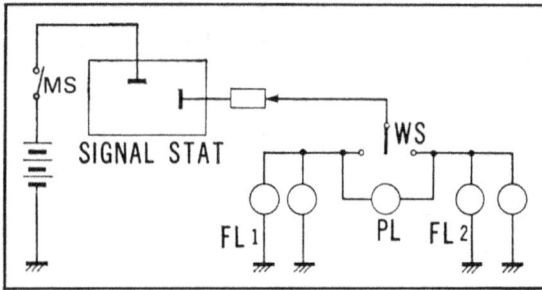

Fig. 6-78. Wiring diagram of signal stat

D. Reassembly

Perform the reassembly in the reverse order of removal.

6. Winker Relay

A. Description

On current models except those for the "US" a capacitor type flasher relay is used and on the "US" model, a Single-Stat 142" relay shown below.

In the capacitor (open-circuit) type relay, the contact points are repeatedly closed to permit the current to flow from the capacitor to the flasher bulb intermittently.

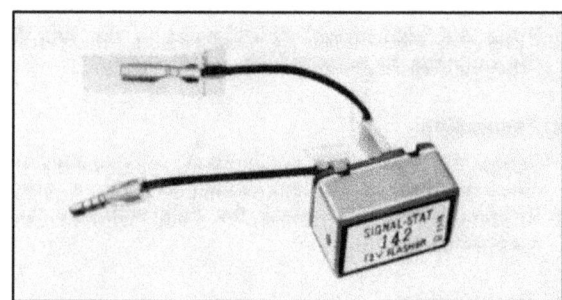

Fig. 6-76. Signal-stat flasher relay

B. Removal

Open the seat and disconnect the flasher unit leads at the connector and then remove the flasher unit.

C. Inspection

1. Make sure that the turn signal light bulb of the proper rating is used. If bulbs of different rating are used, the flashing rate will be affected.
2. Check the operation of the flasher relay.

    When the turn signal light flashing rate is not uniform, the flasher relay should be checked. Disconnect the leads from the left terminal of the relay and connect it to a 12V-10 or 18 or 25W bulb. If the flashing rate is between 65 to 90 cycles per minute, the relay is satisfactory.

    NOTE:
    During the test make sure that the flasher is properly ground.

3. Switch on the turn signal switch and if the lamp stays on continuously and accompanied by a buzzing noise in the relay, check to make sure that the relay is properly grounded or that the ground lead is not broken.
4. When the flasher switch is turned on, and the lamp does not flash, flasher bulb is probably defective. Check the bulb immediately.

D. Reassembly

Perform the installation in the reverse order of removal.

6·7 SWITCHES

1. Ignition Switch

A. Description

This switch controls all electrical circuits of the machine, including lighting circuits, and is operated by a key inserted into it. The positions and operations of this switch are as outlined below:

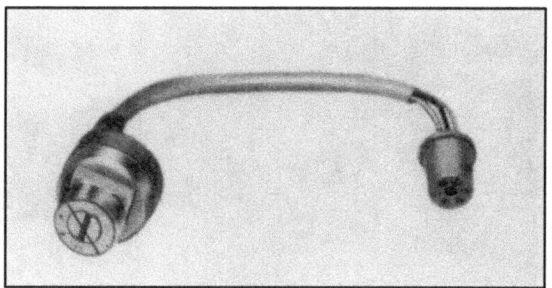

Fig. 6-79. Ignition switch

	BAT (red)	IG (black)	TL1 (brown/white)	TL2 (brown)	Function	Key removal
OFF					Electrical equipment are inoperative and the engine cannot be started.	Removal
I	O——O		O———O		Electrical equipment are operative, the engine will start.	No removal
II	O———————————————O				Parking light is operative, engine cannot be started.	Removal

B. Removal

1. Open the seat and remove the fuel tank.
2. Disconnect the ignition switch leads at the coupler.
3. Remove the ignition switch mounting nut and remove the ignition switch.

C. Inspection

1. Continuity test

   Perform a continuity check to determine if there is a break in the switch lead or defective condition of the contacts. Insert the leads into the X terminal of the tester, turn the selector knob to the continuity position and then turn the ignition switch to the ON position using the key. Apply the test leads across the points to be checked; if the red continuity lamp is lit, the continuity condition is satisfactory. If the lamp does not come on, it indicates an open circuit.

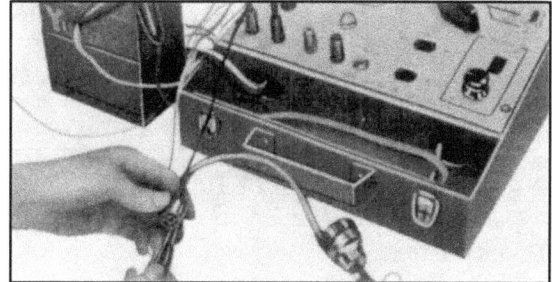

Fig. 6-80. Continuity test of the ignition switch

D. Reassembly

Perform the installation in the reverse order of the removal.

2. Stoplight Switch

A. Description

The stoplight switch is a pull-type switch operated by the brake pedal. (Fig. 6-81)

B. Removal

Disconnect the wiring and remove the stoplight switch from the bracket.

C. Inspection

1. Adjusting the position of the stoplight switch operation.
1) First, check the adjustment of the rear brake pedal in accordance with the procedure on page 100 to make sure that the brakes are properly adjusted.
2) Turn on the ignition key (ignition position "Red" dot).
3) Adjust the stoplight switch ① so that the stoplight will come on when the brake pedal is depressed to the point where the brake just starts take hold. If the stoplight switch is late in switching ON the stoplight, screw in the switch lock nut Ⓐ, and if the stoplight comes on too early, screw out the switch lock nut Ⓑ.

① Stoplight switch ② Lock nut
Fig. 6-81.

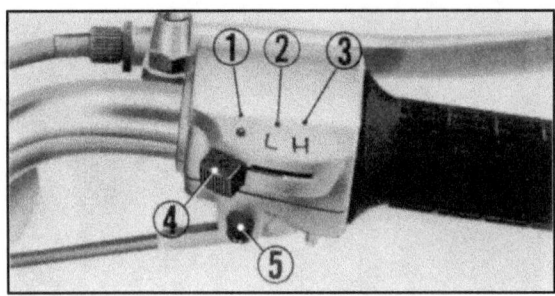

① "OFF" position ② "Low beam" position
③ "High beam" position ④ Headlight control switch
⑤ Starter button
Fig. 6-82.

D. Reassembly

Perform the installation in the reverse of the removal.

3. Starter Switch Button and Lighting Switch

A. Description

The starter switch button and lighting switch (headlight control switch) are built into the right handle bracket.

B. Removal

1. Remove the front brake mounting bolts and remove the front brake lever.
2. Unscrew the two switch mounting screws and separate the upper and lower switch halves.
3. Disconnect the throttle cable end from the throttle control and remove the throttle cable connector from the switch lower side.
4. Disconnect the wiring connectors within the headlight.

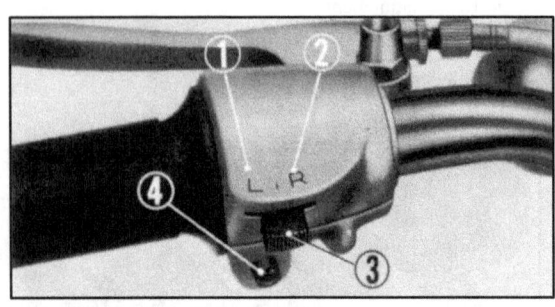

① "Left turn signal" ② "Right turn signal"
③ Turn signal control switch ④ Horn button
Fig. 6-83.

C. Reassembly

Perform the reassembly in the reverse procedure of disassembly.

NOTE:

When installing the switch lower half on the handle, make sure that the pin is inserted into the handlebar stop hole and it is tightened together with the switch upper half.

D. Inspection

1. Check to make sure that the respective switch positions are functioning properly. Turn the ignition key to the ON position and set the headlight control switch to the red dot (① position); the headlight and taillight should not be ON.

   In the L position (② position), the headlight will be ON low beam; in the H position (③ position) the headlight high beam will ON. Further, the taillight will be ON in both the H and L positions.

2. Push the starter button and check to see if the starting motor turn over.

4. Turn Signal and Horn Control Switch

A. Description

The turn signal and horn control switches are built into the left end of the handlebar. The upper button controls the turn signal switch and the lower one the horn control switch.

B. Disassembly

1. Unscrew the clutch lever mounting bolt and remove the clutch lever.
2. Unscrew the two switch mounting screws and disassemble the switch upper and lower halves.
3. Disconnect the electrical connectors located within headlight case.

C. Inspection

1. Turn the ignition switch to the ON position and set the turn signal control switch to the L position (① position). The turn signal light on the left side should be flashing and when the switch to the R position (② position), the right hand turn signal light should be flashing.
2. Set the ignition switch to the ON position and when the horn button is pressed, the horn should operate.

D. Reassembly

Perform the reassembly in the reverse of the disassembly.
NOTE:

When assembling the switch lower half on the handle, make sure that the pin is inserted into the handlebar stopper hole and then tighten together with the switch upper half.

5. Neutral Switch

A. Description

The neutral switch which simulates that the gear change pedal is in neutral position is mounted on one end of the gear shift drum. It closes and opens the circuit to the neutral pilot lamp.

B. Inspection

1. Check to make sure that the green neutral pilot comes on when the gear is shifted into the neutral position by the gear change pedal.
2. Check the operation and condition of the neutral switch.

C. Removal

1. Remove the left crankcase rear cover.
2. Unscrew the neutral switch mounting screws and the switch can be removed from the gear shift drum.

D. Reassembly

Perform the installation in the reverse order of the removal.

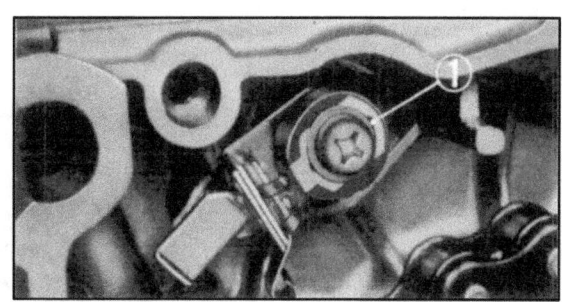

Fig. 6-84. Neutral switch

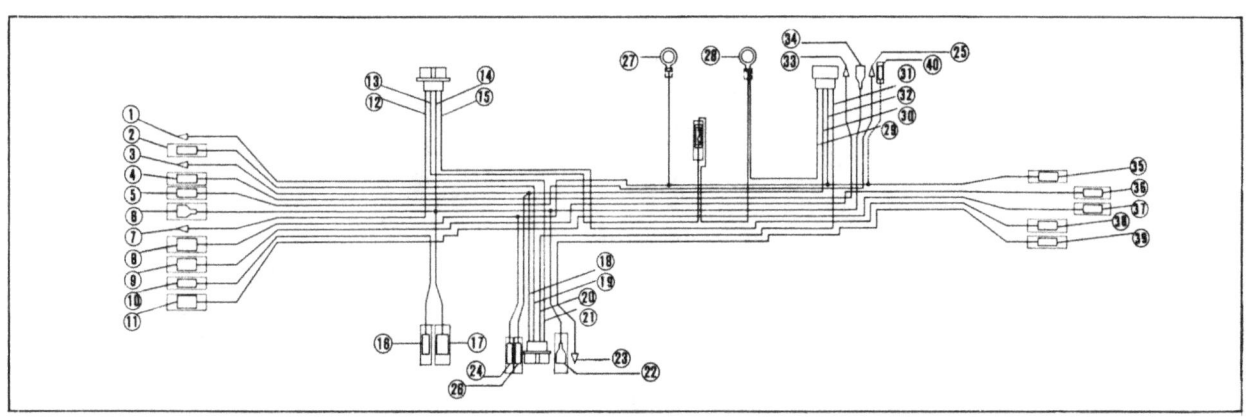

Fig. 6-85. Wiring diagram

	Lead color	Connection
①	Light green/Red	Neutral pilot lamp
②	White/Yellow/Tube	Lighting dimmer switch
③	Yellow	Lighting dimmer switch
④	Yellow/Red	Starter button switch
⑤	Gray	Winker switch
⑥	Black	Lighting dimmer switch/neutral pilot lamp
⑦	Brown/White	Speedometer lamp/lighting dimmer switch
⑧	Green	High beam lamp/head lamp/front winker lamp
⑨	Blue	R. front winker lamp/winker switch/winker pilot lamp
⑩	Light green	Horn button switch
⑪	Orange	L. front winker lamp/winker switch/winker pilot lamp
⑫	Red	
⑬	Brown/White	Ignition switch coupler
⑭	Black	
⑮	Brown	
⑯	Light green	Horn
⑰	Black	Horn/ignition coil
⑱	Yellow	
⑲	White	A.C. generator coupler
⑳	Pink	
㉑	Light green/Red	
㉒	Black	Stop switch
㉓	Green/Yellow	Stop switch
㉔	Green	Pointless regulator
㉕	Gray	Winker relay
㉖	Yellow	Regulator
㉗	Green	Battery ⊖ terminal
㉘	Red (red/white)	Battery ⊕ terminal
㉙	Red/White	
㉚	Yellow	
㉛	Pink	Selenium rectifier coupler
㉜	Green	
㉝	Yellow/Red	Starter solenoid switch
㉞	Black	Winker relay/starter solenoid switch
㉟	Green	Taillight base
㊱	Blue	R. Rear winker lamp
㊲	Orange	L. rear winker lamp
㊳	Brown	Taillamp
㊴	Green/Yellow	Stop switch
㊵	Green	Winker relay (not for SIGNAL-STAT winker relay).

6. Wiring Harness

A. Description

The wire leads in the wiring harness are colored for easy identification of their connections for servicing.

B. Removal

1. Open the seat and remove the fuel tank.
2. Remove the headlight rim and disconnect the connectors within the headlight case.
3. Disconnect the ignition switch and selenium rectifier leads at the coupler.
4. Disconnect the coupler at the frame center.
5. Disconnect the leads at the rear fender.
6. The wiring harness can be removed from the frame.

C. Inspection

1. Abrasions and breaks in the covering of the electrical wiring may render the electrical equipment inoperative, therefore, check to see that there is no damaged wiring.
2. Broken wires should be repaired and all joints checked to make sure that the connections are sound.

D. Reassembly

Perform the installation in the reverse order of the disassembly.

7. ENGINE (SL350)

GENERAL DESCRIPTION OF THE SL350

With the exception of the primary kick mechanism, the carburetor setting and the dismounting and remounting procedures, the engine is identical to the CB/CL350 series.

7·1 DISMOUNTING THE ENGINE

1. Drain the engine oil by removing both the drain plug and the filler cap.
2. Turn the fuel cock to the STOP position. Disconnect the fuel line from the cock. Raise the seat, move the tank to the rear to disengage it from the fuel tank rear cushion, and then separate the tank from the frame by removing it towards the rear.
3. Remove the gear change and kick starter pedals. Remove the mufflers and take off the left rear crankcase cover. (Fig. 7-1)
4. Disconnect the drive chain at the connecting link. (Fig. 7-1)
5. Remove the carburetors by loosening the carburetor insulating band screws. (Fig. 7-2)
6. Disconnect the wiring harness.
7. Remove the contact breaker cable connection and the high tension terminal assemblies from the spark plug.
8. Disconnect the tachometer cable at the engine.
9. Remove the nine engine hanger bolts (at the bottom of crankcase, on top of cylinder head, at the top rear of crankcase) and then dismount the engine from the right side.

7·2 REMOUNTING THE ENGINE

1. The engine can be easily remounted by sliding the rear of the engine in place from the crankcase side.
2. Installing the rear upper crankcase mounting bolt first will permit easy alignment of the remaining crankcase mounting bolts, first the lower and then the cylinder head upper mounting bolts.

NOTE:

Torque all engine hanger bolts to 25.3~32.5 ft-lbs (250~350 kg-cm).

3. The installation details for the engine remounting are performed in the reverse order of the removal procedure.

NOTE:

1. The drive chain joint clip ① should be facing in the correct direction, the closed end of the link clip should point toward the direction of the normal chain rotation. (Fig. 7-4)
2. The steel ball ① must be in the clutch lever ② housing when installing the left crankcase rear cover. (Fig. 7-5)

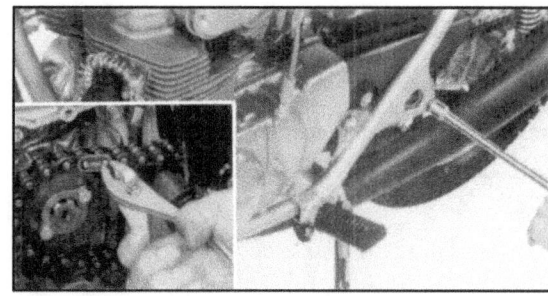

Fig. 7-1. Removing the muffler

① Carburetor insulating band screw
Fig. 7-2.

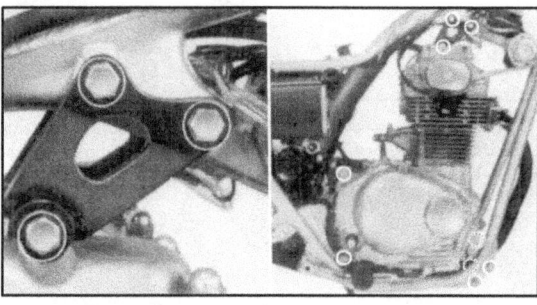

Fig. 7-3. Engine hanger bolts

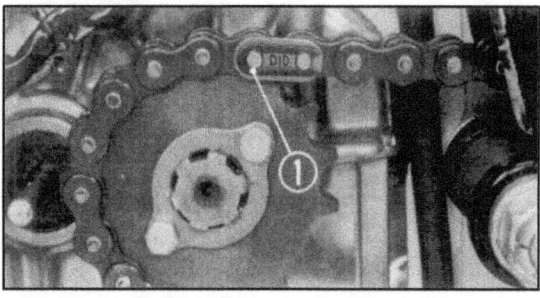

① Drive chain joint clip
Fig. 7-4.

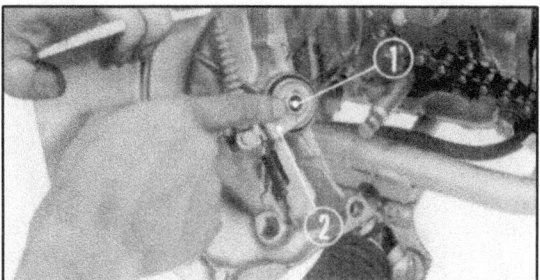

① Steel ball ② Clutch lever
Fig. 7-5.

7·3 PRIMARY KICK STARTER

Since SL350 transmission incorporates a primary kick, the engine can be started with the gears engaged by disengaging the clutch. The kick gear will directly engage the crankshaft through the primary starter idle gear which rotates freely on the countershaft.

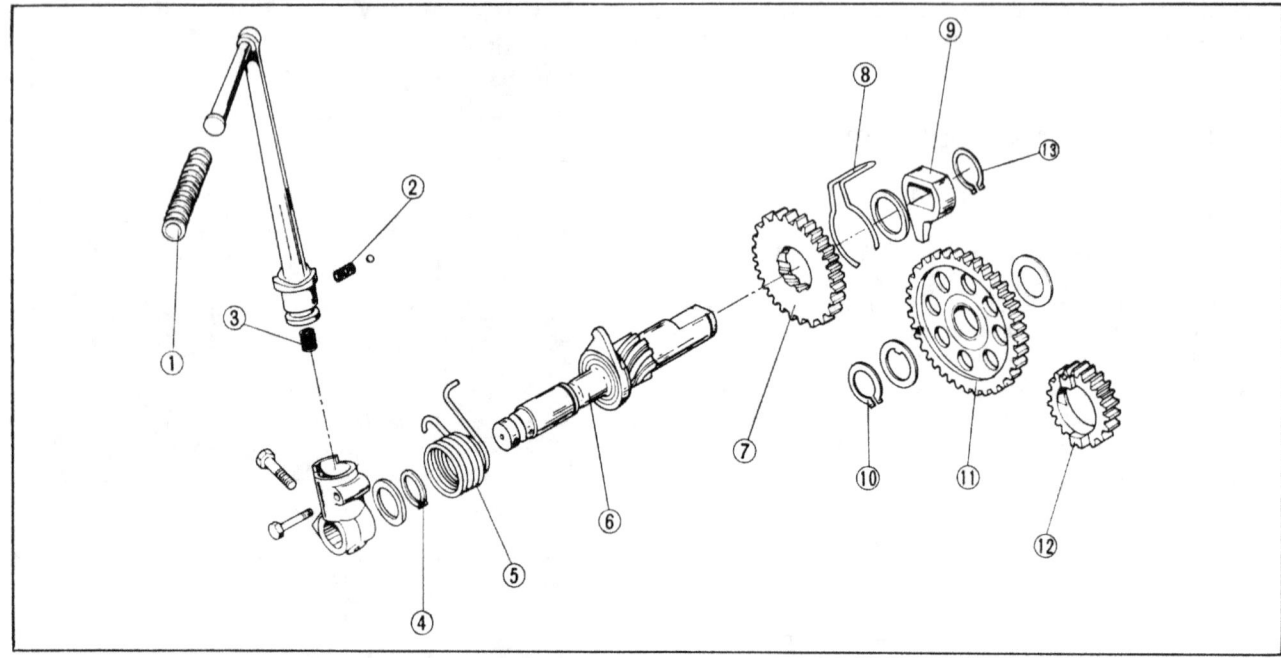

① Kick starter rubber   ② Kick starter stopper spring   ③ Kick starter knuckle spring   ④ 18 mm, circlip
⑤ Kick starter spring   ⑥ Kick starter spindle complete   ⑦ Kick starter pinion   ⑧ Friction spring
⑨ Kick spindle stopper   ⑩ 20 mm, circlip   ⑪ Kick starter idle gear   ⑫ Kick starter gear
⑬ 20 mm, clip
Fig. 7-6.

A. Disassembly

1. Separate the upper and lower crankcase and then remove the kick starter spindle.
2. Remove circlips and disassemble the kick starter spindle.

B. Inspection

1. Inspect the gear teeth and kick spindle stopper for wear or damage. If damaged, replace with new one.

C. Reassembly

Reassemble the kick starter components in the reverse order.

NOTE:
Do not forget to assemble 18 mm and 20 mm circlips.

7·4 CARBURETOR

A. Specifications

The carburetor specifications are summarized below.

Item \ Model	SL350		
Setting mark	A		
Venturi bore dia	24.0 mm (0.944 in)		
M.J. (Main jet)	#120		
A.J. (Air jet)	#150		
J.N. (Jet needle)	2.515 mm (0.099 in) 2°00′		
Throttle valve	2.5×1.8×0.2		
S.J. (Slow jet)	#40	AB_1	0.6 mm (0.023 in)×2
		AB_2	0.6 mm (0.023 in)×2
		AB_3	0.6 mm (0.023 in)×2
Float height	25 mm		

B. Carburetor Circuits

1. Starting circuit

When the engine is started while it is cold, a richer fuel-air mixture is required. The choke valve is provided for this purpose. Raise the choke lever, and the choke valve is closed to reduce the amount of incoming air, causing the richer mixture to be drawn into the engine. A relief valve is attached to the choke valve to prevent the engine from stalling due to excessive fuel. The relief valve is controlled by the negative pressure created by air drawn into the main bore.

2. Low-speed circuit

The low-speed circuit is designed to supply the proper amount of mixture for the engine at idle and extremely low speeds.

The fuel in the float chamber enters the slow jet. The fuel metered by the slow jet is mixed with the air bled by the slow air jet. The mixture is jetted into the main bore through the by-pass.

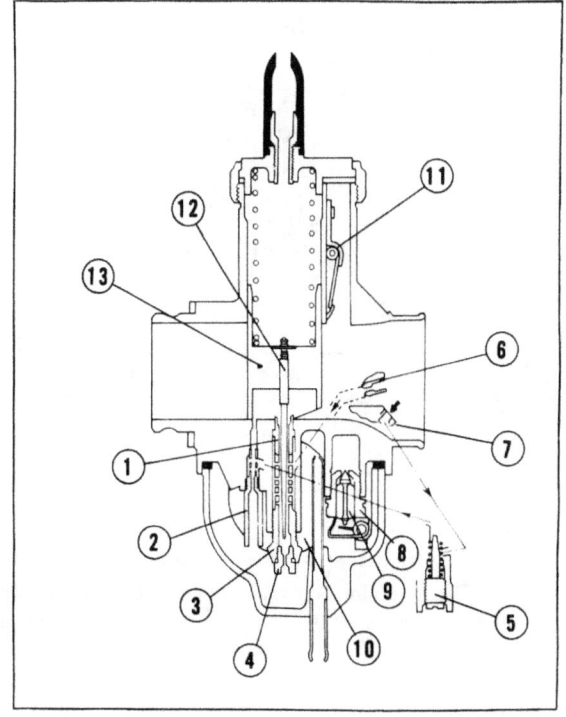

① Needle jet ② Slow jet ③ Needle jet holder
④ Main jet ⑤ Air screw ⑥ Main air jet
⑦ Slow air jet ⑧ Valve seat ⑨ Float valve
⑩ Float ⑪ Choke valve ⑫ Jet needle
⑬ Throttle valve
Fig. 7-7A.

3. Main circuit

The main circuit is designed to supply the proper amount of mixture for the engine at medium and high speeds. The fuel in the float chamber enters the main jet. The fuel metered by the main jet is mixed with the air bled by the main air jet in the needle jet holder. The mixture is jetted into the main bore through the needle jet. The lower part of the jet needle is tapered to regulate the amount of mixture.

4. Float circuit

In order to keep the operating characteristics of the carburetor and its atomization of fuel as nearly constant as possible, it is essential that the level of the fuel for the jet is always maintained at the same level. This is accomplished by means of a float system or circuit. The fuel flows into the float chamber from the fuel tank through the fuel joint and the clearance between the float valve and seat. As the fuel level rises, the float moves up on the fuel. When the float valve comes in contact with its seat, the supply of fuel is shut off. On the other hand, as the level drops, the float moves down and again the fuel enters the float chamber between the valve and seat. By repeating this cycle, the level of the fuel in the float chamber is always maintained at the same level.

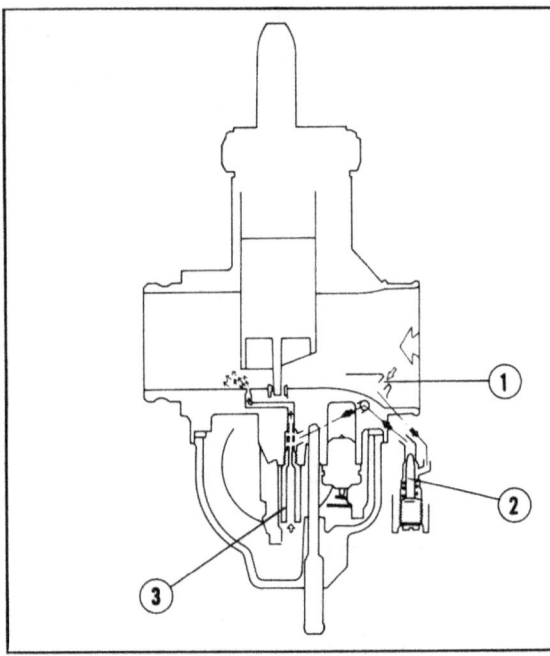

① Slow air jet   ② Air screw   ③ Slow jet
Fig. 7-8B.

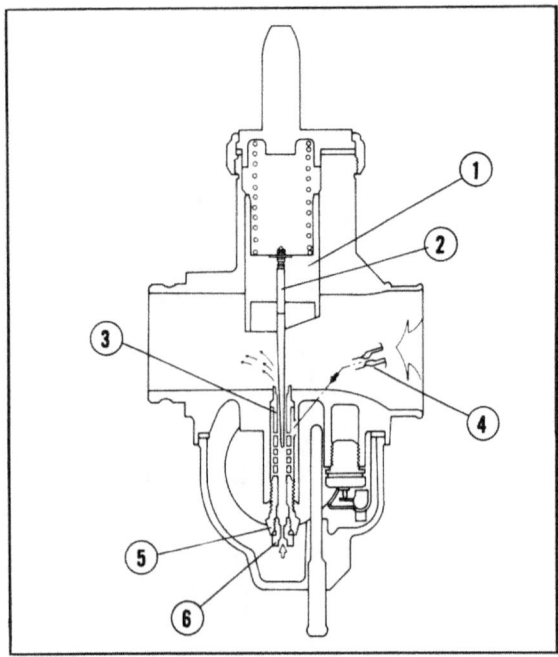

① Throttle valve   ② Jet needle   ③ Needle jet
④ Main air jet   ⑤ Needle jet holder   ⑥ Main jet
Fig. 7-9.

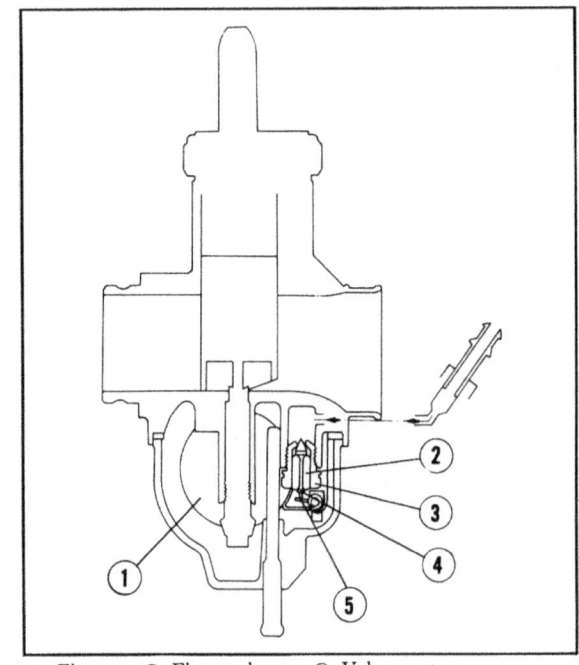

① Float   ② Float valve   ③ Valve seat
④ Float lip   ⑤ Float arm
Fig. 7-10.

Carburetor Adjustments
- Before adjusting the carburetor, check to be sure that the engine and electrical systems are in good condition.
- When disassembling and cleaning the carburetor for adjustment, take care not to lose, contaminate or drop any component parts. Remove dirt from the parts using compressed air.

1. Idle speed adjustment

    This adjustment is made by means of the air screw and throttle stop screw.
    1) Turn the air screw in fully and then back it off the specified number of turns.
    2) Start the engine and turn the throttle stop screw to obtain the specified idle speed.
    3) Under the condition ② above, turn the air screw in either direction to obtain the maximum speed at which the engine can run smoothly.
    4) Back the throttle stop screw off to obtain the specified idle speed.
    5) Turn the air screw in either direction to check to see if the engine runs smoothly.

2. Float level adjustment

    Incorrect float level may result in poor acceleration, excessive fuel consumption, etc. If necessary, adjust the float level in the following procedure.
    1) Remove the float chamber body and place the carburetor as shown.
    2) Finger-move the float and find the position where the float valve pin comes in contact with the float lip. In such a position, measure "H" with a measurement gauge.
    3) If the "H" measurement is out of specification, adjust the float lip.

CAUTION:

Since the float valve is spring loaded, this measurement should be carefully made.

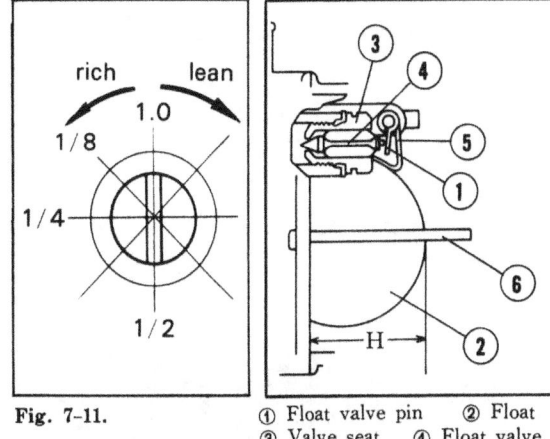

Fig. 7-11.

① Float valve pin ② Float
③ Valve seat ④ Float valve
⑤ Float lip ⑥ Measurement gauge

Fig. 7-12.

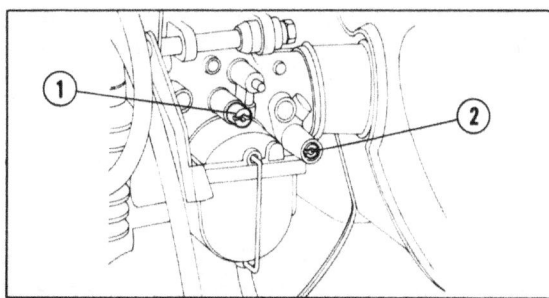

① Idle speed screw ② Air screw
Fig. 7-13.

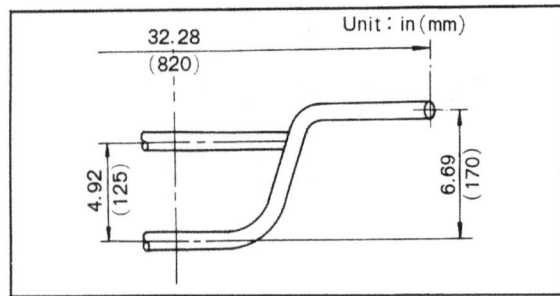

Fig. 8-1. Handlebar

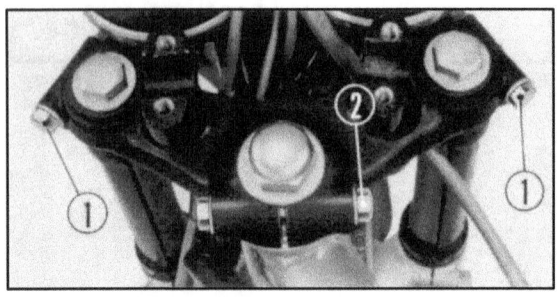

① Fork mounting bolt ② Steering stem setting bolt
Fig. 8-2. Fork top bridge

8. FRAME

8·1 HANDLEBAR

A. Description

The handlebar is a ladder type similar to that used on the CL350. As the seat height is 2.36 (60 mm) lower the handlebar is designed slightly lower for use especially suited to on and off road riding and to lessen riding fatigue from long road work (Fig. 8-1).

Removal, inspection, and installation are the same for the CL350, therefore, refer to section of CB, CL250·350.

8·2 FORK TOP BRIDGE

A. Description

The fork top bridge and the handle pipe upper holder are painted flat black to prevent annoying reflection. Further, to provide good steering stability on rough roads, the fork top bridge is used to clamp the top of the front fork. The fork top bridge is made larger, incorporating two mounting bolt holes and a steering stem setting bolt hole. (Fig. 8-2)

8·3 FRONT CUSHION

A. Description (Piston valve type)

○ The front fork is assembled into a complete unit by the fork bottom bridge, axle and the fork top bridge and their respective mounting bolts. This three-point mounting design provides a highly rigid unit for good stability. The front cushion is a telescopic type with a 6.7 in (170 mm) range of travel.

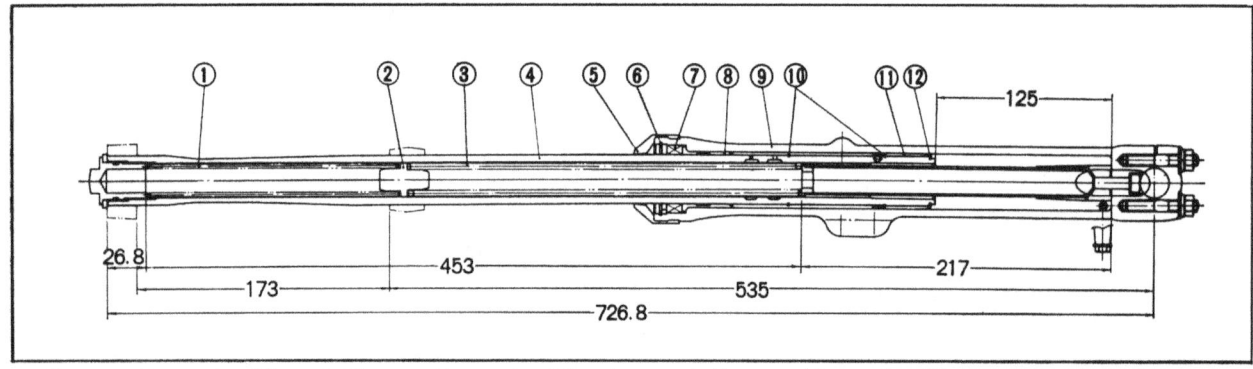

① Front cushion spring (A) ② Front cushion spring joint piece ③ Front cushion spring (B) ④ Front fork pipe
⑤ Front fork dust seal ⑥ Internal snap ring ⑦ Front fork oil seal ⑧ Front fork pipe guide
⑨ Front fork bottom case ⑩ Fork piston stopper ring ⑪ Front fork piston ⑫ Fork piston snap ring
Fig. 8-3. Sectional view of front cushion

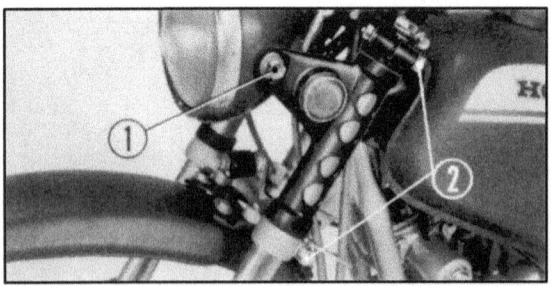

① Headlight mounting bolts ② Front fork fixing bolts
Fig. 8-4.

B. Disassembly

1. Raise the front wheel off the ground by placing a support under the engine.
2. Remove the front brake and speedometer cables from the front wheel.
3. Remove the front wheel.
4. Remove the headlight mounting bolts ①. (Fig. 8-4)
5. Loosen the front fork fixing bolts ② and remove the front fork assembly from the frame. (Fig. 8-4)
6. Remove the front fork top bolt and drain the oil.
7. Remove the front fork dust seal.

8. Remove each fork dust seal, 48 mm internal snap ring and oil seal.
9. Pull out the front fork pipe from the front fork bottom case.
10. Remove the front fork piston.

C. Inspection

1. Front fork bottom case
   Check for cracks and distortion. The cylinder case interior is checked with a cylinder gauge ①. (Fig. 8-7)

mm (inch)

Item	Standard value	Serviceable limit
Cylinder diameter	37.5~37.539 (1.4763~1.4779)	37.680 (1.4834)

Replace if beyond the serviceable limit.

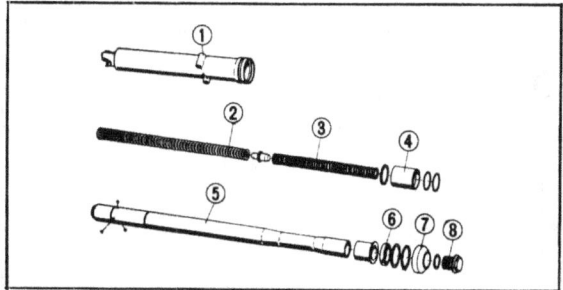

① Front fork bottom case
② Front fork cushion spring (B)
③ Front fork cushion spring (A)
④ Front fork piston ⑤ Front fork pipe
⑥ Front fork oil seal ⑦ Front fork dust seal
⑧ Front fork bolt
Fig. 8-6. Component parts of front fork

2. Front fork piston
   Check the piston ① for wear and scratches. Measure the piston dia. with a micrometer ②. If worn or damaged, replace with new one. (Fig. 8-8)

mm (inch)

Item	Standard value	Serviceable limit
Piston diameter	37.395~37.42 (1.4722~1.4732)	37.385 (1.4718)

D. Reassembly

Perform the reassembly in the reverse order of disassembly.

NOTE:

1. It is recommended that all set, stopper and snap rings be replaced with new items.
2. Apply petroleum resistant grease between the main and dust lips of the front oil seal. Install the oil seal ① into the front wheel bottom case with the oil seal driving guide ② (Tool No. 07947-2730100) and weight ③ (Tool No. 07797-2920300). (Fig. 8-9)

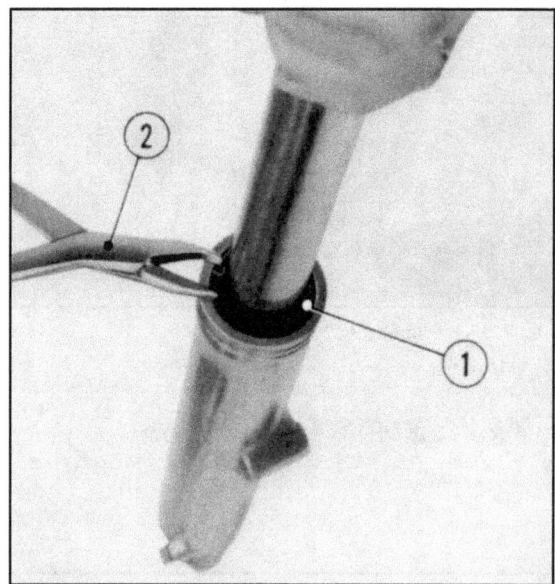

① Internal snap ring ② Special pliers
Fig. 8-5.

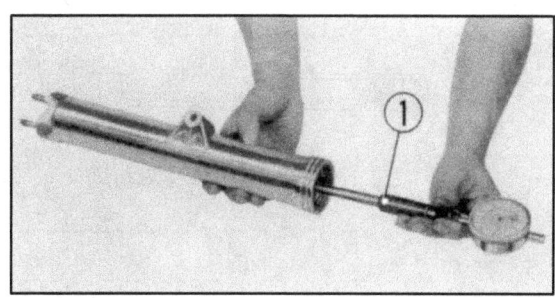

① Cylinder gauge
Fig. 8-7.

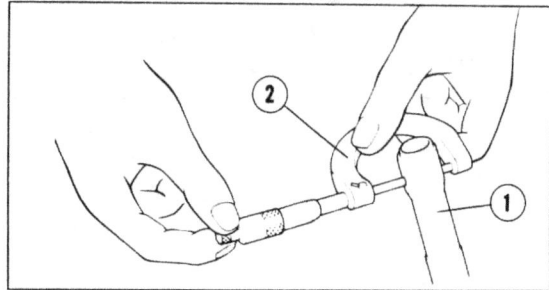

① Fork piston ② Micrometer
Fig. 8-8.

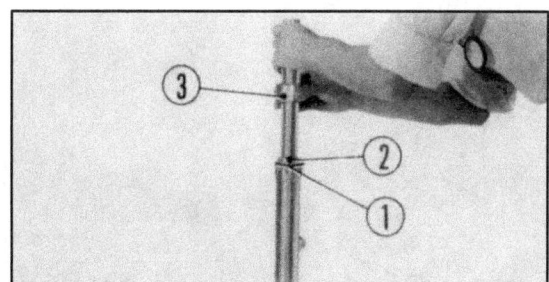

① Oil seal ② Oil seal driving guide
③ Oil seal driving weight
Fig. 8-9.

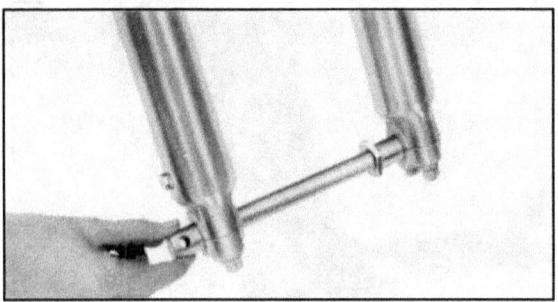

Fig. 8-10. Aligning both front axle holes

3. Install the snap ring into the retainer groove.
4. Assemble the cushion spring into the case.
5. After installing the front fork to the frame, fill the fork cylinder with 11~11.6 cu-in (180~1900 cc) **SAE 10W-30** oil.
6. If the front fork mounting is misaligned, the steering will pull to one side; therefore, before installing the wheel, align both front axle holes by inserting a shaft through the axle holes. (Fig. 8-10)

4. FRONT FORKS (free valve type)

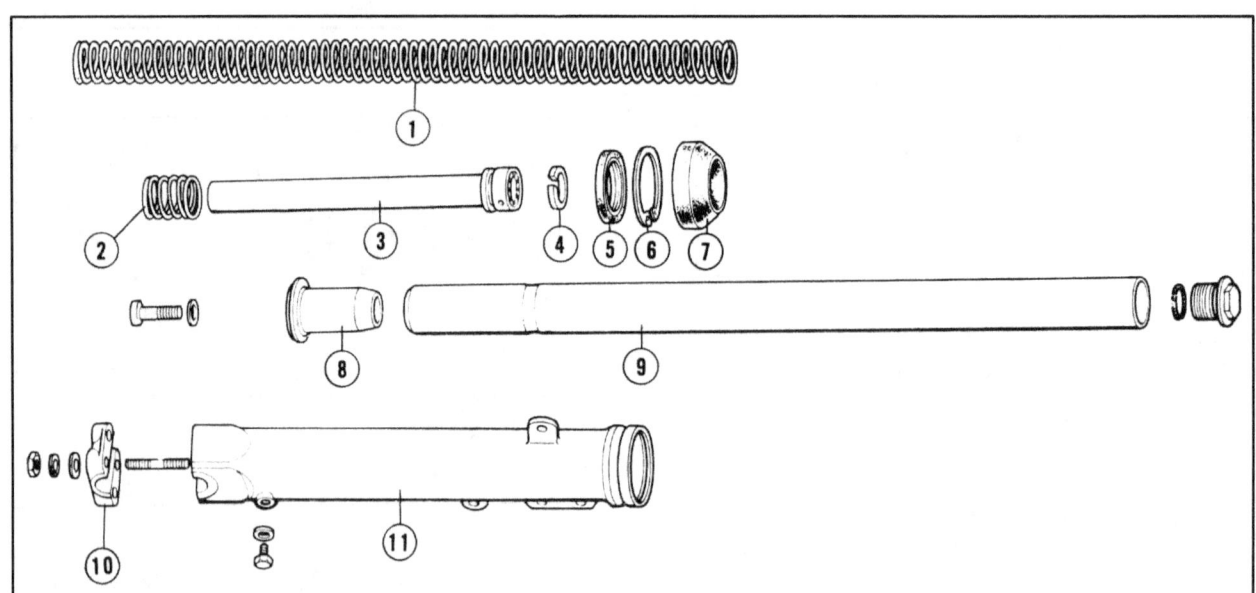

① Front cushion spring
② Front rebound spring
③ Bottom pipe
④ Piston ring
⑤ 35-48-11 oil seal
⑥ Internal 48 mm cir-clip
⑦ Front fork dust seal
⑧ Oil lock piece
⑨ Fork pipe
⑩ Front axle holder
⑪ Bottom case

Fig. 8-11.

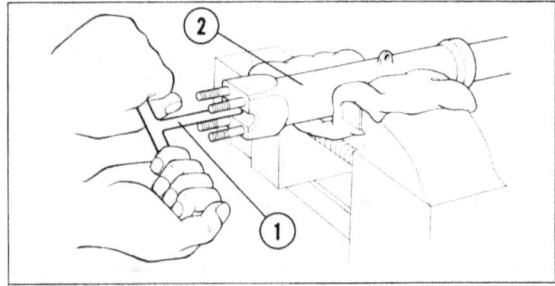

① Hollow set wrench ② Front fork bottom case
Fig. 8-12.

Disassembly

The free valve type front forks should be disassembled in the same manner as the piston type up to step 6.

1. With the front fork bottom case held in a vice, remove each socket bolt with the Hollow set wrench (Tool No. 07917-3230000).
   Then separate the front fork pipe from the fork bottom case.

2. Remove each front fork dust seal, 48 mm internal snap ring and oil seal.

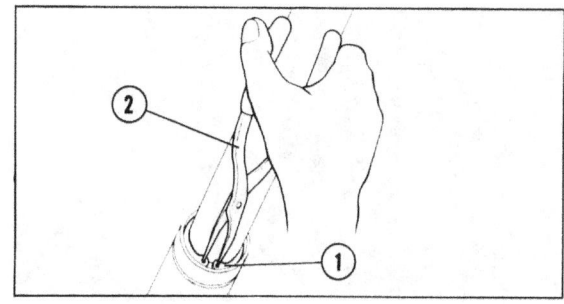

① 48 mm internal snap ring   ② Front fork dust seal
Fig. 8-13.

Inspection

1. Check the front fork piston rings for wear.
2. Check the front shock absorber springs A and B for tension. Also measure the spring free length.
3. Check the fork bottom cases for wear, scores, scratches or cracks.
4. Check the front fork pipes for wear, scores, scratches, cracks or rust. If rust formation is noticed on the pipes, completely remove it with a fine emery cloth.
5. Check the oil seals for scores, scratches or damage.

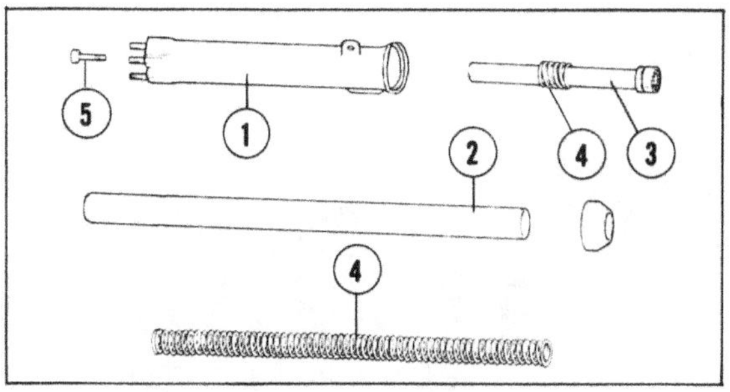

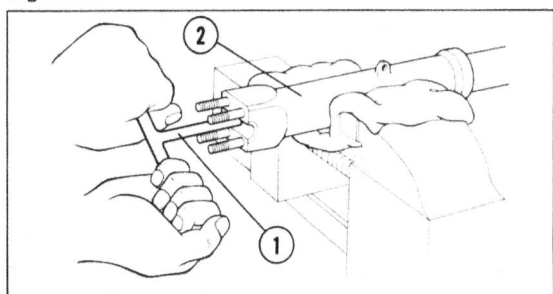

① Front fork bottom case   ② Front fork pipe
③ Bottom pipe   ④ Front suspension springs
⑤ Front fork bolt
Fig. 8-14.

Assembly

- To assemble, reverse the disassembly procedures.
1. As shown in Fig. 8-14, install each front fork pipe to the fork bottom case and tighten it with the socket bolt securely.
   When tightening, apply a coat of locking sealant to the socket bolt.

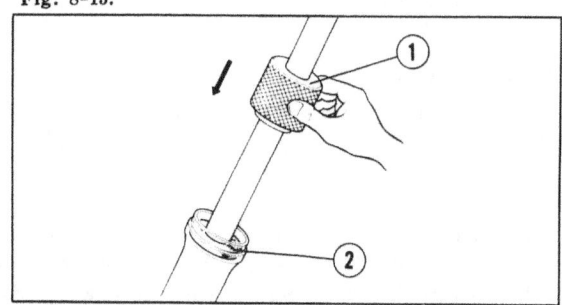

① Hollow set wrench   ② Front fork bottom case
Fig. 8-15.

2. Apply a coat of grease to each oil seal lip. Then insert the oil seal with the fork seal driver (Tool No. 07947-3290000).
   Do not forget to install the snap ring.
3. Fill the fork pipes with premium quality automatic transmission fluid (ATF) up to the specified level.
   (See page 68).

① Fork seal driver   ② Oil seal
Fig. 8-16.

8·4 STEERING STEM

A. Description

The steering stem is mounted into the frame head pipe supported by the upper and lower steering balls. An oil damper bracket which mounts the optional steering oil damper is installed on the right side of the fork bottom bridge together with the horn. Its function is to improve steering, prevent handle vibration, and dampen shock when travelling on rough roads. A steering lock is incorporated into the fork bottom bridge, identical to the CL350, and it can be removed as a complete assembly by inserting the key, turning counterclockwise and pulling. When performing the installation, do not forget to install the steering lock spring.

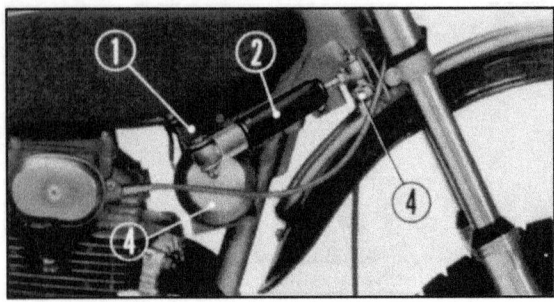

① Steering oil damper bracket ② Steering oil damper
③ Horn ④ Fork bottom bridge
Fig. 8-17. Steering oil damper (option)

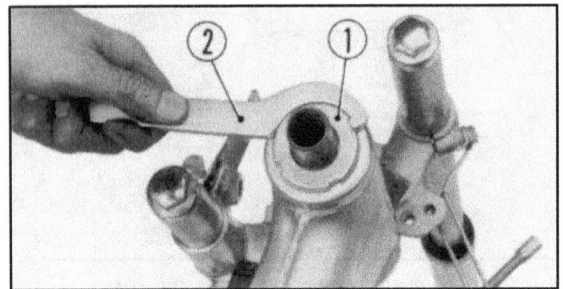

① Steering stem top nut ② Hook spanner
Fig. 8-18.

B. Disassembly

1. Disconnect the front brake cable at the brake arm and the clutch cable at the lower end. Disconnect the throttle cable at the carburetor and the wiring harness located within headlight case. Remove handlebar by unscrewing the four 8 mm bolts from the handle pipe holder clamps.
2. Remove the front wheel.
3. Remove the top bridge plate.
4. Remove the steering oil damper (option) from the bottom bridge plate and the damper bracket with horn.
5. Remove the headlight and front fork.
6. Remove the steering stem top nut ① using a hook spanner (Tool No. 07902-2000000) and pull the stem out the bottom. (Fig. 8-18)

NOTE:

Do not drop the steel balls during the steering stem removal.

C. Inspection

1. Check the steering stem for any bend or deformation. Straighten the bent stem with a press and then check it with a dial gauge. If badly damaged, replace with new one.
2. Check the steel balls for wear and cracks. If heavy steering is experienced while riding, it is probably due to either the worn steel balls or the broken balls. Replace the balls to correct the trouble.
3. Check the steering oil damper for dents, damage or fluid leakage. If defective, it must be repaired or replaced.

D. Reassembly

Perform the reassembly in the reverse order of disassembly, however, special attention must be given to the following points.

NOTE:

1. Use sufficient grease when installing the steel balls of 1/4 in (6.35 mm) dia. into the ball races (18 for the upper and 19 for the lower races). When removing the steering stem, care should be taken not to drop the steel balls.
2. When mounting the steering stem, the steering stem top nut should be tightened so that only slight pressure is applied and there is no slackness in the steering cones. To check tightness of the steering, tilt the front wheel to either side slightly and let the handle start moving by its own weight. If the handle does not move by itself or there are gaps between races, readjust the steering stem top nut.

8·5 FUEL TANK

A. Description

The fuel tank is mounted on the frame body directly above the engine and is installed on the frame body and mounted on a rubber cushion. A flip open type of tank cap is used to facilitate refueling.

Removal and installation procedures are identical to the CL350, therefore, refer to the section of CB, CL250·350.

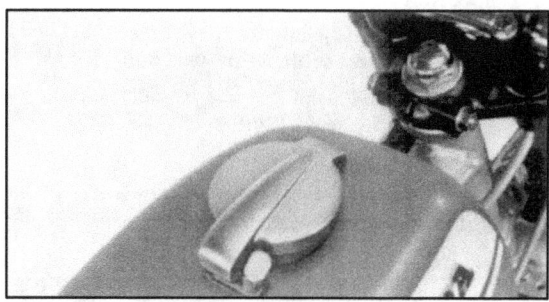

Fig. 8-19. Fuel tank

8·6 FRAME

A. Description

The frame is of a double cradle tubular steel construction. This design is particularly suited for rough road. A fender stay is welded on the rear extension of the half frame for mounting the rear fender.

① Head pipe
② Main pipe
③ Rear fender stay
④ Sub tube
⑤ Center pipe
⑥ Sub tube holder
⑦ Front down tube
⑧ Lower cross member

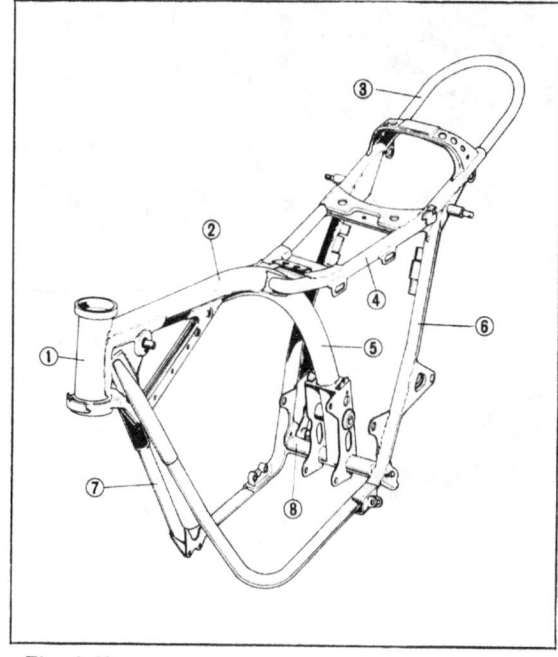

Fig. 8-20.

B. Disassembly

1. Engine dismounting
   Refer to engine dismounting section on page 127.

2. Seat
   Unlock the seat latch, open the seat and remove the two lock pins and bolts at the seat hinge. Then separate seat from the frame.

3. Fuel tank
   When dismounting the engine, the fuel tank is also removed at the same time. Refer to page 127.

4. Air cleaner
   Remove the two air cleaners as described on page 138.

5. Steering handle, front suspension and wheel
   Remove these parts as described on page 132~135.

6. Rear wheel
   Remove the rear wheel as described on page 141.

7. Rear cushion
   Remove the rear cushion as described on page 140.

8. Rear fork
   Remove the rear fork as described on page 139.

C. Inspection

1. Inspect the weld joints for any breaks or cracks and the steering pipe for twist and bends. Weld the cracks, straighten the minor dents or twisting.
2. Check the frame paint coating for rust spots. Paint the worn or scratched parts.

D. Reassembly

Perform the assembly in the reverse order of disassembly.

① Seat latch
Fig. 8-21.

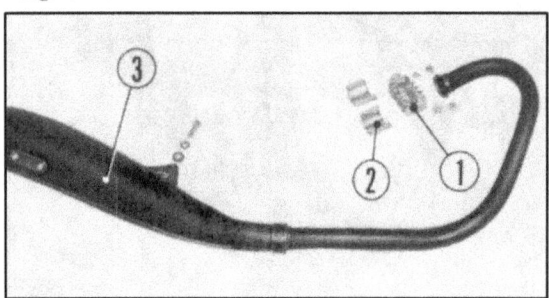

① Exhaust pipe joint flange
② Exhaust pipe joint collar ③ Muffler assembly
Fig. 8-22.

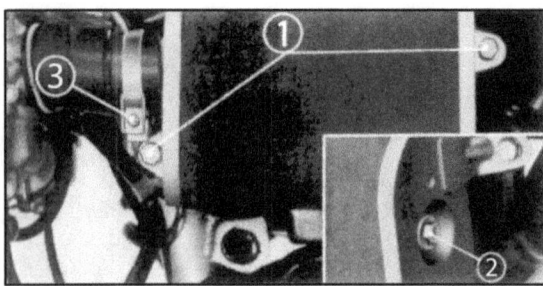

① Air cleaner fixing bolts ② Air cleaner fixing bolt
③ Connecting tube screw
Fig. 8-23.

8·7 SEAT

A. Description

The center of the seat is made into a depression changing gradually from a flat surface to a series of ridges covered with vinyl. This provides good seat holding on rough roads: also, the sponge rubber cushion used in the seat absorbs shock and vibration for more comfortable riding.

The seat is unlocked and raised toward the right side for access to the battery, selenium rectifier and the winker relay for inspection. Refer to the 250·350 Shop Manual relay for inspection.

8·8 MUFFLER

A. Description

The exhaust pipes are mounted to their respective right and left cylinder heads with exhaust pipe joints and 8 mm bolts and nuts.

The muffler and the exhaust pipe are an integral unit which is mounted to the units on the muffler bracket with a 10 mm hex. bolt. A US Forestry Service approved spark arrester is installed within the muffler to prevent the emmission of hot sparks when riding through forest and mountainous regions.

Refer to the 250·350 Shop Manual for removal, inspection and installation procedure.

NOTE:

Disconnection of the muffler and exhaust pipe or disassembly of the muffler cannot be done.

8·9 AIR CLEANER

A. Description

Two air cleaner elements are attached, one on each side of the frame. Both elements are made of uretane foam which requires cleaning at specified intervals.

B. Disassembly

1. Remove the air cleaner cover by pulling it off at the rubber mount.
2. Unscrew air cleaner fixing bolts ①, ② and connecting tube screw ③ and then withdraw the cleaner from the frame. (Fig. 8-23)

C. Inspection

1. If the element is dirty, wash it in solvent or gasoline and allow to dry throughly. Then follow by squeezing out the excess oil and assembling it into the air cleaner case. If broken or damaged, replace with new one. (Fig. 8-24)
2. Check the air cleaner case for cracks or other damage. If badly damaged, replace with new one.

D. Reassembly

Perform the reassembly in the reverse order of disassembly.

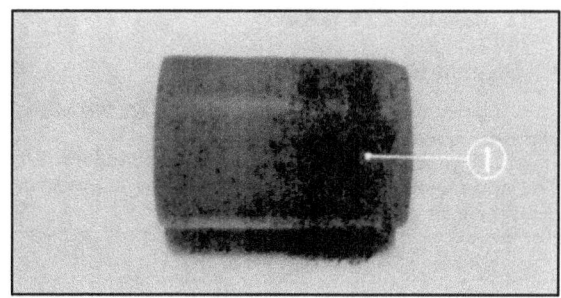

① Air cleaner element
Fig. 8-24.

8·10 REAR FORK

A. Description

The rear fork supports the wheel and pivots at the rear fork pivot bolt to provide a swing action.

It is constructed of steel tubing for greater strength and durability and mounted through a pivot bushing on lock side and lubricated with grease for smooth operation.

B. Disassembly

1. Place a block under the engine to raise the rear wheel off the ground.
2. Remove the chain, the rear wheel and the drive chain guard.
3. Pull out the rear fork pivot bolt ① and remove the rear fork ②. (Fig. 8-25)

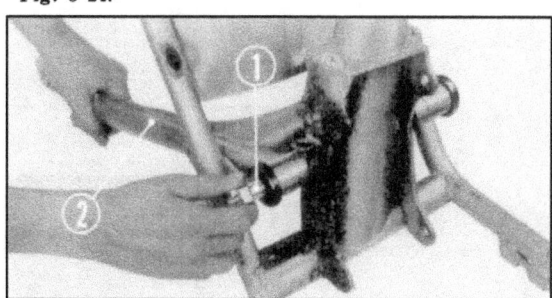

① Rear fork pivot bolt ② Rear fork
Fig. 8-25.

C. Inspection

1. The rear fork should be inspected for distortion. Insert the rear fork pivot bolt through both pivot holes in the rear fork and check the rear fork for alignment.
2. Measure the inside diameter of the rear fork pivot bushing and replace if beyond the serviceable limit.

mm (inch)

Item	Standard value	Serviceable limit
Inside diameter of bushing	20.000~20.033 (0.787~0.789)	20.18 (0.795)

D. Reassembly

1. Apply a liberal amount of grease on the pivot collar and assemble it into the rear fork. Insert the pivot bolt from the right side, and then install and tighten the 14 mm self lock nut. Tightening torque is 65.0~79.5 lb-ft (900~1200 kg-cm).
2. Install the drive chain guard and the rear wheel.
3. Install the drive chain, the rear brake pedal and drive chain tensioners.

8·11 REAR CUSHION

A. Description

A De Carbon type damper containing nitrogen gas under high pressure is contained within the cylinder to maintain pressure against the oil.

This prevents bubbles from being produced in the oil during compression. It assures positive damping action. The spring force can be adjusted to three positions according to carring load and riding condition. The stroke of the rear cushion is 3.62 in. (92 mm).

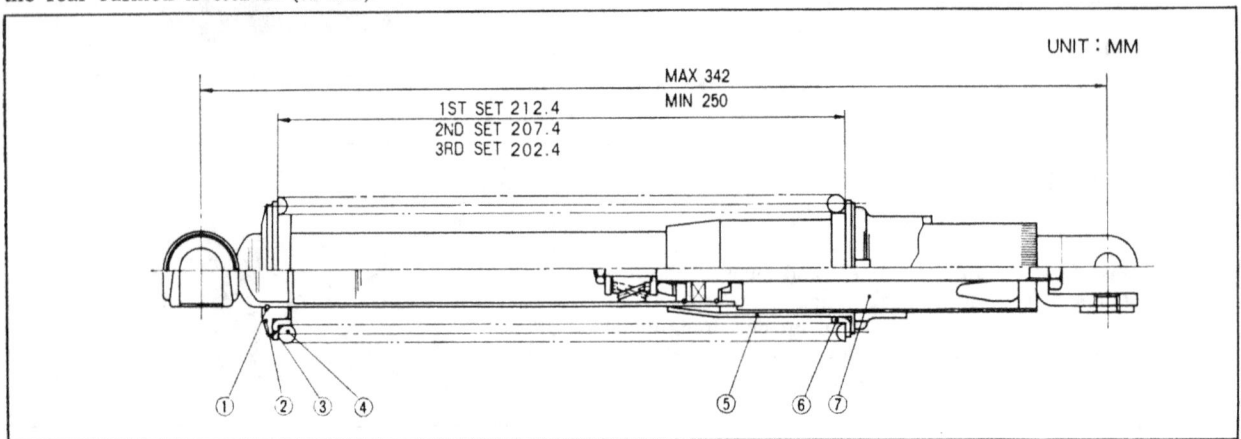

① Clip ② Rear shock spring seat stopper ③ Rear shock spring upper seat
④ Rear shock spring ⑤ Rear shock spring guide ⑥ Rear shock spring lower seat
⑦ Rear shock damper unit
Fig. 8-26. Sectional view of rear suspension

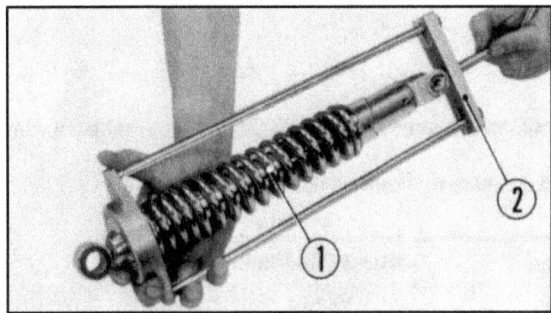

① Rear shock spring
② Suspension disassembling and assembling tool
Fig. 8-27.

B Disassembly

1. Remove the blind nut from the upper mounting bolt of each rear shock spring. Remove the lower mounting bolt and withdraw the rear shock spring.
2. Remove the spring ① from the shock spring unit by using the rear suspension disassembling and assembling tool (Tool No. 07959-3290000) ②. (Fig. 8-27)
   Turning the handle of the special tool clockwise will gradually compress the spring, permitting the removal of the spring upper seat.
   As the handle is turned counter clockwise, the special tool can be separated from the cushion spring allowing the damper unit to be disassembled.

C. Inspection

1. Check the body of the damper for dents or damage, for fluid leakage or lack of damping effect. If any of these defects are found, replace the whole unit as the damper is not repairable.

CAUTION:

The cylinder is pressurized by nitrogen gas to approximately 568.8 psi (40 atm.), therefore, no attempt should be made to disassemble the cylinder.

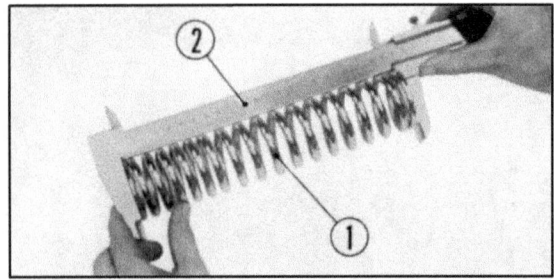

① Rear suspension spring ② Vernier caliper
Fig. 8-28.

2. Check the free length of the spring ① with a vernier caliper ②. (Fig. 8-28) If it measures less than the specified value, the spring should be replaced.

mm (inch)

Item	Standard value	Serviceable limit
Spring free length	222.9 (8.77)	217 (8.54)

3. Damping force connot be measured, therefore the test is performed by compressing the rear damper unit by hand; normal operating condition is indicated by a greater resistance on the extension stroke than on the compression stroke.

D. Reassembly

Install the rear suspension spring onto the rear damper unit with the tapered end of the coil toward the top.
Perform the reverse order of disassembly.

> • The model SL250K2 uses rear shock absorbers of the double tube type. For the operation see page 81.

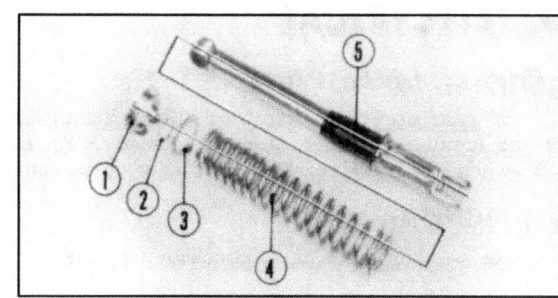

① Rear suspension spring seat stopper ② Clip
③ Rear suspension spring upper seat
④ Rear suspension spring ⑤ Rear damper unit
Fig. 8-29. Component parts of rear cushion

8·12 FRONT WHEEL

A. Description

Pratically all of the parts such as the wheel bearings, wheel hub, brake backing plate, brake drum and shoes, spokes and etc., are the same as those for the CL250.

The major differences are in the knobby tires (3.25~19-4 PR) used on the SL350 for better hold when travelling over rough roads.

The procedure for the removal and installation of the front wheel assembly, bearing removal, serviceable limit of the drum wear, brake shoe and tire replacements are the same as for the other series and should be referred to the 250·350 Shop Manual.

B. Tire Recommendation

The following tire is recommended for use with the SL350.

Brand	Manufacturer	Size	Air pressure (cold)
Front: B.S. Trail wing	Bridgestone Tire Co., Japan	3.25~19	21.5 psi
Rear: B.S. Trail wing	Bridgestone Tire Co., Japan	4.00~18	21.5 psi

This tire was specially developed for the SL350 and features susperior road holding for both off-the-road and on the highway.

8·13 REAR WHEEL

A. Description

Similar to the front wheel, the parts for the rear wheel are the same as those used on the CL350 with the exception of the knobby tire and rim designed for the installation of two bead spacers for off-the-road riding. Disassembly, inspection, repair and reassembly, is the same.

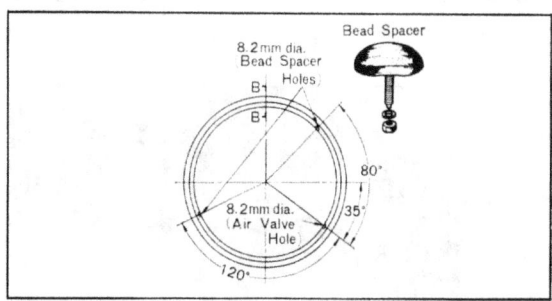

Fig. 8-30. Tube air valve hole and bead spacer holes

9. ELECTRICAL

GENERAL DESCRIPTION

All parts used in the electrical system are the same as the same as those used in the CL350, with the exception of the ignition coil, horn and speedometer. As safety and emergency feature, the ignition circuit is exposed and a kill switch has been incorporated to shut off the engine. Description of the special parts.

9·1 IGNITION COIL

The wires in the harness connecting the fuse, condenser and breaker points are of a larger size.

9·2 HORN

The center distance of the horn bracket mounting holes has been made greater to permit the used of the same bolts for mounting the steering damper bracket.

9·3 SPEEDOMETER

The design of the dial plate has been changed to indicate the speed ranges for on-the-road riding, however, the speedometer main unit has not been changed.

Refer to the 250·350 Shop Manual for information of the diassembly, inspection and rassembly of the respective components.

9·4 STARTER LIGHTING EMERGENCY SWITCH

The starter lighting emergency switch is located on top of the right handle bracket. (Fig. 9-1)

A. Disassembly

1. Separate the switch bracket by removing the two switch mounting screws ①. (Fig. 9-2)
2. Disconnect the throttle cable.
3. Disconnect the wiring harness within the head light case and remove the switch assembly.

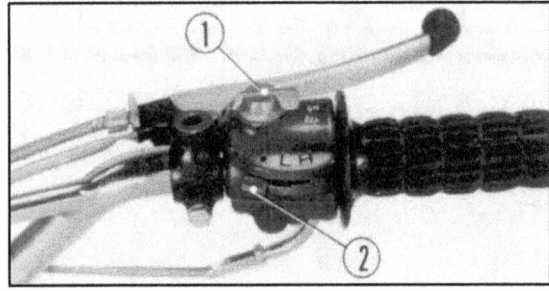

① Emergency switch ② Headlight control switch
Fig. 9-1.

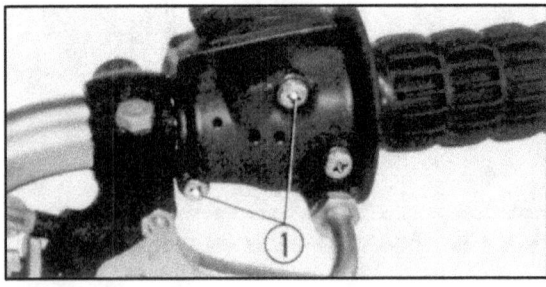

① Switch mounting screw
Fig. 9-2.

B. Inspection

1. Start the engine, first make sure the engine can be stopped by switching off the emergency switch. If the respective switch positions are not functioning properly, the switch or wiring is defective.

   If the wiring is correct, check by the testing conductivity of wires with the switch. If the conductivity is not correct, replace the switch with new one.

2. Switch on the main key switch and check to see that the headlight control switch is functioning properly by setting the respective switch positions. If its positions are not functioning properly, the switch or wiring is defective. If both the wiring and conductivity are correct, replace the switch with new one.

C. Reassembly

Perform the reassembly in the reverse order of disassembly.

NOTE:

When installing the switch lower housing on the handle bar, make sure that the locating pin is inserted into the handle bar stop hole and tightened together with the switch upper housing.

WIRING DIAGRAM

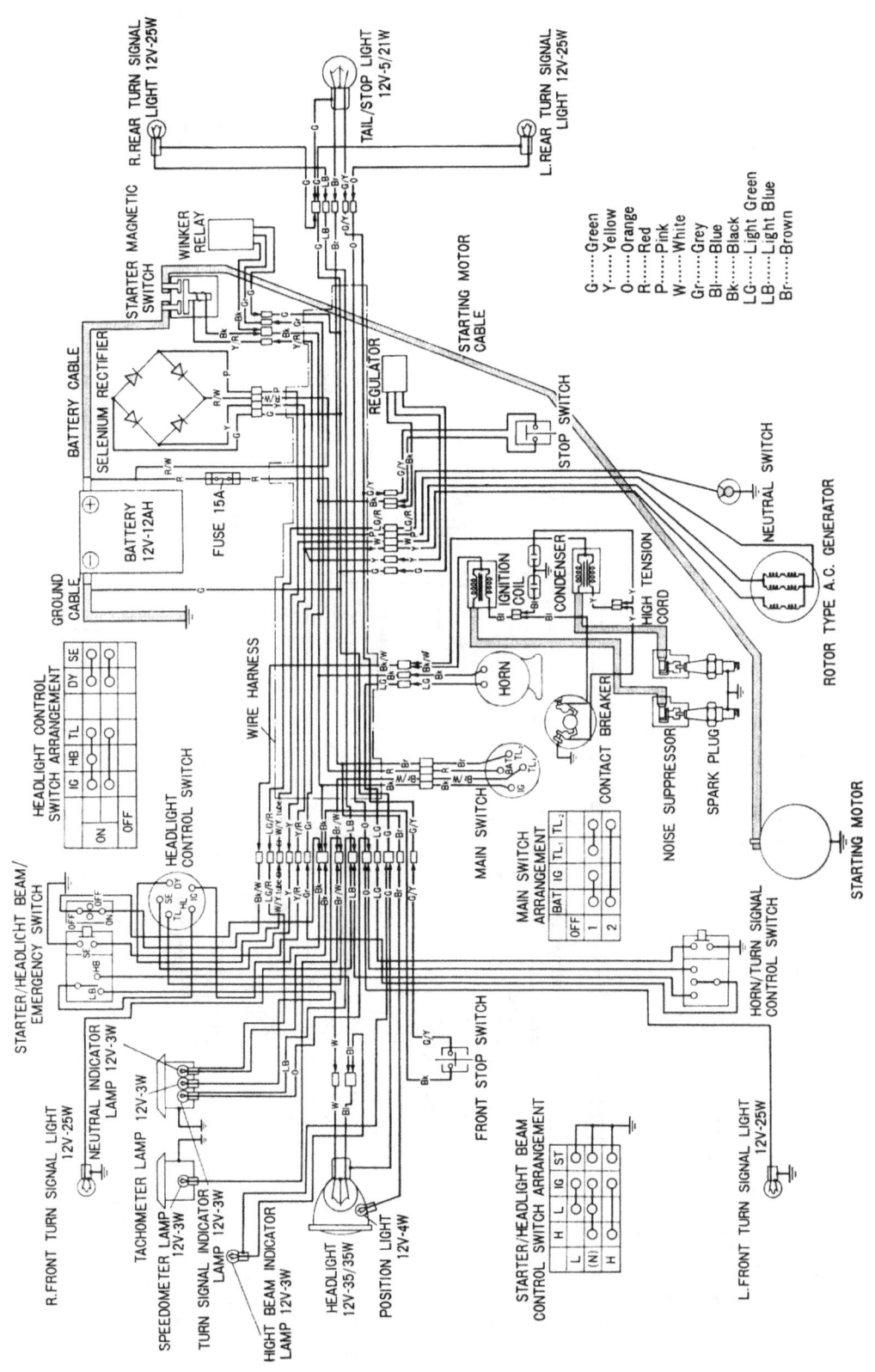

CB250K4 WIRING DIAGRAM (U.K. Type)

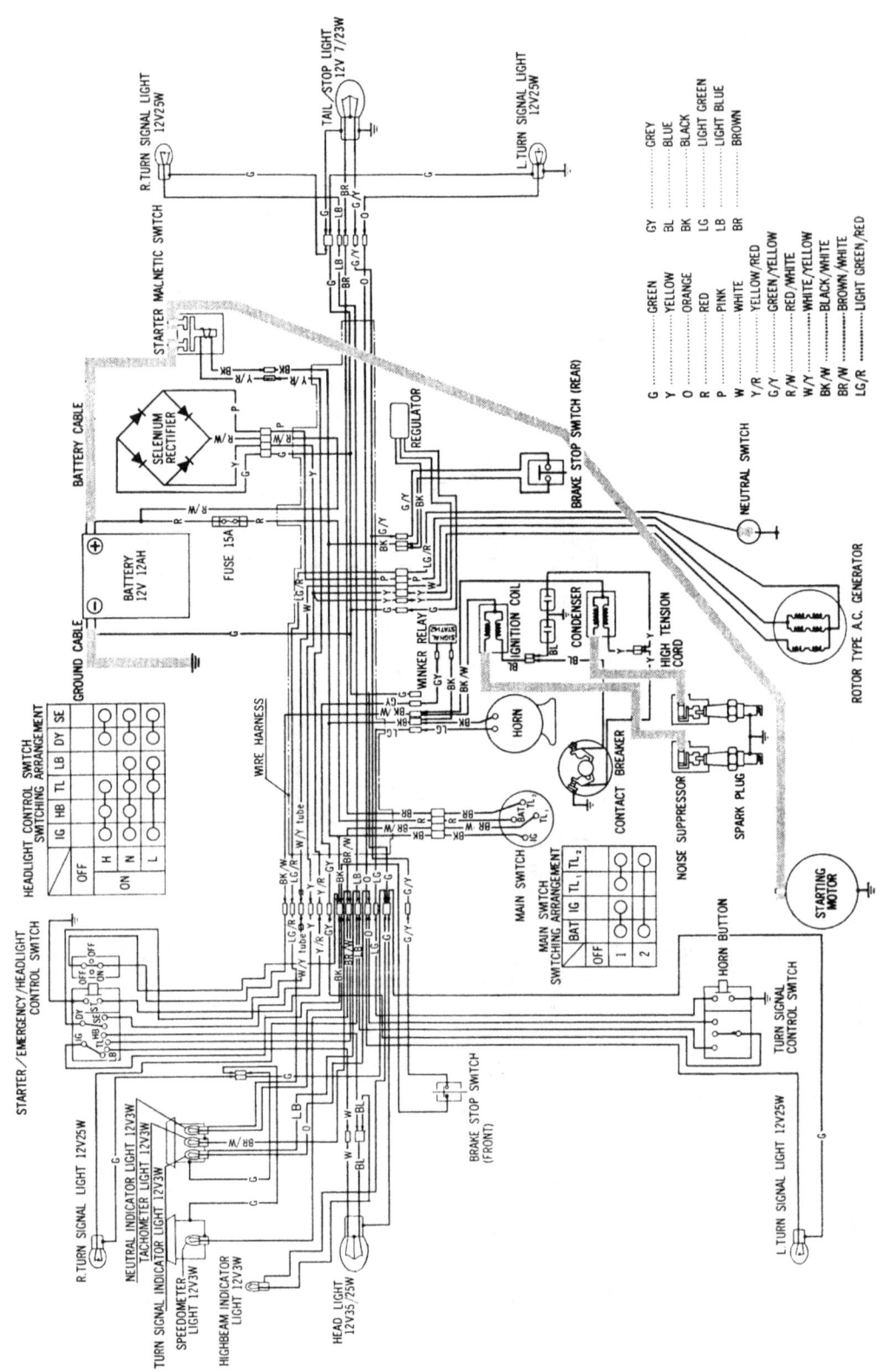

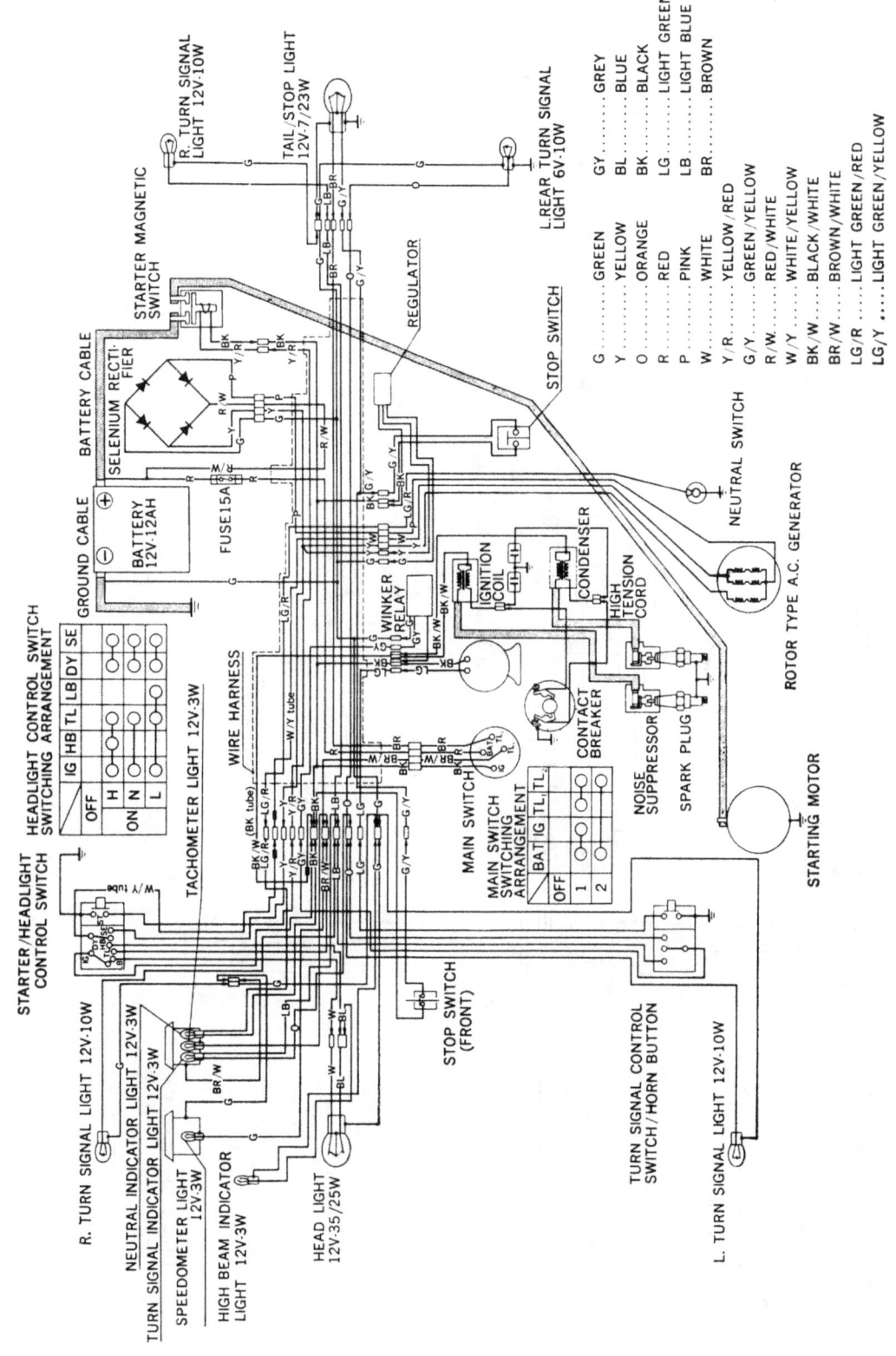

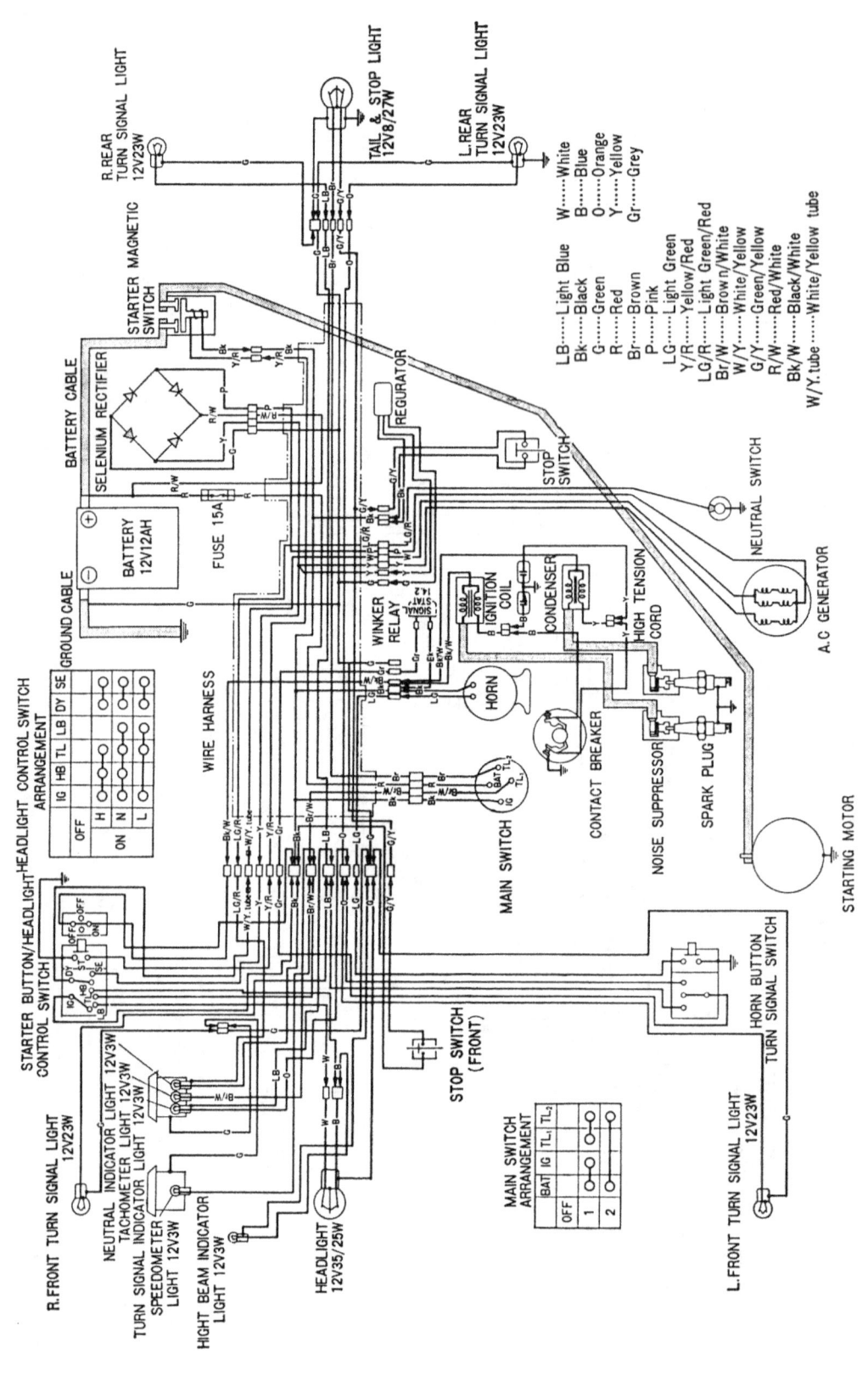

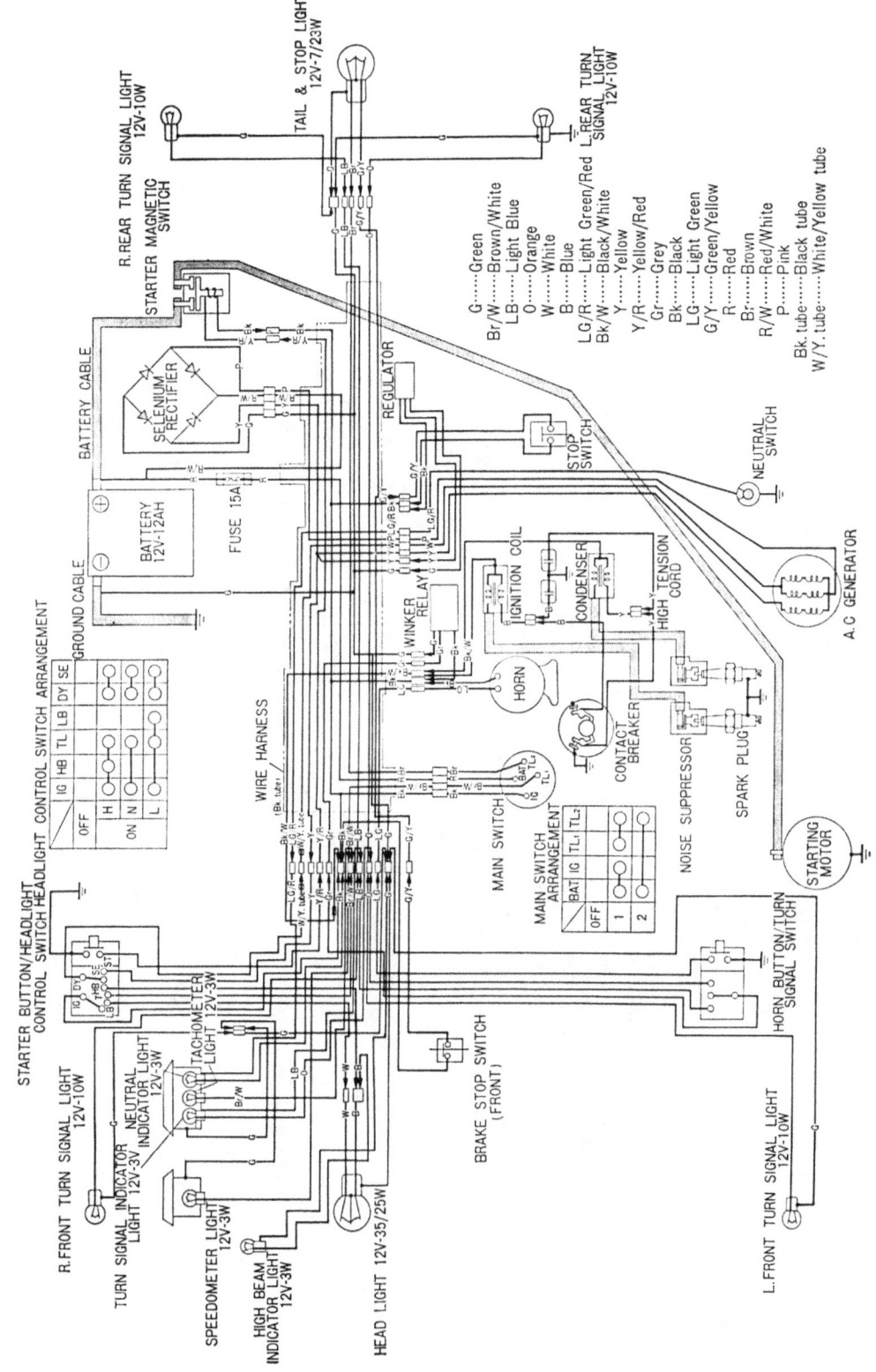

SL350K2 WIRING DIAGRAM (U.S.A. Type)

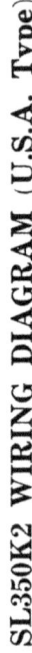

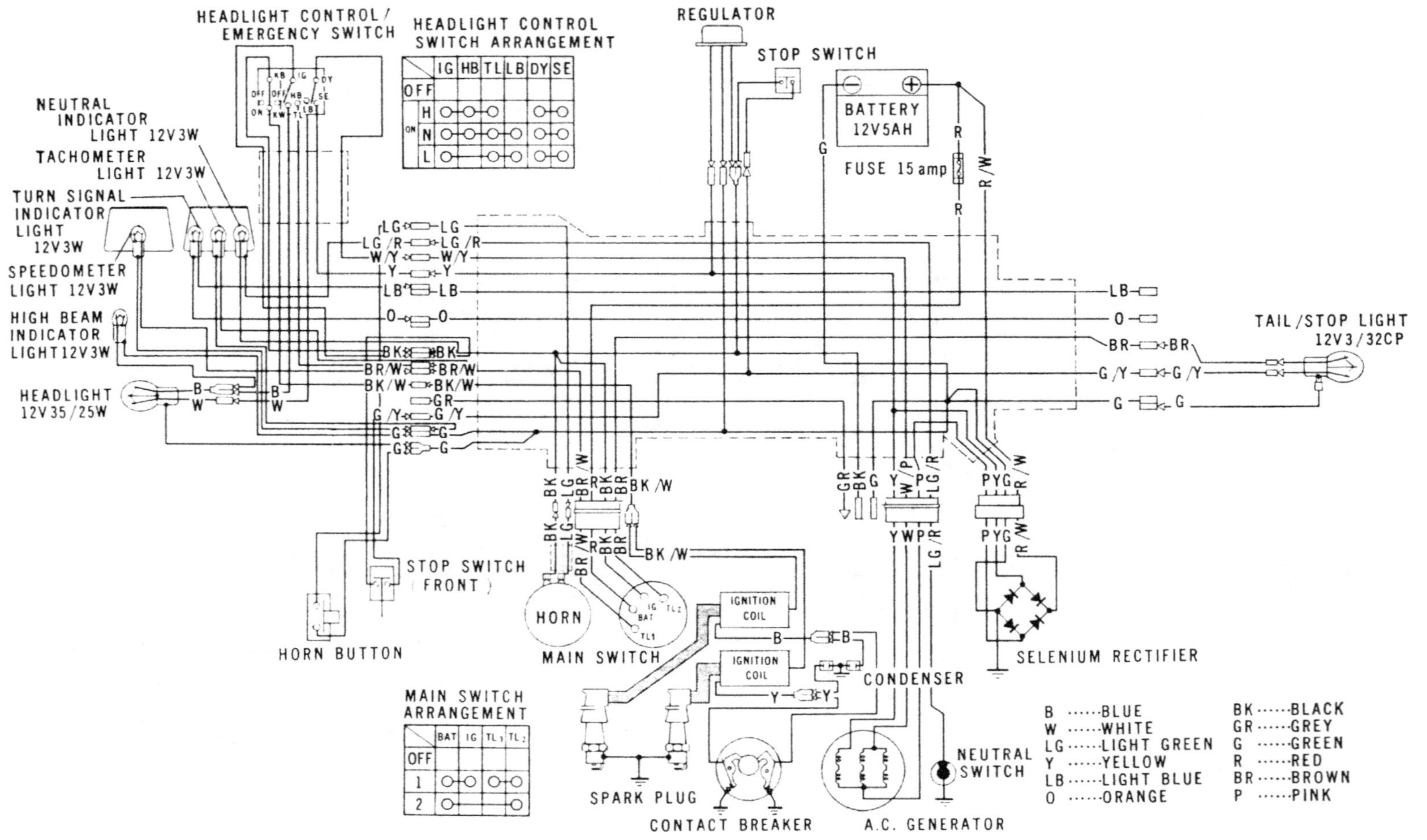

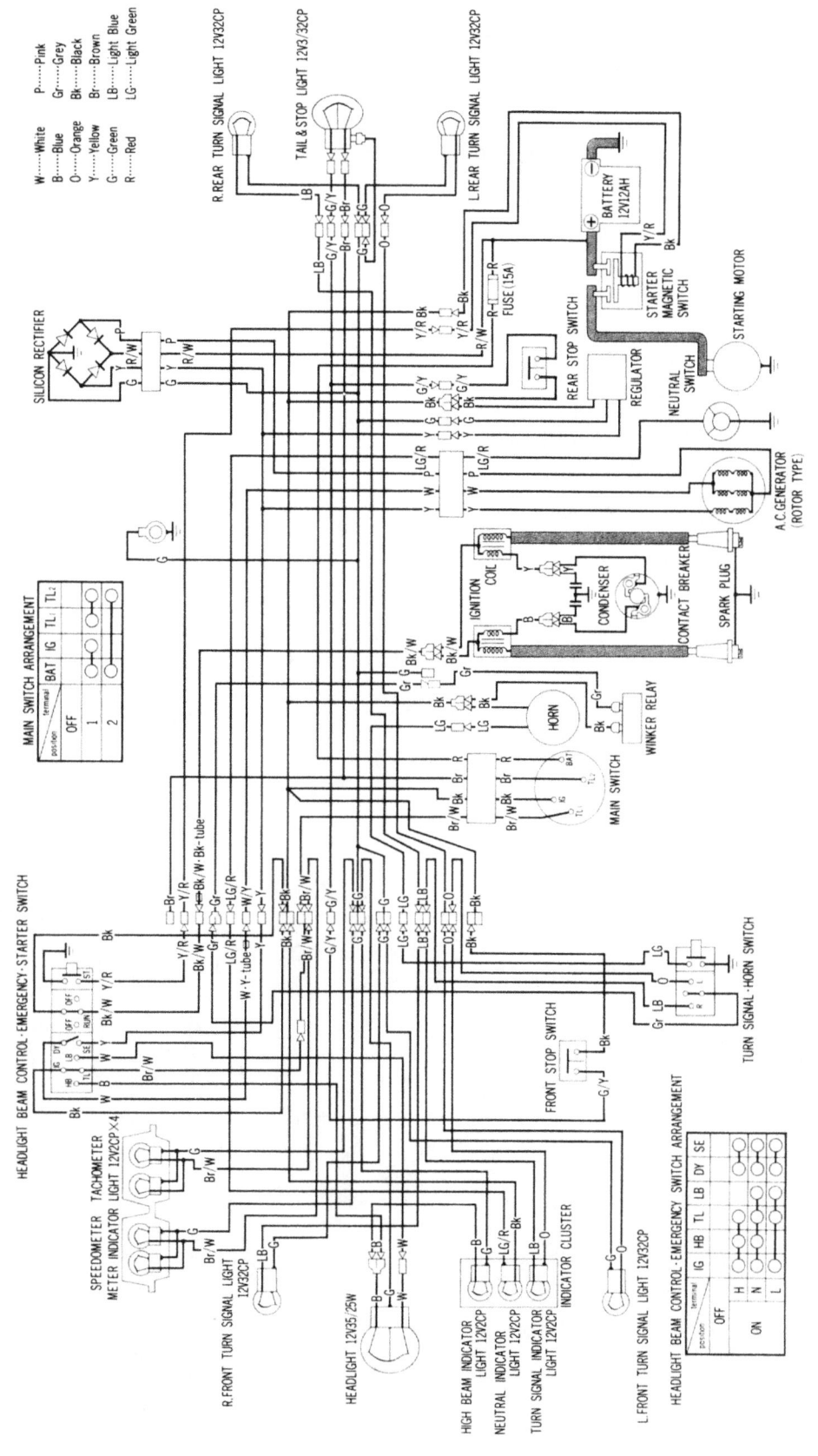

MEMO

10. MAINTENANCE

10·1 MAINTENANCE SCHEDULE

Perform the periodic inspections on the scheduled mileage shown in the chart to maintain the motorcycle in the peak of condition and be assured of extended trouble free service.

MAINTENANCE SCHEDULE This maintenance schedule is based upon average riding conditions. Machines subjected to severe use, or ridden in unusually dusty areas, require more frequent servicing.	INITIAL SERVICE PERIOD 500 miles	REGULAR SERVICE PERIOD Perform at every indicated month or mileage interval, whichever occurs first.			
		1 month 500 miles	3 months 1,500 miles	6 months 3,000 miles	12 months 6,000 miles
ENGINE OIL—Change.	●		○		
CENTRIFUGAL OIL FILTER—Clean.					○
OIL FILTER SCREEN—Clean.					○
SPARK PLUGS—Clean and adjust gap or replace if necessary.				○	
*CONTACT POINTS AND IGNITION TIMING—Clean, check, and adjust or replace if necessary.	●			○	
*VALVE TAPPET CLEARANCE—Check, and adjust if necessary.	●			○	
*CAM CHAIN TENSION—Adjust.	●			○	
PAPER AIR FILTER ELEMENT—Clean.	(Service more frequently if operated in dusty areas)			○	
PAPER AIR FILTER ELEMENT—Replace.					○
*CARBURETORS—Check, and adjust if necessary.	●			○	
THROTTLE OPERATION—Inspect cable. Check, and adjust free play.	●			○	
FUEL FILTER SCREEN—Clean.				○	
FUEL LINES—Check.				○	
*CLUTCH—Check operation, and adjust if necessary.	●			○	
DRIVE CHAIN—Check, lubricate, and adjust if necessary.	**●	○			
*BRAKE SHOES—Inspect, and replace if worn.				○	
BRAKE CONTROL LINKAGE—Check linkage, and adjust free play if necessary.	●			○	
*WHEEL RIMS AND SPOKES—Check. Tighten spokes and true wheels, if necessary.	●			○	
TIRES—Inspect and check air pressure.	●	○			
FRONT FORK OIL—Drain and refill.	***●				○
FRONT AND REAR SUSPENSION—Check operation.	●			○	
REAR FORK BUSHING—Grease. Check for excessive looseness.				○	
*STEERING HEAD BEARINGS—Adjust.					○
BATTERY—Check electrolyte level, and add water if necessary.	●		○		
LIGHTING EQUIPMENT—Check and adjust if necessary.	●	○			
ALL NUTS, BOLTS, AND OTHER FASTENERS—Check security and tighten if necessary.	●	○			

Items marked * should be serviced by an authorized Honda dealer, unless the owner has proper tools and is mechanically proficient. Other maintenance items are simple to perform and may be serviced by the owner.

** INITIAL SERVICE PERIOD 200 MILES.

*** INITIAL SERVICE PERIOD 1,500 MILES.

10·2 TIGHTENING TORQUE STANDARD

No.	Location	Part tightened	Tightening torque
①	Front brake arm (panel side)	Front brake torque bolt	180~250 kg. cm
②	Front brake arm (fork side)	Front brake torque bolt	180~250 kg. cm
③	Front fork top bridge	16 mm front fork bolt	700~800 kg. cm
④	Front cushion under holder	8 mm front cushion under holder nut	180~250 kg. cm
⑤	Front wheel axle	12 mm front axle nut	550~650 kg. cm
⑥	Steering stem	24 mm steering head stem nut	800~1200 kg. cm
⑦	Steering bottom bridge	8 mm steering stem bottom bridge bolt	180~250 kg. cm
⑧	Handle pipe holder	8 mm × 32 mm hex. bolt	180~250 kg. cm
⑨	Engine mounting	10 mm engine mounting nut (NH10)	350~450 kg. cm
⑩	Rear fork pivot bolt	14 mm self-locking nut	550~700 kg. cm
⑪	Rear cushion	NCA 10 mm cap nut 10 × 32 hex. bolt	350~450 kg. cm 350~450 kg. cm
⑫	Rear wheel axle	16 mm rear axle nut	800~1000 kg. cm

10·3 TROUBLE SHOOTING

When trouble develops, the most important thing is to first locate the cause of the trouble. The chart shows the procedure, sequence to follow, and the most direct method to perform the correct diagnoses. The diagnosing procedures and the probable causes are shown separately for each trouble, and therefore, the appropriate corrective action can be taken for the respective cause.

The O in the chart indicates [   ], and the indicates the motorcycle which has had the trouble corrected.

A. Engine does not start or hard starting

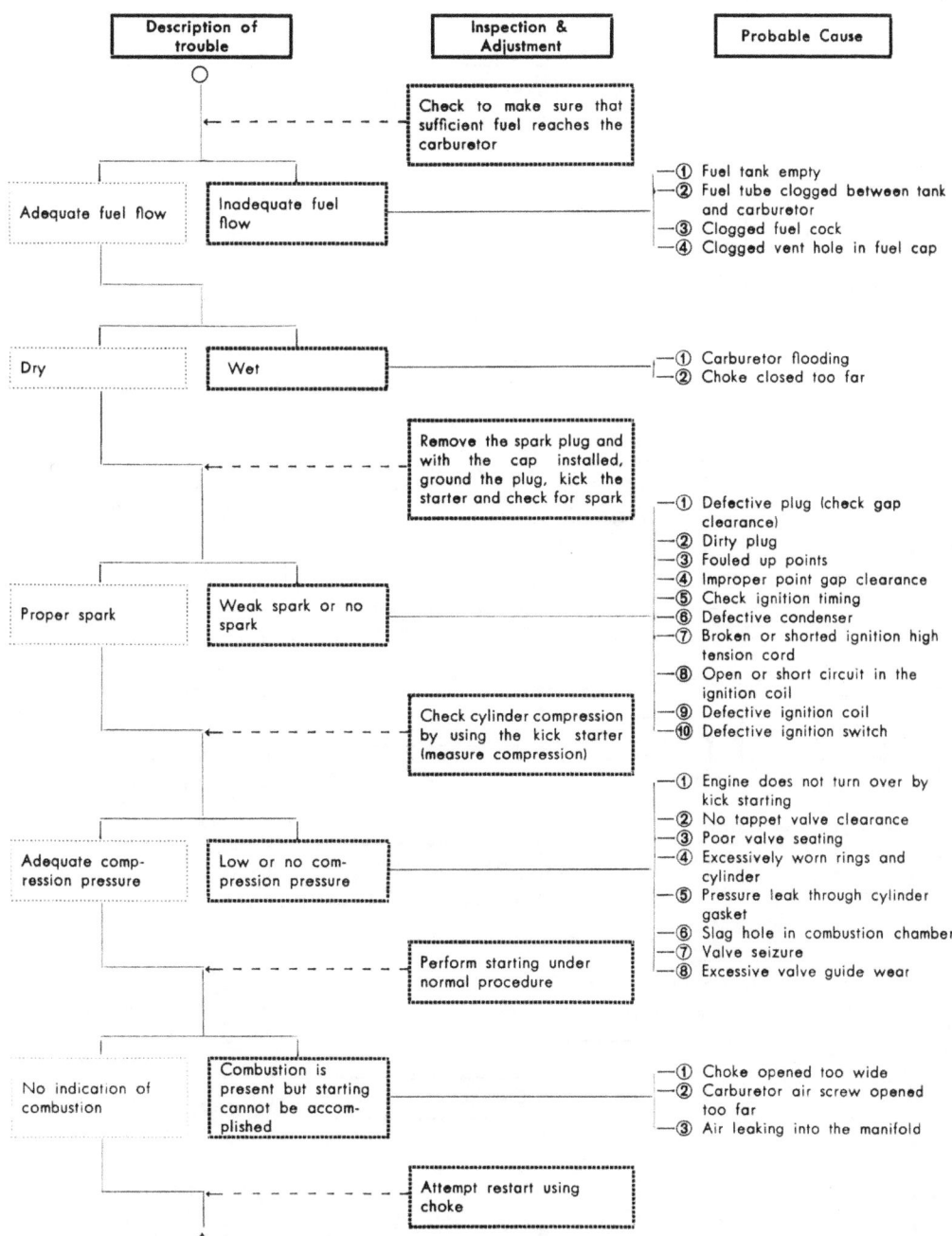

B. Loss of speed and drop in power

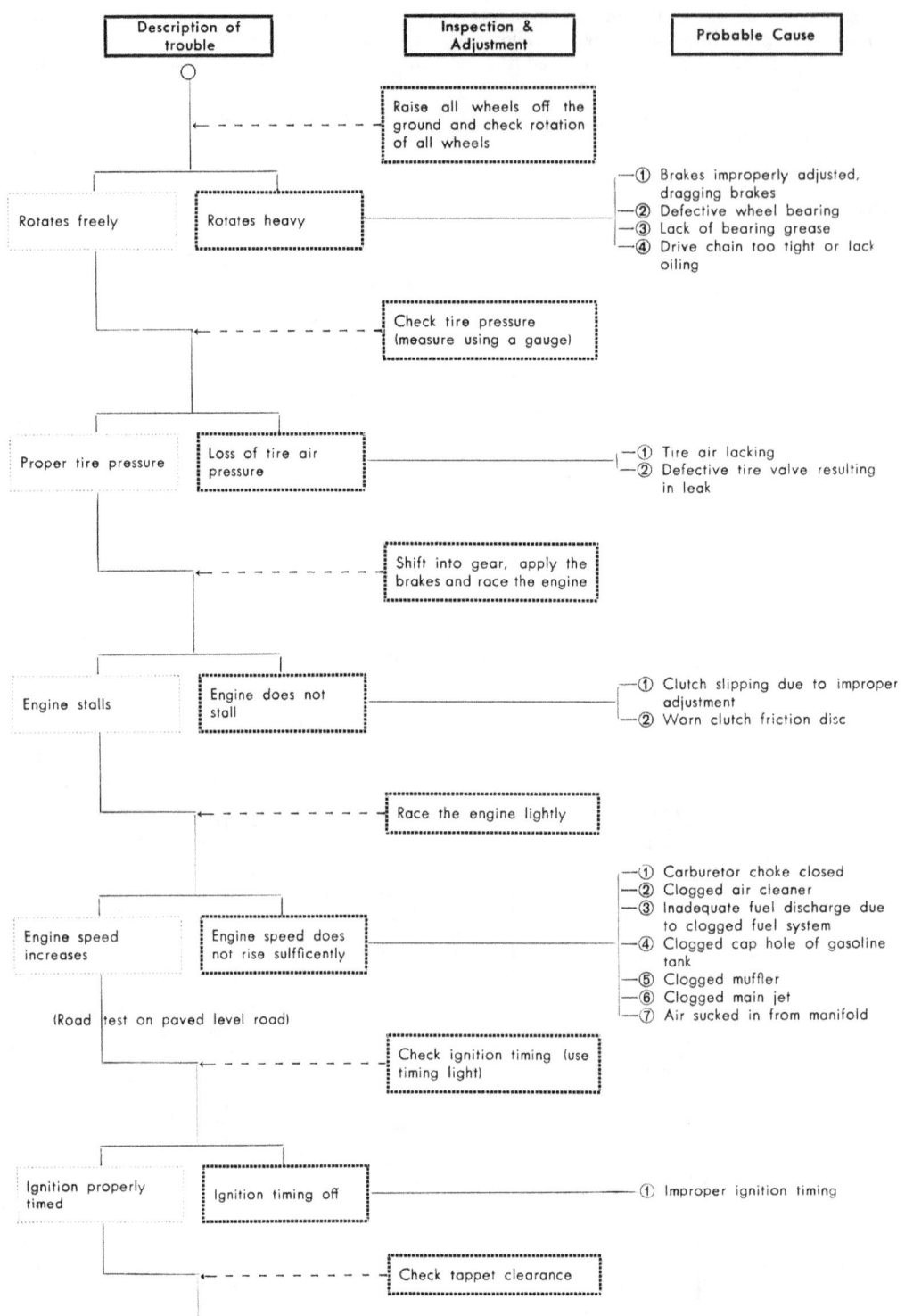

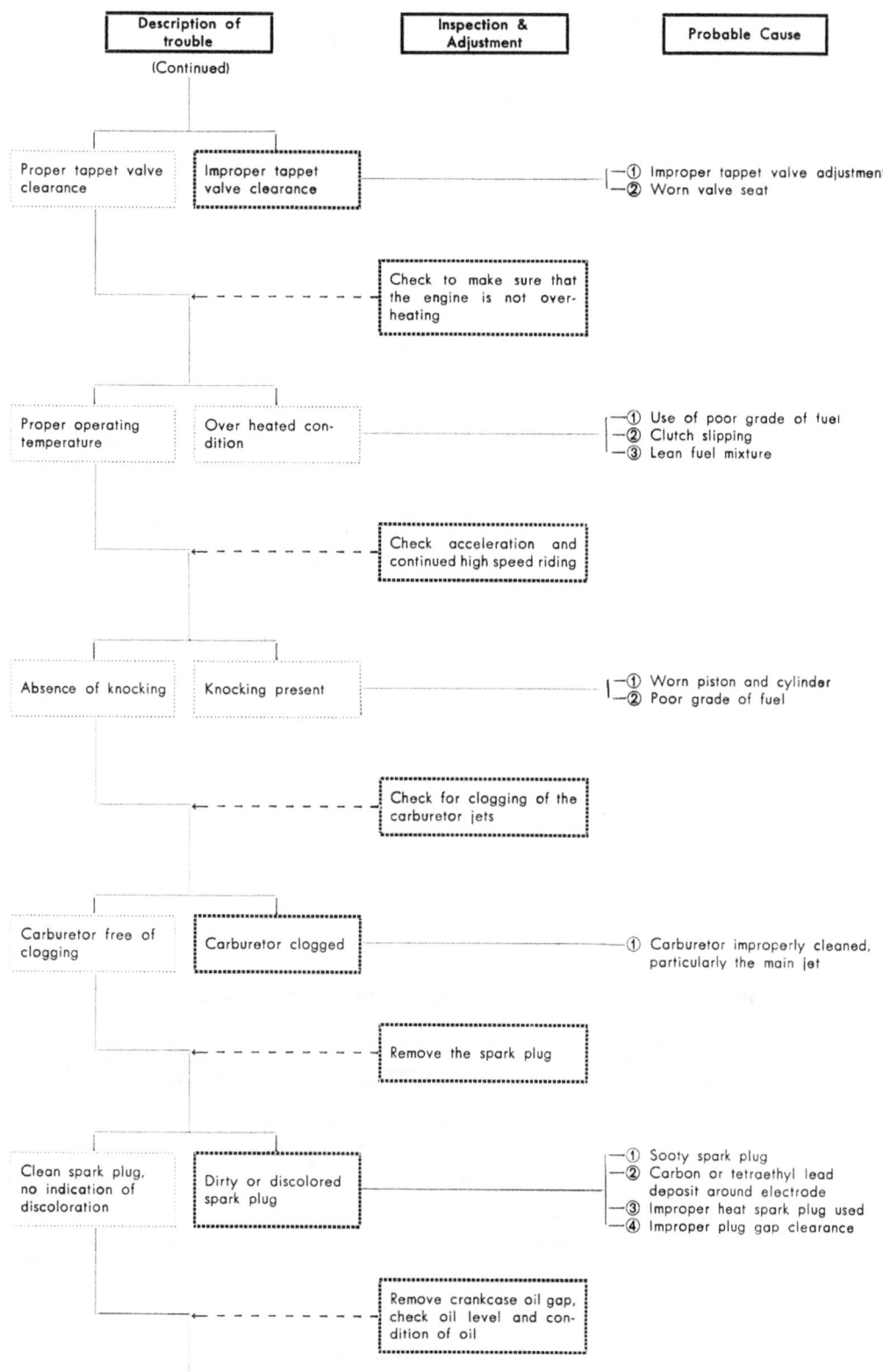

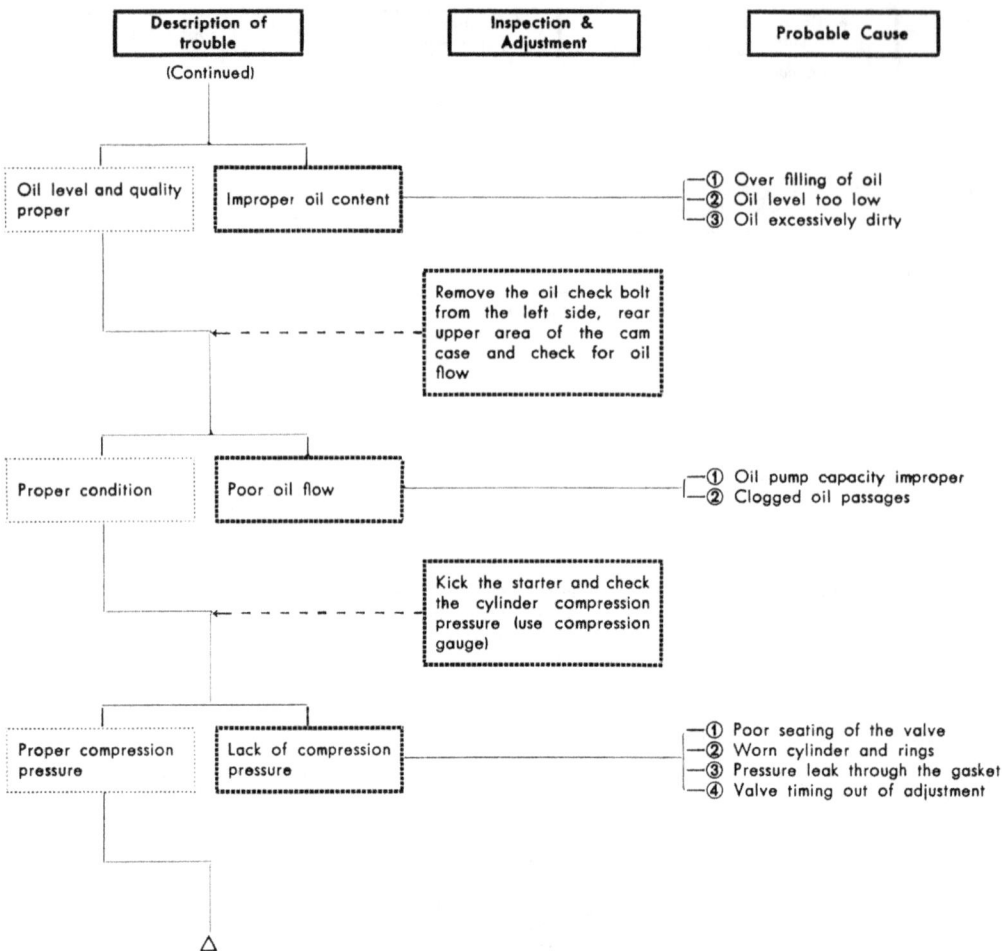

C. Improper running of engine (Particularly at low speed and idling)

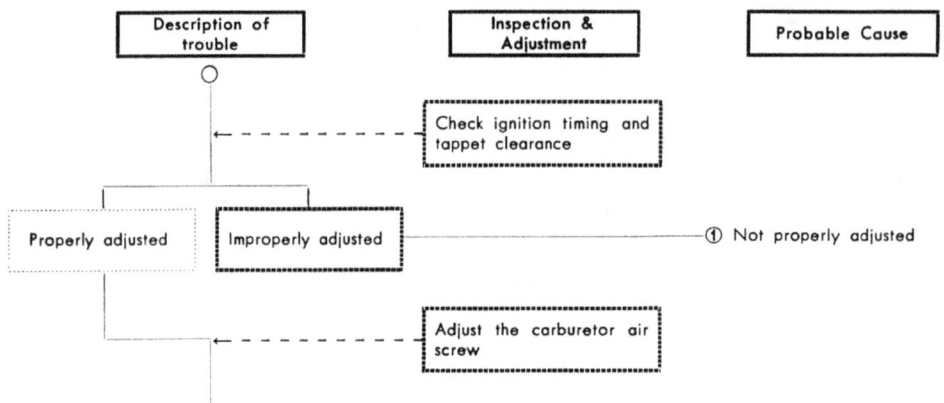

157

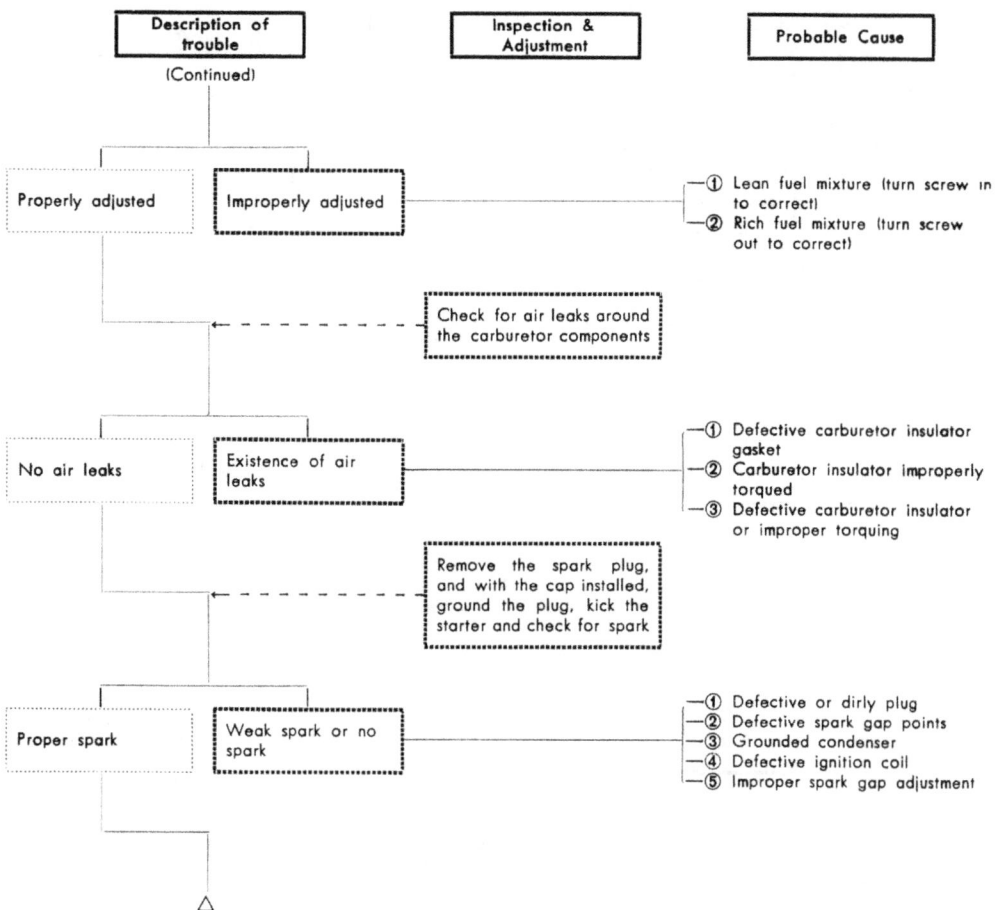

D. Improper running of engine (high speed)

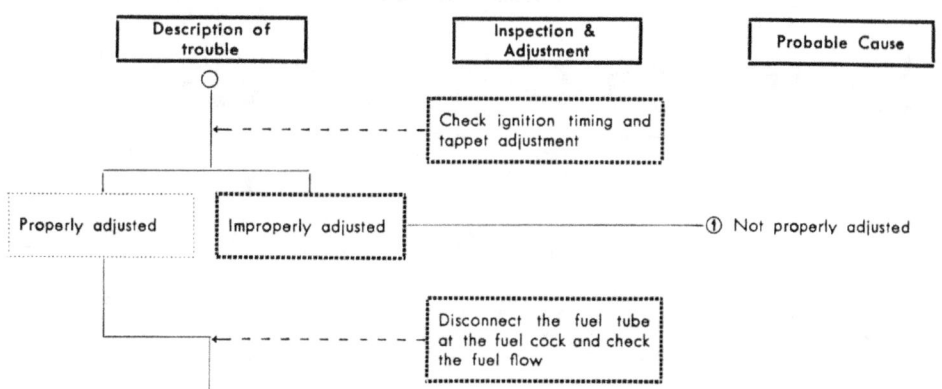

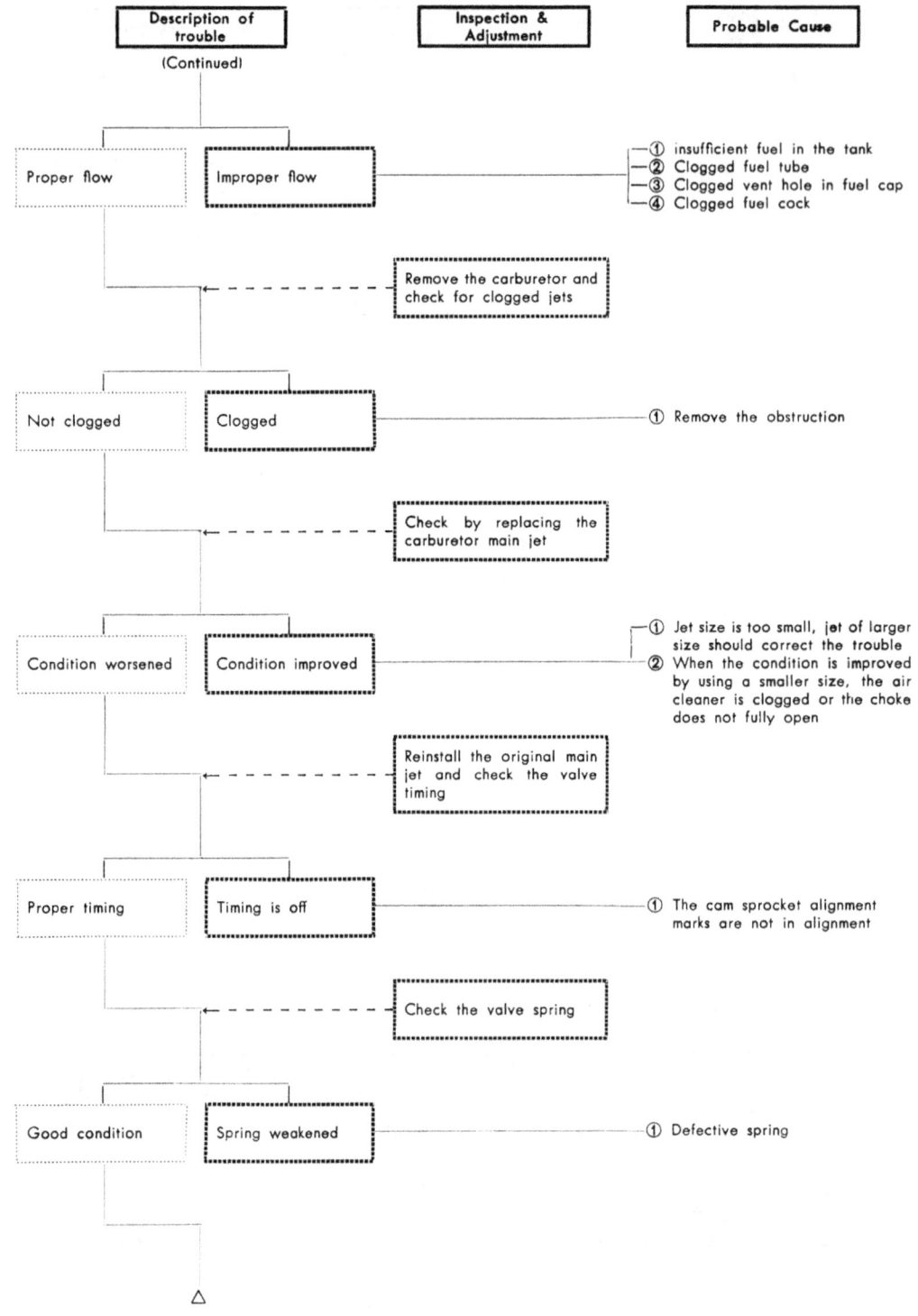

E. Excessive oil consumption

Exhaust smoke

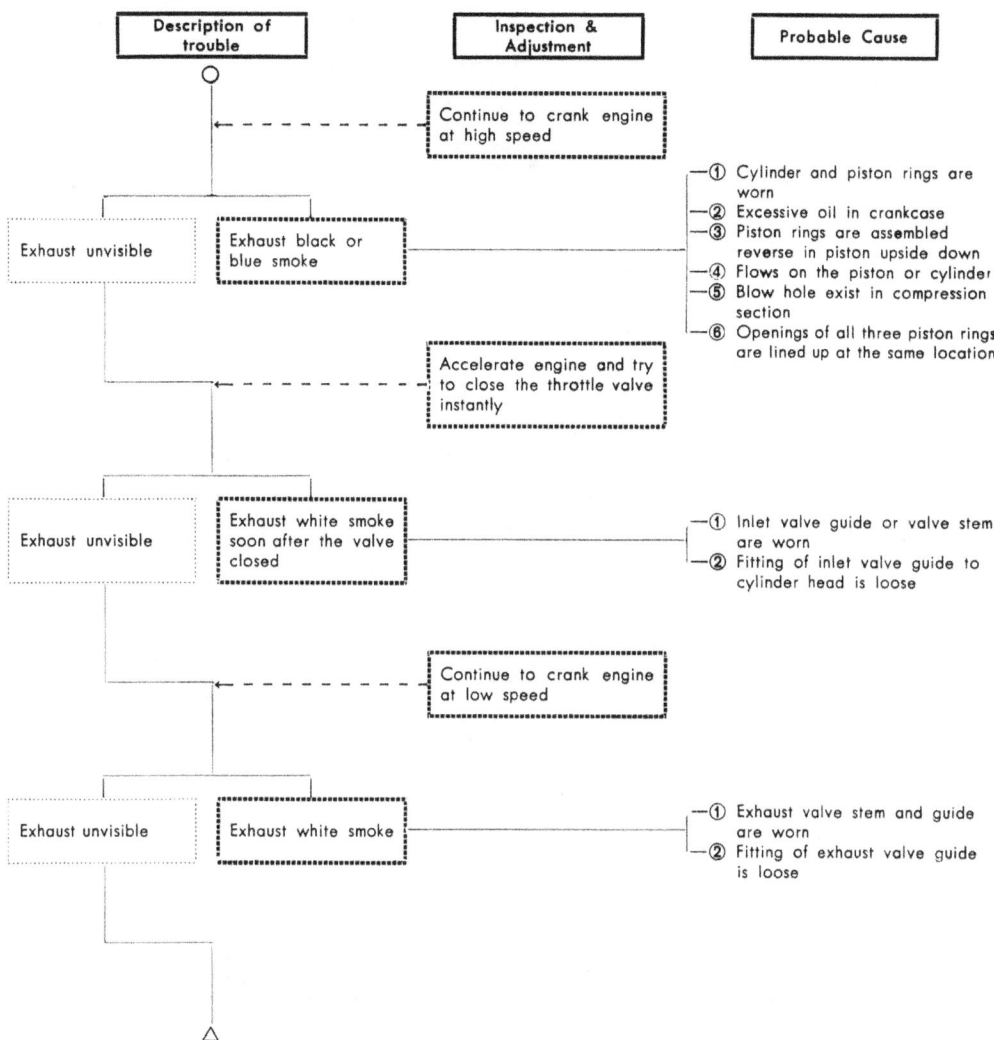

F. Clutch operates faulty

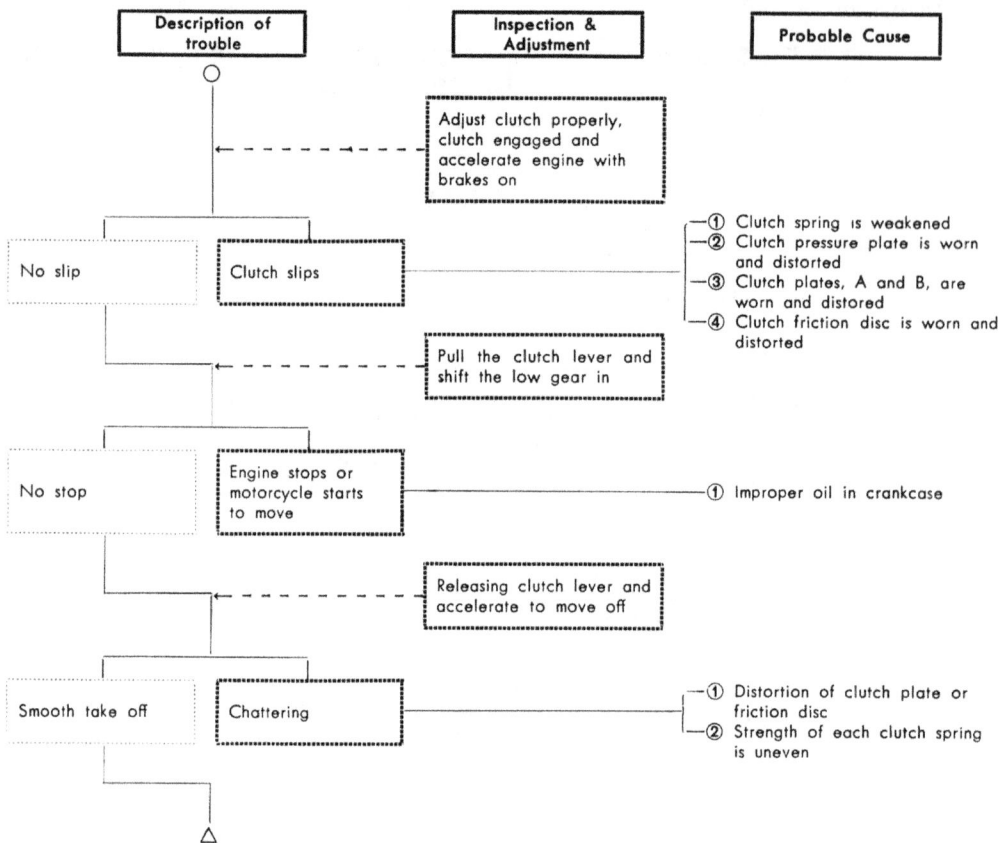

G. Shift operates faulty

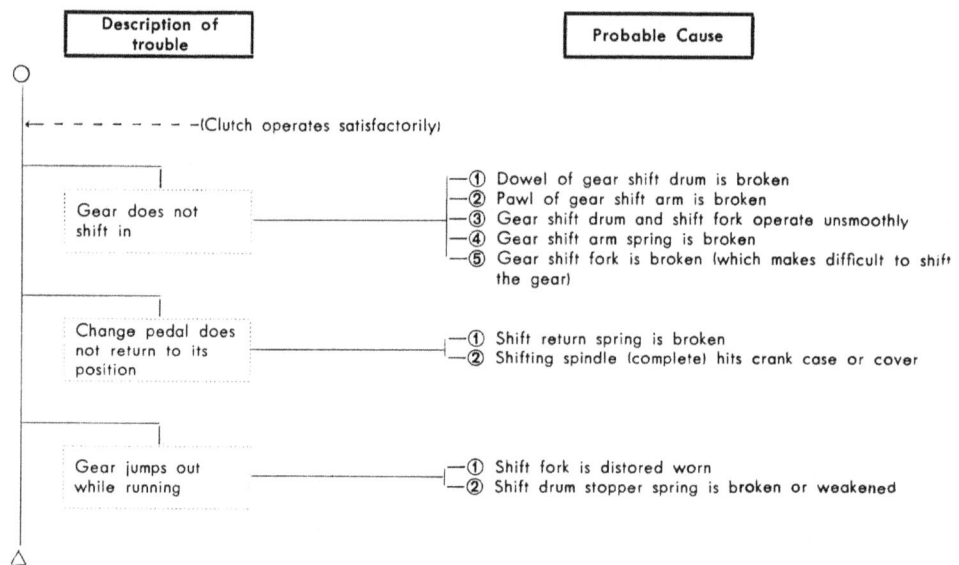

H. Engine runs with unusual noise

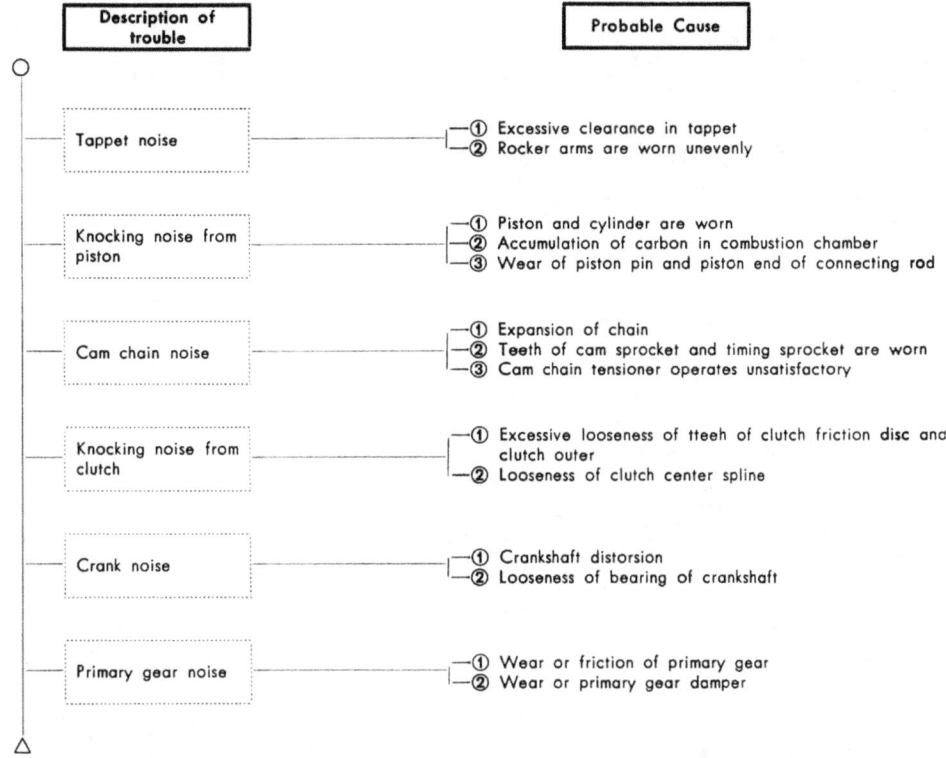

I. Vehicle steers faulty

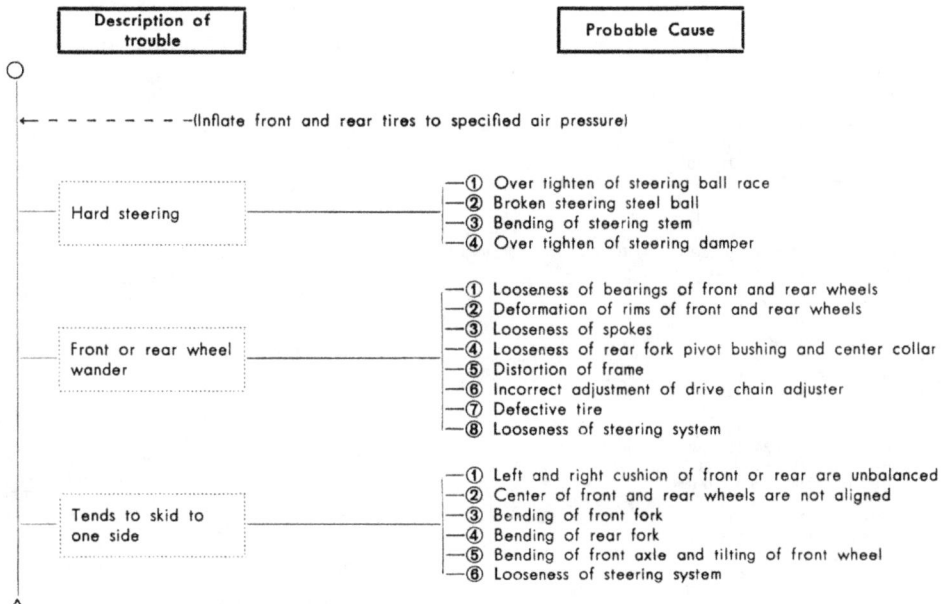

VELOCEPRESS MANUALS – MOTORCYCLE BY MAKE

AJS 1932-1948 SINGLES & TWINS 250cc THRU 1000cc (BOOK OF)
AJS 1945-1960 SINGLES 350cc & 500cc MODELS 16 & 18 (BOOK OF)
AJS 1955-1965 SINGLES 350cc & 500cc (BOOK OF)
AJS 1957-1966 FACTORY WSM - ALL SINGLES & TWINS
ARIEL UP TO 1932 (BOOK OF)
ARIEL 1932-1939 PREWAR MODELS (BOOK OF)
ARIEL 1933-1951 (WORKSHOP MANUAL)
ARIEL 1939-1960 4 STROKE SINGLES (BOOK OF)
ARIEL 1958-1964 LEADER & ARROW (BOOK OF)
BMW R26 R27 (1956-1967) FACTORY WORKSHOP MANUAL
BMW R50 R50S R60 R69S (1955-1969) FACTORY WORKSHOP MANUAL
BRIDGESTONE 90 SERIES FACTORY WSM & PARTS CATALOGUE
BRIDGESTONE 175 SERIES FACTORY WSM & PARTS CATALOGUE
BRIDGESTONE 350 SERIES FACTORY WSM & PARTS CATALOGUES
BSA SERVICE SHEETS MASTER CATALOGUE ALL MODELS 1945-1967
BSA BANTAM D1 TO D7 1948-1966 FACTORY SERVICE SHEETS MANUAL
BSA BANTAM ALL MODELS FROM 1948 ONWARDS (BOOK OF)
BSA BANTAM D14 FACTORY WORKSHOP & INSTRUCTION MANUAL
BSA SINGLES & V-TWINS UP TO 1927 (BOOK OF)
BSA SINGLES & V-TWINS UP TO 1930 (BOOK OF)
BSA SINGLES & V-TWINS UP TO 1935 (BOOK OF)
BSA SINGLES & V-TWINS 1936-1939 (BOOK OF)
BSA C10, C11 & C12 1945-1958 FACTORY SERVICE SHEETS MANUAL
BSA OHV & SV SINGLES 250-600cc 1945-1959 (BOOK OF)
BSA C15 & B40 1958-1967 FACTORY SERVICE SHEETS MANUAL
BSA OHV & SV SINGLES 250cc (ONLY) 1954-1970 (BOOK OF)
BSA B31, B32, B33 & B34 1945-60 FACTORY SERVICE SHEETS MANUAL
BSA OHV SINGLES 350 & 500cc 1955-1967 (BOOK OF)
BSA M20, M21 and M33 1945-1963 FACTORY SERVICE SHEETS MANUAL
BSA TWINS A7 & A10 1948-1962 FACTORY SERVICE SHEETS MANUAL
BSA TWINS A7 & A10 1948-1962 (BOOK OF)
BSA TWINS A50 & A65 1962-1965 FACTORY WORKSHOP MANUAL
BSA TWINS A50 & A65 1962-1969 (SECOND BOOK OF)
DOUGLAS 1929-1939 PREWAR ALL MODELS (BOOK OF)
DOUGLAS 1948-1957 POSTWAR ALL MODELS FACTORY SHOP MANUAL
DUCATI 160cc, 250cc & 350cc OHC MODELS FACTORY SHOP MANUAL
HONDA 50 ALL MODELS UP TO 1970 INC MONKEY & TRAIL (BOOK OF)
HONDA 90 ALL MODELS UP TO 1966 (BOOK OF)
HONDA 125-150cc TWINS C/CS/CB/CA FACTORY WORKSHOP MANUAL
HONDA 250-305 TWINS C/CS/CB 1959-1967 FACTORY WSM
HOHDA 250-350 TWINS CB/CL/SL 1968-1973 FACTORY WSM
HONDA 450 CB/CL 1965-1974 K0 TO K7 WORKSHOP MANUAL
HONDA C100 SUPER CUB FACTORY WORKSHOP MANUAL
HONDA C110 SPORT CUB 1962-1969 FACTORY WORKSHOP MANUAL
HONDA TWINS & SINGLES 50cc THRU 305cc 1960-1966 (BOOK OF)
HONDA TWINS ALL MODELS 125cc THRU 450cc UP TO 1968 (BOOK OF)
INDIAN PONYBIKE, BOY RACER & PAPOOSE ILL PARTS LIST & SALES LIT
J.A.P. ENGINES 1927-1952 & MOTORCYCLES 1934-1952 (BOOK OF)
MATCHLESS 1931-1939 ALL MODELS 250cc THRU 990cc (BOOK OF)
MATCHLESS 1945-1956 350 & 500cc SINGLES (BOOK OF)
MATCHLESS 1955-1966 350 & 500cc SINGLES (BOOK OF)
MATCHLESS 1957-1966 FACTORY WSM - ALL SINGLES & TWINS
NEW IMPERIAL ALL SV & OHV FROM 1935 ONWARDS (BOOK OF)
NORTON 1932-1939 PREWAR MODELS (BOOK OF)
NORTON 1932-1947 (BOOK OF)
NORTON 1938-1956 (BOOK OF)
NORTON 1955-1963 MODELS 19, 50 & ES2 (BOOK OF)
NORTON 1955-1965 DOMINATOR TWINS (BOOK OF)
NORTON 1960-1970 TWIN CYLINDER FACTORY WORKSHOP MANUAL
NORTON 1970-1975 COMMANDO FACTORY WORKSHOP MANUAL
NORTON 1975-1978 MK 3 COMMANDO FACTORY WORKSHOP MANUAL
PANTHER 1932-1958 LIGHTWEIGHT MODELS 250 & 350cc (BOOK OF)
PANTHER 1938-1966 HEAVYWEIGHT MODELS 600 & 650cc (BOOK OF)
RALEIGH MOTORCYCLES 1919-1933 (BOOK OF)
ROYAL ENFIELD 1934-1946 SINGLES & V TWINS (BOOK OF)
ROYAL ENFIELD 1937-1953 SINGLES & V TWINS (BOOK OF)
ROYAL ENFIELD 1946-1962 SINGLES (BOOK OF)
ROYAL ENFIELD 1958-1966 250cc & 350cc SINGLES (SECOND BOOK OF)
ROYAL ENFIELD 736cc INTERCEPTOR FACTORY WORKSHOP MANUAL
RUDGE 1933-1939 (BOOK OF)
SUNBEAM 1928-1939 (BOOK OF)
SUNBEAM 1946-1957 S7 & S8 (BOOK OF)
SUZUKI 50cc & 80cc UP TO 1966 (BOOK OF)
SUZUKI T10 1963-1967 FACTORY WORKSHOP MANUAL
SUZUKI T20 & T200 1965-1969 FACTORY WORKSHOP MANUAL
SUZUKI TWINS 1962 ONWARDS 125-500cc WORKSHOP MANUAL
TRIUMPH 1935-1939 PREWAR MODELS (BOOK OF)
TRIUMPH 1935-1949 (BOOK OF)
TRIUMPH 1937-1951 (WORKSHOP MANUAL)
TRIUMPH 1945-1955 FACTORY WORKSHOP MANUAL
TRIUMPH 1945-1958 TWINS (BOOK OF)
TRIUMPH 1956-1969 TWINS (BOOK OF)
VELOCETTE 1925-1970 ALL SINGLES & TWINS (BOOK OF)
VILLIERS ENGINE UP TO 1959 INC. 3 WHEELERS (BOOK OF)
VILLIERS ENGINE UP TO 1969 (BOOK OF)
VINCENT 1935-1955 (WORKSHOP MANUAL)
YAMAHA 1961-1967 YA5 & YA6 (WORKSHOP MANUAL & ILL PARTS LIST)
YAMAHA 1971-1972 JT1& JT2 (WORKSHOP MANUAL & ILL PARTS LIST)

VELOCEPRESS TECHNICAL BOOKS – MOTORCYCLE

1930'S BRITISH MOTORCYCLE CARBS & ELEC COMPONENTS (BOOK OF)
1930'S BRITISH MOTORCYCLE ENGINES (OVERHAUL & MAINTENANCE)
1930'S BRITISH MOTORCYCLE GEARBOXES & CLUTCHES (BOOK OF)
CATALOG OF BRITISH MOTORCYCLES (1951 MODELS)
LUCAS ELECTRONICS BRITISH M/CYCLES REPAIR & PARTS (1950-1977)
MOTORCYCLE ENGINEERING (P.E. Irving)
MOTORCYCLE ROAD TESTS 1949-1953 (Motor Cycle Magazine UK)
SPEED AND HOW TO OBTAIN IT (Motor Cycle Magazine UK)
TUNING FOR SPEED (P.E. Irving)
WIPAC SERVICE MANUAL NUMBER 3

VELOCEPRESS MANUALS – SCOOTERS BY MAKE

BSA SUNBEAM SCOOTER WORKSHOP MANUAL 1959-1965
BSA SUNBEAM SCOOTER 1959-1965 (BOOK OF)
LAMBRETTA 1947-1957 ALL 125 & 150cc MODELS (BOOK OF)
LAMBRETTA 1957-1970 LI & TV MODELS (SECOND BOOK OF)
NSU PRIMA 1956-1964 ALL MODELS (BOOK OF)
TRIUMPH TIGRESS SCOOTER WORKSHOP MANUAL 1959-1965
TRIUMPH TIGRESS SCOOTER (BOOK OF)
VESPA 1951-1961 (BOOK OF)
VESPA 1955-1963 125 & 150cc & GS MODELS (SECOND BOOK OF)
VESPA 1955-1968 GS & SS (BOOK OF)
VESPA 1963-1972 90, 125 & 150cc (THIRD BOOK OF)

VELOCEPRESS MANUALS – MOPEDS & MOTORIZED BICYCLES

CYCLEMOTOR (BOOK OF)
NSU QUICKLY 1953-1963 ALL MODELS (BOOK OF)
PUCH MAXI N & S MAINTENANCE & REPAIR (3 MANUAL COMPILATION)
RALEIGH MOPEDS 1960-1969 (BOOK OF)

VELOCEPRESS MANUALS - THREE WHEELER'S

BOND MINICAR THREE WHEELER 1948-1967 (BOOK OF)
BMW ISETTA FACTORY WORKSHOP MANUAL
BSA THREE WHEELER (BOOK OF)
RELIANT REGAL THREE WHEELER 1952-1973 (BOOK OF)
VINTAGE MORGAN THREE WHEELER (BOOK OF)

VELOCEPRESS MANUALS – AUTOMOBILE BY MAKE

ALFA ROMEO GIULIA WORKSHOP MANUAL 1300 TO 2000cc 1962-1975
ALFA ROMEO GIULIA TECH MANUAL CARBURETED CARS FROM 1962
ALFA ROMEO GIULIA TECH MANUAL FUEL INJECTED CARS FROM 1969
ALFA ROMEO GIULIETTA & GIULIA 750 & 101 SERIES 1955-1965 WSM
AUSTIN-HEALEY SPRITE & MG MIDGET WORKSHOP MANUAL 1958-1971
BMW 600 LIMOUSINE FACTORY WORKSHOP MANUAL
BMW 600 LIMOUSINE OWNERS HAND BOOK & SERVICE MANUAL
BMW 2000 & 2002 1966-1976 WORKSHOP MANUAL
CORVAIR 1960-1969 WORKSHOP MANUAL
CORVETTE V8 1955-1962 WORKSHOP MANUAL
FIAT 500 FACTORY WORKSHOP MANUAL 1957-1973
FIAT 600, 600D & MULTIPLA FACTORY WORKSHOP MANUAL 1955-1969
JAGUAR E-TYPE 3.8 & 4.2 SERIES 1 & 2 WORKSHOP MANUAL
JAGUAR MK 7, 8, 9 & XK120, 140, 150 WORKSHOP MANUAL 1948-1961
METROPOLITAN FACTORY WORKSHOP MANUAL
MGA & MGB OWNERS HANDBOOK & WORKSHOP MANUAL
MG MIDGET TC, TD, TF & TF1500 WORKSHOP MANUAL
PORSCHE 356 1948-1965 WORKSHOP MANUAL
PORSCHE 911 2.0, 2.2, 2.4 LITRE 1964-1973 WORKSHOP MANUAL
PORSCHE 911 2.7, 3.0, 3.2 LITRE 1973-1989 WORKSHOP MANUAL
PORSCHE 912 WORKSHOP MANUAL
TRIUMPH TR2, TR3, TR4 1953-1965 WORKSHOP MANUAL
VOLKSWAGEN TRANSPORTER, TRUCKS & WAGONS 1950-1979 WSM
VOLVO 1944-1968 ALL MODELS WORKSHOP MANUAL

VELOCEPRESS TECHNICAL BOOKS - AUTOMOBILE

FERRARI 250/GT SERVICE AND MAINTENANCE
FERRARI GUIDE TO PERFORMANCE
FERRARI OWNER'S HANDBOOK
FERRARI TUNING TIPS & MAINTENANCE TECHNIQUES
HOW TO BUILD A FIBERGLASS CAR
HOW TO BUILD A RACING CAR
HOW TO RESTORE THE MODEL 'A' FORD
MASERATI OWNER'S HANDBOOK
OBERT'S FIAT GUIDE
PERFORMANCE TUNING THE SUNBEAM TIGER
SOUPING THE VOLKSWAGEN
SOLEX CARBURETORS (EMPHASIS ON UK & EU AUTOMOBILES)
SU CARBURETORS (EMPHASIS ON UK AUTOMOBILES)
WEBER CARBURETORS (EMPHASIS ON ALFA & FIAT)

VELOCEPRESS BOOKS & GUIDES - AUTOMOBILE

ABARTH BUYERS GUIDE
COMPLETE CATALOG OF JAPANESE MOTOR VEHICLES
FERRARI 308 SERIES BUYER'S AND OWNER'S GUIDE
FERRARI BERLINETTA LUSSO
FERRARI BROCHURES AND SALES LITERATURE 1946-1967
FERRARI BROCHURES AND SALES LITERATURE 1968-1989
FERRARI SERIAL NUMBERS PART I - ODD NUMBERS TO 21399
FERRARI SERIAL NUMBERS PART II - EVEN NUMBERS TO 1050
FERRARI SPYDER CALIFORNIA
HENRY'S FABULOUS MODEL "A" FORD
MASERATI BROCHURES AND SALES LITERATURE

VELOCEPRESS BOOKS – RACING

CARRERA PANAMERICANA - MEXICAN ROAD RACE (BOOK OF)
DIALED IN - THE JAN OPPERMAN STORY
IF HEMINGWAY HAD WRITTEN A RACING NOVEL
VEDA ORR'S NEW REVISED HOT ROD PICTORIAL

AUTOBOOKS WORKSHOP MANUALS & BROOKLANDS ROAD TEST PORTFOLIOS

FOR A COMPLETE LISTING OF THE AUTOBOOKS & BROOKLANDS TITLES THAT WE CURRENTLY HAVE AVAILABLE, PLEASE VISIT OUR WEBSITE.
www.VelocePress.com

www.ingramcontent.com/pod-product-compliance
Lightning Source LLC
Chambersburg PA
CBHW080746250426
43673CB00062B/1922